KNIFE SKILLS
ILLUSTRATED

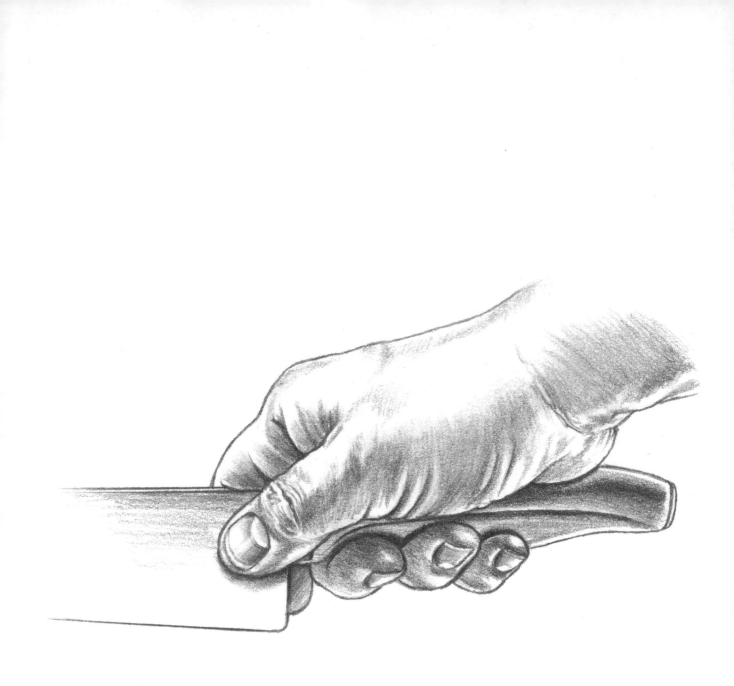

KNIFE SKILLS
ILLUSTRATED
A User's Manual

Peter Hertzmann

ORIGINAL ART BY ALAN WITSCHONKE ILLUSTRATION

W. W. Norton & Company

NEW YORK · LONDON

For information about permission to reproduce
selections from this book, write to
Permissions, W. W. Norton & Company, Inc., 500 Fifth Avenue,
New York, NY 10110

Manufacturing by The Courier Companies, Inc.
Book Design by Chalkley Calderwood
Production: Andrew Marasia, Sue Carlson

Library of Congress Cataloging-in-Publication Data

Hertzmann, Peter.
Knife skills illustrated : a user's manual / Peter Hertzmann ;
    original art by Alan Witschonke.
       p. cm.
    Includes index.
    ISBN-13: 978-0-393-06178-9 (hardcover)
    ISBN-10: 0-393-06178-7 (hardcover)
    1. Carving (Meat, etc.) 2. Knives. I. Title.
    TX885.H47 2007
    642'.6—dc22

                                    2006100808

W. W. Norton & Company, Inc.
500 Fifth Avenue, New York, N.Y. 10110
www.wwnorton.com

W. W. Norton & Company Ltd.
Castle House, 75/76 Wells Street, London W1T 3QT

 3 4 5 6 7 8 9 0

for Jill

CONTENTS

KNIFE SKILLS
ILLUSTRATED

INTRODUCTION

I LIKE TO THINK THAT I HAVE ALWAYS LEARNED FROM MY MISTAKES, BUT IT CERTAINLY didn't appear that way for the first part of my life when it came to using a knife. It seemed that whenever I picked one up to prepare dinner, I'd leave a bit of myself behind. As an eleven-year-old Boy Scout, I managed to earn my cooking merit badge even though the stew meat was tough and flavorless, the potatoes were still crunchy, the bread dough was raw in the center, and I cut myself with my pocketknife during the preparation. The *Boy Scout Handbook* had instructions on how to whittle sticks safely, but it provided no instructions on how to whittle an onion. I had no idea of what I was doing wrong. It's hard to learn from your mistakes if you don't know why you are making them.

Most of my serious cooking as a teenager was performed outdoors, so the mess I created was absorbed by nature, but when I went off to college and decided to live by myself, the responsibility for preparing my meals and cleaning the resulting mess became all mine. My father gave me a copy of the *I Hate to Cook Cookbook* as a going-away gift. It had a recipe for a baked chicken breast that was well within my abilities: place a half chicken breast in a baking dish, season with salt and pepper, drizzle with white wine, and bake for 30 minutes at 350°F. All I had to do was open the package and place the half chicken breast in the dish. No cutting was required, and thus little opportunity for bloodletting mistakes.

I began to learn about knives, and about how to cut food without cutting myself, over the next decade as I gradually expanded my knowledge of cooking and built on the skills required to move beyond my baked-chicken past. I became especially interested in Chinese cooking, learning about every aspect of it that I could. I took cooking classes. I studied Chinese-American history, Chinese history, and Chinese culture. I did anything that would advance my knowledge of Chinese food and cooking.

I made friends with a family who ran a Chinese restaurant in my neighborhood. The father had been a chef of some renown in his native Taiwan, and on days when I worked late and happened to stop by the restaurant just before closing time, I would be invited to eat with the family and staff. I tasted many dishes at these meals—home-style dishes prepared on a higher level—that I would never have experienced during a normal restaurant visit or by cooking from books. These opportunities continued over the years as various Chinese-American friends introduced me to their most recent or exciting restaurant, store, or other food-related find.

In the mid-1980s, I started studying with Martin Yan, who at the time operated a small cooking school near my home in addition to hosting his weekly television program. It was from Martin that I finally learned how to hold a knife, or at least a Chinese slicing cleaver, and how to cut an onion without cutting myself. He was always quick to show the "pinch grip," the proper way of holding the cleaver: you pinch the blade with your thumb and forefinger and wrap only the other three fingers around the handle. Martin would do a demonstration where he asked a student to hold the cleaver as he or she normally did—which usually was with all five fingers wrapped around the handle. After instructing the student to hold the cleaver as tight as possible, Martin would grip the top of the blade and easily twist the cleaver in the student's hand. He then instructed the student to hold the cleaver with a pinch grip. This time, Martin couldn't twist the blade, because it was now held in a stable manner. He didn't have to show me twice. From then on, I held my cleaver with a pinch grip.

Martin also showed me how to use the flat surface of the second part of my forefinger or middle finger to guide the blade of the cleaver while cutting. With a little instruction and lots of practice, I became proficient with my cleaver, and my fingers rarely came in contact with its sharp edge. I had seen the error of my ways.

A decade later, after my first trip to France—when my tastes and cooking had moved halfway around the globe—I found it quite simple to apply to French cooking what I'd learned while cooking Chinese food. For the first five or so years of my foray into French cuisine, I continued to use my Chinese cleaver for most of my cutting.

When I was learning Chinese cooking, I purchased a small sharp-tipped paring knife to carve vegetables for use in decorating dishes. Now that I was learning French cooking, I was using this knife routinely alongside my cleaver for tasks that were too awkward with the cleaver, such as peeling vegetables. And I realized that I was holding the paring knife and vegetables for French cooking the same way I had held them for Chinese-style vegetable carving.

In 2000, I had a chance to work in a French restaurant kitchen for five weeks (what the French call a *stage*, or period of training). It was during this *stage* that I switched to a traditional chef's knife. I spent five

weeks working in eastern France with the cooks of the Michelin one-star restaurant Le Château d'Amondans, and I learned to use a chef's knife for most tasks. There were three blade sizes to choose from: ten, twelve, and fourteen inches long. When the sous-chef, and my principal teacher on that visit, Taïchi Megukami, gave me instructions, he would grab whichever knife was handy and demonstrate how he wanted something cut. He would then hand me the knife so I could attempt to duplicate what he had done with the rest of the particular ingredient requiring my attention. I must have been able to learn from my mistakes at that point, because the chef, Frédéric Médigue, allowed me to do five more *stages* at the restaurant before it closed at the end of 2003.

My first purchase after I returned home from my original French-kitchen experience was a ten-inch-long chef's knife. That and my pointy little paring knife are still what I use every day in my own kitchen.

Ever since my Chinese cooking period, I've taken every opportunity to observe other cooks at work and to learn from them. I've worked in a half-dozen or so kitchens in France, and in each one, I had to learn the chef's preferred technique for each task. One year, I learned three different ways to shuck scallops, each kitchen insisting its way was the best. A year later, I was able to teach the three methods to a cook who had no idea how to shuck scallops.

In short, over the years, I've learned that there is often more than one right way of doing something, though I've also learned that there are wrong ways too. And one commonality I've noticed among chefs, teachers, and other cooks is that, for the most part, they have never received formal instruction in how to use their knives. If they went to a cooking school—and most of them didn't—maybe they were exposed to some knife skills instruction, but once that was over, they were left to their own devices. As a master chef in Alsace (a region in eastern France) confided to me one afternoon, he depended heavily on the young cooks in the restaurant because he'd "have a problem cutting his way out of a paper bag!" He could build and run one of the top restaurants in France, but his knife skills were below par.

Most of us, though, don't have a staff to cut our ingredients for us, so we need to have good knife skills. Having good knife skills will not make you a great cook, but it will make it easier for you to become one. Good knife skills can even help the home chef who only prepares Sunday breakfast make it better.

I have been involved in teaching knife skills at a local cooking school for the past couple of years. I've become aware of how little people know about knives and how to use them, but, more important, I've also seen how eager people are to learn. During each class, students are introduced to a variety of topics, such as what knives to own and how to care for them. After a lecture and demonstration, students practice doing the basic cutting techniques they've just witnessed. It's during the hands-on portion of the class that each student receives individual instruction about how to hold and use knives. Some students are stubborn and want to do everything the same way they have all their lives, but these students are in a minority. Most immediately start breaking the habits they've picked up over their lifetimes. With these students, it's as if a whole new world has been opened to them during our three hours together.

But there's always been something missing from the classes. There's never been a guide that students could take home with them to help them recall what they had learned. That is the main reason why I wrote this book.

Chances are, when you start using this book, you'll do so with the kitchen knives you already have on hand. The first chapter will help you understand those knives better. You'll learn how to make a knife sharp, and how to keep it that way. You'll learn what type of cutting surface is best. And if you later decide to replace your knives, there's information here as to how to choose new ones.

The cutting techniques presented in chapters 2 and 3 provide step-by-step instructions for cutting most of

the fruits, vegetables, meats, poultry, and fish that you encounter daily. With experience, you'll discover that any food items not directly covered can be handled similarly to ones that are. You'll also find that each item you pick up to cut will be unique. At times, you will have to modify these instructions slightly to accommodate this uniqueness.

The step-by-step instructions are accompanied by illustrations drawn to enhance the instructions. Most of the time the technique is depicted from your point of view, so you can see exactly where your hands should be and how the knife should be used. Occasionally an additional view is provided so you can better see how to produce a good result.

In some cases, multiple techniques are detailed for achieving the same cut. For example, there are three different methods included for dicing an onion. The first is the traditional way you will see in other books or on television. I developed the other two methods because I find the traditional method difficult for beginners to learn, and often for even experienced cooks to master. The third method is especially useful when you need to dice only a small amount of onion, not an entire half. I have, of course, seen other methods demonstrated for dicing onions, but I believe these produce the best results and allow for the widest variety of cuts.

Why learn how to cut fruits and vegetables now that markets are beginning to sell many of these precut? The answer is that the quality of precut fruits and vegetables falls far short of what you can produce at home with your own two hands. One of the problems is that many precut vegetables are cut into a variety of sizes, which means that there are smaller pieces that will cook faster than the larger ones. When you cut the vegetable yourself, you are able to cut it into evenly sized pieces that will all cook at the same rate. The quality of the food you place on your table will improve with your knife skills. With a little hands-on practice, you will never even stop to consider these prepackaged bits. You'll soon even learn that they won't even provide a time savings. The problems with precut meats and fish are less than those with fruits and vegetables, but by learning some simple butchering techniques, you can improve the quality of the meat and fish you cook too.

With good knife skills, cooking becomes fun. Cutting carrots is no longer a chore, but a meditation. Slicing an onion no longer brings tears of anguish, but those of joy. Disjointing a chicken is no longer punishment, but pleasure. With good knife skills, preparing food becomes a time of great satisfaction indeed!

chapter 1
THE BASICS

INSIDE THIS CHAPTER

HOW KNIVES WORK

THE NEXT TIME YOU SIT DOWN FOR A MEAL AND PICK UP YOUR KNIFE AND FORK, think about how you use them. When there's a piece of meat or vegetable on your plate that needs cutting, do you push the knife cleanly through or saw back and forth? You probably saw back and forth. Most dinner knives are not particularly sharp, so you may switch over to a "steak knife" with a sharper blade. How do you use this sharper blade? You still saw back and forth. So why is it that when you pick up a chef's knife, you want to push the blade through the food without sawing back and forth? When cutting fruits and vegetables, the knife is almost always used with a back-and-forth motion. In rare instances, a small knife held with a couple of fingers wrapped around the blade is used without a sawing motion.

When the fine cutting edge of a knife comes in contact with a substantially less hard material, the very edge of the blade exerts an extremely high force on the softer material. This force is concentrated at the contact point, and the surface of the softer material is pierced. Once the surface gives way, the area immediately below it is exposed to this same force and it yields as well. As this effect cascades through the softer material, it parts along a plane, and what is referred to as a cut is made.

When the skin of a tomato meets the edge of a blade head-on, a substantial amount of force may be required to push the blade through the tomato without squashing it. But if the blade is moved back and forth across the skin, much less force is required. This is because the edge

of the blade, which appears to the eye to be smooth and sharp, is actually quite jagged when viewed on a microscopic level. This jaggedness greatly increases the force at the points of contact and the knife moves through the tomato with greater ease. This process is true for cutting all foods, not just tomatoes.

By cutting with a sawing motion, your knife will always work better and cutting will be easier.

KNIFE·ANATOMY

A STUDENT ONCE TOLD ME THAT A KNIFE HAS ONLY TWO PARTS: THE PART YOU HOLD and the part you don't. While there is an element of truth in that statement, describing a knife this way is like saying humans are simply featherless bipeds.

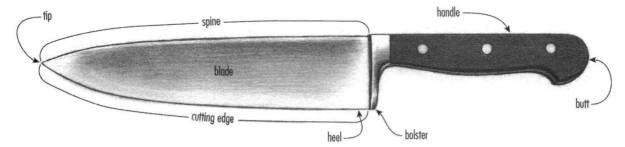

The blade of a knife, although it is a single piece of metal, has a number of components. The most important is the cutting edge, the portion of the blade that does the work. The actual configuration of the cutting edge may not be visible to the naked eye. There are a number of possible configurations, but the most common are the single bevel and the double bevel. The single bevel is as one might imagine—the metal is beveled an equal amount on both sides of the blade.

The total angle of the bevel on most commercially available knives is about 50 degrees. The smaller this angle is, the sharper the knife will be. But the smaller the included angle, the easier it is to damage the cutting edge. Manufacturers have settled on the value of 50 degrees as a good compromise between sharpness and durability, but the preferred included angle is actually about 40 degrees or less. Japanese sushi knives, which are beveled on only one side and designed only for right-handed use, often have an included angle of about 25 degrees. This form of bevel is sometimes called a chisel bevel. By grinding a double bevel on the edge of a knife, the manufacturer can produce a thinner overall blade while still having the angle at the very edge be about 50 degrees. In this instance, the overall bevel may be about 20 to 30 degrees, and the very edge is ground to the wider angle. The edges can also be ground to convex curves that form an angle that combines the advantages of the double bevel with a single smooth curved edge, but this type of edge is more difficult to sharpen. The majority of knives manufactured for kitchen use have a single bevel.

At the point of the blade where the two sides of the bevel meet, there is a microscopic piece of metal called a burr. The burr forms when a knife is sharpened, because the process pushes a small line of metal from the surface being ground just past the absolute edge. If no burr is raised during the sharpening process, the blade was probably not ground all the way to the edge. As the blade is ground first on one side, then the other,

KNIFE ANATOMY (*continued*)

the burr is pushed from one side to the other. Although it is unlikely that you can see the burr, it is always easy to feel with your fingers. When doing so, draw your finger or thumb across the edge of the blade moving away from the blade. Don't try to feel the burr by running your finger up and down the edge of the blade: that's called slicing, and it is not what you want to do! On a perfectly sharpened knife, the burr will feel equal on both sides.

All of the above refers mainly to knives with plain edges. Some knives have serrated cutting edges that make the knife resemble a saw. Serrated blades are best for cutting hard or hard-surfaced food, such as crusty breads, or crumbly foods, such a cake that is to be sliced horizontally. Serrated edges are usually ground only on one side of the blade, because it is difficult to grind the bevel on both sides of the blade so the points of the serration line up. Being ground on only one side means the blade will produce a curved cut in the direction opposite to the side with the serrations. Serrated blades will dull over time and need to be sharpened like any other knives.

wavy serrations   sawtooth-like serrations   grantons—not serrations

There are two types of serrated edges. The first has a wavy appearance and is found on both expensive and inexpensive knives. The second looks something like a saw and is commonly used for inexpensive knives. Knives with what are called grantons ground into the side of the blade near the cutting edge are not serrated knives. The grantons do not extend all the way to the cutting edge and do not affect the way the edge works. For more information on grantons, see page 19.

Three kinds of metal are used to make knife blades: carbon steel, stainless steel, and high-carbon stainless steel. Generally, carbon steel is harder than high-

carbon stainless steel, which, in turn, is harder than stainless steel. Why should you care? Because the harder the steel, the sharper the edge can be. Does that mean the best knives are made of carbon steel? Yes and no. Although carbon steel can be ground to a keener edge, a carbon-steel blade will oxidize easily even if the knife is washed and dried thoroughly and often. This is mainly a cosmetic issue—an oxidized blade looks dull and mottled—but the acids in foods corrode the cutting edge, dulling it and making sharpening difficult.

The inexpensive knives sold in the housewares section of your local supermarket are stainless steel. Plain stainless steel is the softest material used to make kitchen knives. When people began to replace their old carbon-steel knives in the 1950s with "modern" knives, they were made from stainless steel. But it is difficult to grind a sharp edge into this material and even more difficult to maintain the edge once obtained.

Today, good-quality knives are usually manufactured from high-carbon stainless steel. High-carbon stainless steel is a compromise material in that it doesn't oxidize like carbon steel, but it can be ground to a keener edge than plain stainless steel. In the kitchen, the edge will probably outlast one on a carbon-steel knife. There are a variety of different materials that different manufacturers use to "dope" the steel in order to obtain high-carbon stainless steel for producing their knives. There is also a series of manufacturing processes they run through to produce the final hardness. However, other than offering some fancy marketing terms, manufacturers do not provide much information that allows for comparison between the high-carbon stainless steels used by the different brands. This usually isn't a concern because in the hands of most people, the differences will be negligible. But how can you tell the difference between a stainless-steel blade and a high-carbon stainless-steel blade? With a magnet: a high-carbon stainless-steel blade is ferrous enough to hold a magnet whereas a plain stainless-steel blade is not.

One other material is now being used for knife blades—ceramic. These ceramics are not the same type used to produce dinner plates, but are very hard industrial ceramics, usually zirconium carbide and zirconium oxide, that can be fashioned into extremely thin, sharp blades. Ceramic knives are very light and a bit fragile. They do not like to be dropped on the counter or floor. If they do become dull, they require special sharpening equipment, so they are usually returned to the manufacturer for sharpening. Luckily, they hold their edge extremely well, so this is not often required. There are manufacturing limitations to the ceramic material, so these knives are not available with blades much longer than six inches.

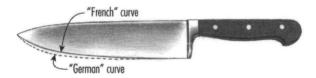

When large, commonly available knives such as ten-inch chef's knives are compared, it becomes apparent that the curvature of the cutting edge varies from manufacturer to manufacturer. French and Japanese knives tend to have less curvature than those manufactured in Germany or the United States. The straighter designs require less "rocking" of the blade when slicing to ensure good contact between the knife and the cutting board, so a straighter edge will result in less fatigue for the user and less strain on the wrist.

The blades of modern kitchen knives are made either by forging or by stamping. Forging was originally one way to increase the surface hardness of the metal. The forging process starts with a thick metal blank that is hammered with multiple dies to achieve its final shape—think of an old-time blacksmith hammering a piece of hot metal into shape. Today, with modern manufacturing methods, manufacturers are able to produce stamped blades with a surface hardness equivalent to that of forged blades. Stamped blades are cut from sheets of metal—think of using a cookie cutter on a sheet of dough. Although some people still insist that forged blades are better, there is scant evidence of that being the case.

Opposite the cutting edge of the knife blade is the spine. Although not as important as the cutting edge in the overall design of the knife, there are a couple of factors to consider. First, the weight of the blade is determined by the thickness of the spine; a thicker spine means a heavier blade. For some types of cutting, such as cutting through cartilage or thin bones, this may be desired, but a thicker blade can make it harder to slice hard foods, such as carrots, without causing the piece being cut to fracture. It is easier to cut thin, even slices from a potato with a thin blade than with a thick one.

The next consideration is whether the spine has a sharp, square edge near the handle or is rounded with the edges softened. This is more of a concern with large knives than small ones. When a knife is held properly, the base of your forefinger is wrapped around the spine. If the edges are sharp, a blister can quickly develop on your finger. Cooks who do a lot of knife work will develop a callus along the thumb side and near the base of the forefinger. Even a thick callus will not protect the cook from a spine with a sharp edge.

The tip of a knife can be described as the juncture of the spine and the cutting edge. Depending on the design and purpose of the knife, the tip may be pointed and sharp or rounded and dull. A sharp tip can be used for puncturing tough materials, such as the skin of some vegetables. It may also be used for cutting thin slices or strips from very thin items, as in cutting thin strips of dough.

Some knives have a series of shallow dimples running next to the cutting edge on each side of the blade. These dimples are called grantons. See the illustration on page 18. Their purpose is to reduce the resistance to movement felt as the knife saws through food. They are typically

KNIFE ANATOMY (*continued*)

found on slicing knives, but a few manufacturers are now making them part of chef's knives.

At the opposite end of the cutting edge from the tip is the heel of the knife. The heel is used mostly for heavy cutting, or when maximum leverage is needed. It is most efficient for making quick, coarse cuts and for jobs that require strength or pressure, such as slicing peppers. Additional force for cutting with the heel is sometimes applied with the palm of the other hand on the spine.

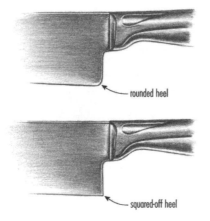

rounded heel

squared-off heel

On knives without a full bolster (see illustration on page 17), the cutting edge at the heel may end in a squared-off configuration. This is typical of many Japanese knives. The preferred configuration is one where the heel is rounded off because it is easy to inadvertently cut yourself on the sharp corner of a squared-off heel.

The bolster is a thickened portion of a knife blade of the place where it meets the handle. Bolsters are a feature of forged blades, where the manufacturing process starts with a thicker piece of metal than would be used for stamped blades. Because the bolster tends to extend down to the cutting edge, sharpening the cutting edge all the way to the end of the heel can be difficult. Some chefs believe that the bolster gives a knife better balance. I think a bolster just gets in the way. Although the bolster helps prevent the user's hand from slipping onto the blade, some knives without a bolster, especially those with molded handles, have a guard at the blade end of the handle that functions in a similar manner.

The part of the blade that extends into the handle is called the tang. Better-quality knives with riveted two-piece handles have a full-length tang that extends all the way to the end of the handle, or the butt. A full extension makes a better-balanced knife. For knives with molded handles, a round pointed rat-tail tang is used. It is contained within the handle and not visible as a riveted handle is.

Handles come in both natural materials, such as wood, and in molded materials, such as plastic. Some knives are now being manufactured with hollow metal handles, which are welded to the blade to give the appearance of the knife being made out of a single piece of metal. Although metal, these hollow handles are often lighter in the hand than their solid counterparts.

A KNIFE DIRECTORY

THE TWO KNIVES THAT EVERY COOK SHOULD OWN, AND THE ONLY TWO THAT ARE mostly used in the technique section of this book, are a chef's knife and a paring knife. A chef's knife, also sometimes called a cook's knife, is the workhorse of the kitchen. It can be used for almost any cutting purpose. This knife has a large blade that is both long and wide. It is almost always used for cutting against a board.

10-inch chef's knife

3½-inch paring knife

A long blade helps reduce the amount of wrist bending required for a particular cut. Slicing with a chef's knife combines moving the cutting edge to and

fro (sawing) and exerting minimal downward pressure. For many smaller vegetables, such as green onions, the tip of the blade is kept in contact with the cutting board for the entire cut while the handle end of the blade is moved up and down and to and fro. The up-and-down motion is accomplished by bending the wrist up and down. The to-and-fro motion is produced by moving the forearm. The two motions together produce the smooth moves of an accomplished cook.

A wide blade makes it easier to produce straight parallel cuts. It also makes it safer to cut following the techniques illustrated in this book since often the first segment of the forefinger is used as a guide for the blade to slide along. With a wide blade, there is both less chance of the cutting edge coming into contact with that finger and greater chance that the side of the blade will always be in contact with this guide finger.

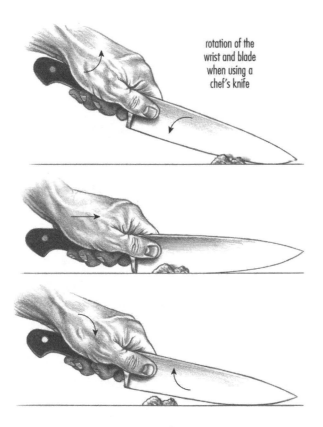

rotation of the wrist and blade when using a chef's knife

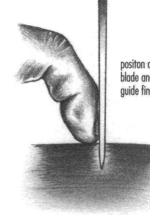

positon of blade and guide finger

A KNIFE DIRECTORY (*continued*)

And a wide blade allows for sufficient space between the fingers of the knife hand and the cutting board. With a narrow blade, the knuckles of your cutting hand will jam against the board during the cutting process because of insufficient space between the bottom of the handle and the cutting edge.

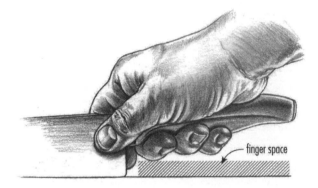

finger space

When choosing a chef's knife, it is important to "test-drive" it before purchase. At a minimum, hold it in your hand using the pinch grip (as described in the next section). Better still, simulate some cutting motions. Even better, cut a carrot or two. The knife should feel good in your hand. You should, of course, consider blade and handle material; blade size, shape, and configuration; spine width and blade length; and price; but feel is most important. If you have been using short-bladed knives all your life, a longer blade may not feel comfortable at first, but with practice, a chef's knife with a ten-inch or longer blade will allow you to achieve better and faster cuts than one with a shorter blade. Do be sure to check out the spine of the knife, where your forefinger will wrap around it. The edges of the spine should be quite smooth, to prevent your finger from blistering.

Recently some chefs have been switching from a chef's knife to a Chinese-style slicing cleaver or the Japanese-style *santoku*. I used a Chinese cleaver for twenty-five years before switching to a chef's knife, and I could do almost anything with it, but I find the extra length of a chef's knife helpful. With a longer blade, the wrist bends less, and so cutting is less tiring. Also, I am better able to achieve very fine, precise cuts with the chef's knife than I ever could with the cleaver. The *santoku* is like the Chinese slicing cleaver but has a narrower blade. This results in a lighter weight knife of the same blade length, but, again, I find the blade of the *santoku* too short for many cutting jobs.

I have found that most home cooks rely on an inexpensive, usually dull, paring knife. This is unfortunate, because after a chef's knife, a paring knife is the most important knife in the cook's arsenal. But whereas a long blade is important in a chef's knife, a short blade is optimal in a paring knife—the shorter, the better. While a paring knife is sometimes held with a pinch grip, it is more often held with one or two fingers wrapped around the blade, so only a little of the blade is exposed. And the shorter the blade, the easier it is to hold when cutting. The blade of a paring knife should be stiff, because the tip is often used laterally, as when peeling an onion or scraping the skin off a piece of ginger.

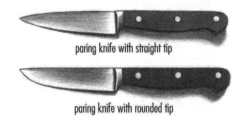

paring knife with straight tip

paring knife with rounded tip

The blade of a paring knife should have as straight a cutting edge as possible, as shown in the upper illustration. If the edge has a curve to it just before the tip, it will be necessary to use the curve, rather than the tip, to lift the skin from an onion. A straight tip can also be used for fine cutting against a board. When there is a curve near the tip, it is difficult to make tight curved cuts unless the blade is held at an elevated angle with respect to the board. The knife sold as a "fluter" actually has a better blade shape for a paring knife than the ones sold as paring knives!

bird's beak paring knife

There is a special type of paring knife called a bird's beak knife, named after the shape of the blade. This type of knife is useful for peeling shucked peas and beans, where the tip is used to pierce the skin. For turning vegetables into interesting shapes as used in classical French cooking, the curved cutting edge makes cutting curve shapes easier. However, it is of little use to the average cook. This type of knife fits best in the "seldom useful" category, whereas a standard paring knife is in the "most useful" category.

Note that with both the chef's knife and the paring knife, the shape of the handle is often of little importance, since with the proper grip, much of the knife hand is holding the blade and bolster, not the handle. As long as the portion of the handle held by the third, fourth, and fifth fingers feels comfortable, the rest of the handle is unimportant—except for its weight. The style of handle that feels right for a chef's knife may feel too heavy attached to a paring knife. Some manufacturers use nearly the same size handle on all blade configurations, but others adjust the handle size to match the blade. Choose each knife on its individual merits and consider what you will be using it for. Avoid knife sets. Don't be afraid to own knives with a variety of handle styles.

The next tier of knives, those that can be described as "often useful," include the slicer and the serrated utility knife. A slicer, sometimes called a carver or carving knife, is used for the slicing cooked meats such as a roasted turkey or ham. The blade is narrow, which reduces the amount of resistance between the blade and the food as the blade is moved to and fro. The narrower the blade, the less contact area and the less surface tension. A chef's knife can substitute for a slicer, but its wider blade produces more resistance. Slicers often have the large shallow dimples called grantons on the sides of the blade to further reduce resistance.

The blade of a slicer is long, to minimize the amount of sawing required when slicing. For best results, it should be at least one and a half times longer than the roast or cut of meat being sliced. When choosing a slicer, buy the longest blade you can find. When you hold it in your hand in the store, hold it like a chef's knife, with a pinch grip, not like a sword. Slicers are generally used to carve meat from a carcass or roast, not against a cutting board, so there isn't much need to test-drive this type of knife further than holding it to judge its balance.

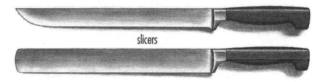

slicers

Some slicers have a pointed tip, like a chef's knife; others have a rounded tip. The ones with a rounded tip, sometimes referred to as ham slicers, have slightly more usable cutting edge, but the tip is less functional. A variation on a rounded-tip slicer, called a salmon slicer, is designed specifically for slicing large fillets of smoked fish into thin slices. The blade of a salmon slicer is much narrower and a bit more flexible than that of a standard rounded-tip slicer. But I have not found any advantage of the salmon slicer over a standard rounded-tip slicer with a granton edge and would categorize it as "rarely useful."

A serrated utility knife is sometimes called a bread knife because that seems to be its principal use, but it is also useful for cutting hard foods such as hard cheeses and for decapitating heads of garlic. A good serrated knife has a long blade because it is really just a cousin of the slicer. A good serrated knife has serrations on

A KNIFE DIRECTORY (*continued*)

both sides of the cutting edge. If the blade is only serrated on one side, it will have a tendency to produce a curved cut when slicing through thick objects. Even though the serrations help when cutting through hard-food items, the blade should be as sharp as possible. Serrated knives do not have to be sharpened as often as other knives, but they do need periodic sharpening. There is a short variation on the serrated utility knife called a tomato slicer, but a sharp chef's knife will cut a tomato, even a soft ripe one, much better than one of these knives. The tomato slicer is marketed to people who don't have a sharp slicer or chef's knife. Place it in the "rarely useful" category.

serrated utility knife

Another knife that is commonly recommended by cooking instructors, but that I find seldom useful, is the boning knife. Most people buy their meat ready to cook and have little need for this knife. But if you spend your spare time dissecting sides of beef, or even occasionally remove the chine bone from a rack of lamb, then a boning knife is a must. A boning knife with a longer blade will provide better reach into a carcass than one with a short blade. Some boning knives have very flexible blades, to make it easier to cut along a bone, but I have never found the increased flexibility to be an advantage. I can bone a whole chicken more quickly and with greater safety with a sharp 3-inch-long paring knife than with an 8-inch-long flexible boning knife.

If you fillet your own fish, a filleting knife moves from the "rarely useful" category to the "often useful" category. A filleting knife is essentially a slicer with a somewhat flexible blade. Some manufacturers produce a filleting knife that has a narrower blade than a slicer of the same length, which improves the knife's performance by reducing drag.

Knife manufacturers also sell a lot of another "seldom useful" knife called a utility knife. Really slicers in miniature, these are popular with people who are afraid of knives with a large blade but realize that they need something bigger than a paring knife. However, any job that can be done with a utility knife can be accomplished with a chef's knife.

If you purchased one each of the complete range of knives that one popular German manufacturer produces in a single handle style, you'd be the proud owner of fifty-three knives. Each knife pattern comes with a variety of different blade lengths. And some patterns are available in multiple flexibilities, or blade thicknesses, or cutting-edge configurations (serrated or plain). But with a few knife skills under your belt, you'll have no need for a large variety of knives—all you need are the chef's knife and paring knife.

When browsing through the knife selection at your local cooking store, you'll also see a variety of other tools in the same display case. There are usually a couple of heavy-bladed cleavers, used for chopping through bone. If you plan to do some butchering, a large one can be very helpful. You'll also find that there is a whole world of butchering knives and accessories made specially for the purpose.

There will also generally be two types of forks on display. A fork with two straight tines is popular with old-time French chefs for turning items in a frying pan. Although it can also be helpful for forming long pasta shapes into "nests" for serving, most people find a pair of cheap tongs more useful than one of these forks. The other type of fork has curved tines and is used to stabilize a piece of meat when carving. If you purchase a slicer and plan to carve the Thanksgiving turkey at the table, buy one of these.

Some knife manufacturers also produce very sharp heavy-duty scissors. These can be very helpful for various tasks in the kitchen. I've even used them for trimming excess skin from boned-out quail breasts—something one does every day! But for heavy-duty cutting of things not best cut with a knife, they can be very helpful, and they are not too expensive. Do use them with respect— I've cut myself with these scissors more than I have with my large chef's knife!

The last item in the display case is usually a steel, in one or more styles. These will be discussed in detail in "Keeping Knives Sharp."

Knife preference is a very personal thing. Test-drive a number of knives before deciding which to buy. Don't be persuaded by special sales or your neighbor's opinion. And select each knife individually: it may turn out that all your knives are from the same manufacturer, or it may not.

EVALUATING KNIVES

Most Useful	Often Useful	Seldom Useful	Rarely Useful
• Chef's knife (8 inches or longer) • Paring knife	• Serrated utility knife (8 inches or longer) • Slicer	• Boning knife • Bird's beak knife • Chef's knife (shorter than 8 inches) • Nonserrated utility knife • Serrated utility knife (shorter than 8 inches)	• Fish filleting knife • Salmon slicer • Tomato slicer

HOW TO HOLD A KNIFE

THE PROPER WAY TO HOLD MOST KNIVES is with a "pinch grip." Pinch the blade just in front of the handle with your thumb and forefinger. Wrap your other three fingers around the handle. Use this grip whether you are cutting perpendicular to, at an angle, or parallel to the cutting board. The pinch grip works both with large and small knives. Any time you are cutting toward a bone, use a pinch grip. Don't hold the knife like a sword, and never place your forefinger on top of the spine.

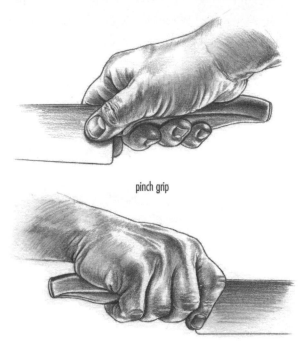

pinch grip

edge directed toward your thumb. The movement of the blade is limited by the ability of your palm to flex. With this "choke grip," only a small portion of the blade is exposed to the food.

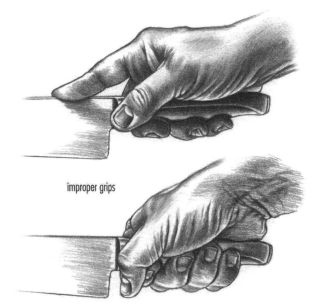

improper grips

When you use a paring knife for peeling an onion or removing the germ from a clove of garlic, hold the knife with your forefinger, and maybe your middle finger, wrapped around the spine of the blade, with the cutting

choke grip

How you stand is almost as important as how you hold the knife. Stand with your weight equally divided between each leg, your back straight, knees slightly bent, and your hips parallel to the cutting board. When cutting on the board, the knife axis should be at an angle of about 45 degrees to your body. The knife should act as an extension of your cutting arm, which should be rotated out about 45 degrees from your body. The same is true for the hand and arm you are using to hold the food being cut. You should wear a good, comfortable pair of shoes with plenty of support. If you stand in this manner, you can do so for hours at a time without pain or stiffness.

If you need to move through kitchen with a knife in hand, always hold it with the tip pointed down and the cutting edge to the rear. And if you drop a knife, never try to catch it.

CARING FOR KNIVES

GOOD KNIVES ARE AN INVESTMENT THAT CAN LAST YOUR ENTIRE LIFE IF YOU CARE for them properly, or can be ruined in a few days if you don't. The cutting edge of any knife can easily be damaged. It should only come in contact with food and the cutting board. When you are not using your knives for a moment during prep, lay them on their sides in a single layer next to or on your cutting board.

Keep a damp kitchen towel next to your cutting board to wipe any food from the blade after each item is cut. Fold the towel into a six- to eight-inch square and hold it flat in the palm of your non-knife hand. Place the knife so its spine is in the center of the towel, fold the towel over the blade so the spine is in the crease of the towel and the cutting edge is pointed away from your hand, and wipe the blade clean.

If there is fat on the blade, you will need to clean the blade under hot running water. Use a sponge folded in the same manner as the towel to wipe the blade. With sufficiently hot water, soap should not be necessary. You can also use a soft nylon brush with a little soap, but never use cleaning abrasives (such as steel wool or Scotch-Brite) on a knife, especially the cutting edge. Dry the blade thoroughly with a clean towel folded as described above.

When you have finished cutting, clean each knife as described above and put it away. Never set a knife with other dirty utensils for cleaning later, and never leave a knife in a dishpan full of soap—someone else may put their hands in the water and be cut. Never place a good knife in a dishwasher, even if the manufacturer claims that it is "dishwasher safe."

When storing knives, do so in a way that both shields the cutting edges from damage and protects anyone from the cutting edges. Restaurants often store knives on a magnetic strip mounted on the wall behind the prep table. These magnetic strips are also available for home use. They work with any carbon-steel blade or high-carbon stainless steel blade. Ordinary stainless steel blades lack sufficient iron to hold to a magnetic surface. Ceramic blades, of course, do not work with magnets.

The wooden storage blocks that many manufacturers sell with their knives are adequate, but they have some limitations. Most blocks will not hold a blade longer than eight inches, so if your blade is longer, the tip jams against the wood in the bottom of the storage slot; this can damage the tip. Although wood is not nearly as rough on the cutting edge as metal would be, knives stored in vertical slots should be inserted with their cutting edges up so the blade rests on its spine.

Wooden drawer inserts allow knives to be placed in a drawer side by side. These inserts have many advantages. They keep the knives off the counter and protected from one another, but they are still easily accessible. The drawbacks to such inserts are that the knives must stored on their cutting edges and that they require a fair amount of drawer space.

There are also inexpensive plastic sleeves that slide over the cutting edge of a knife blade for storage. You can then store a number of knives in a drawer without the edges becoming damaged. Even so, I still recommend that knives be placed only with other knives, not dumped in with other kitchen gadgets in a utility drawer. If you do not have a separate drawer for knives, use a long plastic tray in your drawer to separate the knives from the other tools. I have two such trays, a long one for big knives and a short one for small knives. As an alternative to a plastic sleeve, you can use the cardboard sleeve provided with some knives, but these sleeves will wear out. Whether cardboard or plastic, the sleeve should fit snugly on the blade.

KEEPING KNIVES SHARP

THE CUTTING EDGE ON EVEN THE MOST WELL-MADE knife is not permanent. If you hold a knife properly, give it gentle care, and store it so the blade is protected, the cutting edge still seems to dull with only a little use. Actually, though, with such care, the knife probably isn't dull. The fine burr at the tip of the cutting edge has rolled over the edge, and once it is straightened, the knife will seem sharp again. The process of straightening the burr is called honing.

rolled-over burr on knife edge

In the kitchen, honing is done with a steel. A steel is a metal rod with a handle. Although these are sometimes called sharpening steels, they do not sharpen the cutting edge, because they do not remove any metal—they simply straighten the burr. Steels are made from steel that is harder than the steel used in knife blades. A traditional steel is a round rod with shallow grooves running along its length. Some steels have a flattened cross section. The grooves are ground into the surface in a cross-hatch (diamond) pattern, so these are sometimes called diamond steels. There are also steels coated with industrial diamond dust that, in theory, remove some of the burr while it is being straightened. There are also "steels" made with finely ground ceramic rods.

No matter what type of steel you have, they are all used in the same manner. To straighten the burr on an edge, draw the cutting edge across the steel with the blade held at about a 30-degree angle to the steel. The angle will be 30 degrees if the distance from the spine to the steel is half the distance of that from the spine to the cutting edge.

There are three principal methods of steeling. My preferred method is with the steel held in your non-knife hand, pointed away from your body horizontally and about 45 degrees from being parallel with your shoulders. The knife is held in a pinch grip, with the cutting edge directed toward your body. Starting with the heel of the blade near the tip of the steel, the cutting edge is drawn across the steel while holding the blade at a 30-degree angle to the steel; the blade is moved down the steel so that by the time the tip is drawn across the steel, it is near the handle of the steel. The sides of the cutting edge are steeled alternately, and the process is repeated three to five times. With this technique, the steel will tend to point slightly upward when the blade is on the bottom and slightly downward when the blade is on the top; your wrists will flex and your forearms will rotate to adjust the angle. Even though the cutting edge of the blade is pointing at your belly, the hilt of the steel will protect your body from injury should the knife slip. If your knife has a full bolster, one that extends all the way from the spine to the edge, you will not be able to steel the full heel of the blade.

Some people recommend a variation on the above method, with the cutting edge directed away from the body. I don't like this method, because it is harder to hold the cutting edge at the equivalent angle when switching from one side of the blade to the other. For this method, most of the flexing and rotating is done with the hand holding the knife in an awkward manner.

Yet another variation is to hold the steel vertically with the tip against the work surface. The blade is drawn across the steel with the cutting edge pointed down, switching from side to side after each pass. Again, it is difficult to maintain the same angle on both sides of the blade.

The second and third methods are often suggested by teachers and manufacturers to alleviate your fears of steeling with the blade toward your body. (It is also an attempt to limit their liability.) But it generally does not work as well as the first method.

Some knife manufacturers sell V-shaped devices or little sets of wheels that allow you to steel a blade without having to worry about the angle of the blade. Some of these work better than others. Some are called sharpeners, but, as described above, they only align the burr. If you find one that works for you, great. As with regular steels, if your knife has a full bolster, these devices will not straighten the burr along the entire heel.

How often should you steel your knife? Daily? Hourly? Every two minutes? It all depends on how often you use your knife. Chefs traditionally steel their knives before each use. They then steel the knife again as soon as it begins to feel the least bit dull, which, depending on what is being cut, may be quite often.

Does only a chef's knife need to be steeled? No. All knives except those with serrated blades should be steeled before use. Even your smallest paring knife.

Even if you steel your knives often, you will sooner or later notice that they don't cut as easily as they did when they were new. All knives will eventually dull from use. When this happens, it's time to sharpen your knives. The difference between steeling and sharpening a knife is that steeling only straightens the burr and sharpening actually removes metal from the cutting edge and, in doing so, creates a new burr. After sharpening, a knife should be steeled before use.

Sharpening a knife can be a do-it-yourself project or something you pay an outside service to do. Many chefs believe that only a professional knife sharpener can really do a good job. Finding a truly good professional knife sharpener may be a challenge. Just because someone charges you to sharpen your knives doesn't mean that they are good at it. Many cookware stores offer a knife-sharpening service, but they just pass your knives through a machine without any thought. Knife sharpening is an art. Professional knife sharpeners will use motorized grinders to sharpen your knives. These devices require skill and experience. Ask a local chef or your butcher who sharpens their knives. They have probably tried various services before settling on one.

If you decide that you want to sharpen your knives yourself, there are many methods and tools available. These range from simple sharpening stones to elaborate mechanical contrivances to machines. Whatever method you choose, be sure that it has the ability to grind the blade in varying degrees of coarseness. A damaged blade may require grinding a fair amount of metal. Usually, though, only a touch-up is required. That is done with a very fine, almost smooth grinder that removes very little metal. When purchasing a system, be sure that it is designed to work with your specific knives and that it comes with detailed instructions. Some systems require drawing the blade through a guide, and this may not be possible with a knife that has a full bolster. Others don't work well with short blades. Most cannot do serrated blades, which are best left to the professionals.

KEEPING KNIVES SHARP (*continued*)

My preferred sharpening device is an electric one that has three distinct grinding wheels. The wheels range in coarseness from medium to very fine. Unless the cutting edge is damaged, I usually only need to use the fine and very fine wheels. The machine has guides so the blade is held at the proper angle with respect to the grinding wheel. To use the machine, you draw the blade through a slot in the top of the machine, alternating between either side of the grinding wheel being used.

CUTTING BOARDS

THE MOST CONTROVERSIAL ASPECT OF "KNIFEOLOGY" MAY NOT BE WHICH KNIVES to buy or how to cut with them, but which cutting board to use and how to clean it. When I worked at the Michelin-starred restaurant Le Château d'Amondans in France, we had both wood and plastic cutting boards. We usually used the wooden boards, but whenever one particular health inspector arrived at the front door, we would scurry around to hide the wooden boards and set out the plastic boards. Another inspector rejected the plastic boards and demanded wooden ones. (A third didn't care which board we used but demanded that everyone wear a hat—which we did until she left the building.)

From the standpoint of cutting without damaging the blade of the knife, a wood cutting board made of medium to hard end grain is the best. With an end-grain board, you can see part of the rings of the tree from which the wood was cut. The end grain is easier on the cutting edge than a side grain so your knife will not dull as fast. Boards made from end grain are usually thicker and more expensive than others. Because end-grain boards are usually made from pieces of wood glued together, they are more susceptible to breaking if bumped or dropped. Side-grain boards may begin to chip after extensive use.

The minimum size for a board should be about 18 inches long by 12 inches wide by 1½ inches thick; it should be large enough to easily hold the items you will be cutting without crowding. The board should be heavy enough so it doesn't slide on the work surface. If it does, lay a damp towel flat underneath the board so it won't slide or rock. After each use, wooden boards need to be washed and then set out to dry. They should never be stored wet.

The alternatives to wooden boards are plastic boards made from high-density polyethylene. Like wooden boards, these should be heavy enough so they will not easily shift on the work surface, and they must be anchored with a damp towel. Avoid thin plastic boards or sheets; they move during cutting and rarely sit flat. If a plastic board warps, replace it. I have not read any studies on the effects of plastic boards on a cutting edge, but my sense is that knives dull faster on plastic boards. Plastic boards seem to scratch faster and deeper than wooden boards after heavy use, and they also can stain.

Some health departments require professional food preparers to have separate cutting boards for poultry, meat, fish, and vegetables. They may require that these boards be made of plastic and be color-coded. Their reasoning is that using different boards will prevent cross contamination and that wood cannot be sufficiently cleaned. Neither of these beliefs have been borne out by any studies that I have found. The Hospitality Institute of Technology and Management studied the microbiology of cleaning and sanitizing a cutting board, and their conclusion was that wood and

CUTTING BOARDS (*continued*)

plastic boards could be cleaned equally well.[1] They wrote: "Simply scrubbing the cutting board in flowing water, without the use of a detergent, reduced the bacteria enough that even if there were a heavy load of *Salmonella*, *Campylobacter jejuni*, or other pathogens, there would be so few pathogens remaining that the surface would be considered safe."

I have been using the same cutting board for the last thirty years. It's four-inch-thick stump of wood, typical of what you can see in many Chinese restaurants. The surface is becoming slightly concave from years of use, but it still works great. I clean it only with hot tap water. If some fat has stuck to the surface, I use a nylon brush along with the hot water to scrub the board. After washing, I use my hand to slide any residual water off the surface. I then set it aside to air dry. Over the years, the surface has become so impervious to contamination that even beets fail to stain it.

[1] O. Peter Synder, *The Microbiology of Cleaning and Sanitizing a Cutting Board,* Hospitality Institute of Technology and Management, St. Paul, MN, 1997.

SLICING, CHOPPING, DICING, AND MINCING

P RACTICALLY EVERY RECIPE YOU READ CALLS FOR FOOD TO BE SLICED, CHOPPED, diced, or minced, but what do these terms mean? Each has a general meaning that most people seem to understand instinctively, even if they don't cook often. But many recipes provide little precise information on how thick to slice, how coarse to chop, how large to dice, or how fine to mince. Even if a recipe says, "Cut into thick slices," you don't know how thick to make the slice.

According to American Culinary Federation guidelines, large dice means a ¾-inch cube, medium dice means a ½-inch cube, and small dice means a ¼-inch cube. A *brunoise* means a ⅛-inch cube, and a fine *brunoise* means a ¹⁄₁₆-inch cube. A *bâtonnet* means a ¼-inch-square by 2-inch-long strip, a julienne means a ⅛-inch square by 2-inch-long strip, and a fine julienne means a ¹⁄₁₆-inch square by 2-inch-long strip. When was the last time you saw a recipe call for carrots to be cut into *bâtonnets*? And I do not recall ever knowing a chef who followed these guidelines.

What should you do if the recipe author doesn't provide a dimension for how coarse you should chop and how fine you should mince? Look through the recipe to for clues. It is often preferable for all the ingredients of a recipe to be cut into similar shapes and sizes. It may primarily be my sense of aesthetics, but I believe that uniformity is very important when cutting either a single ingredient or a group of

ingredients. The finished product generally is more attractive if its elements are uniformly cut. And, if all the pieces of an ingredient are the same size, they will cook at the same rate and be done at the same time. If such uniformity makes sense for the recipe, do it. Is the ingredient quickly cooked or slow-cooked over many hours? Quick cooking requires smaller pieces than slow cooking. Is the ingredient used for flavoring and then discarded before serving, as in the case of onions or carrots, for example, in a broth? If so, it can be cut larger and uniformity is probably not required. Is the ingredient used for a decoration or garnish? If so, it should be cut very evenly and probably quite small.

If, on the other hand, the author provides detailed instructions with dimensions, be sure you really know how large an eighth of an inch is. (Assuming, of course, that the author's measurement guidelines are accurate.) A small ruler is a very helpful kitchen gadget.

chapter 2

VEGETABLES & FRUITS

INSIDE THIS CHAPTER

CUTTING ONIONS

THE ONION IS USED IN ALMOST ALL CULTURES. READILY AVAILABLE THE YEAR round, it is inexpensive and versatile. Even though it doesn't cost much, it's a shame that many people waste so much of it when they cut it. The instructions here will help you to maximize the yield from every onion you use.

When dicing an onion, because of its structure, it is impossible to produce uniform cubes. The thickness of an onion's layers partially determine the size of the dice. The skill to be learned here is how to cut an onion so the results appear uniform.

The following section describes two methods for slicing onions. The usual way is to cut the onion crosswise into rounds or half rounds. This technique produces slices of varying size. A superior method is to cut the onion lengthwise from root to stem, which produces slices that appear more uniform. This is sometimes referred to as shredding.

CUTTING ONIONS (*right-hand version*)

Trimming the Root

Hold the onion firmly in your left hand and a sharp paring knife in your right hand, with your forefinger wrapped around the blade. Support your knife hand by resting your right thumb firmly against the side of the onion (1). Cut the tendril-like portion of the root from the onion: using a slight sawing motion, make the cut at the juncture of the skin and the root so that the skin remains intact

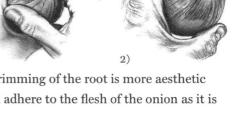

1)   2)

and the root is cut flush with the surface of the onion (2). The reason for trimming of the root is more aesthetic than practical, but sometimes, if it is not trimmed, loose pieces of root will adhere to the flesh of the onion as it is being sliced or diced.

Trimming the Stem

In the same manner, slice off the stem end, removing only the tiniest amount of flesh so there is minimal waste.

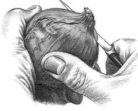

Splitting an Onion

If the onion is not going to be used whole, hold it firmly on a cutting board with the root end up. Using a chef's knife held with a pinch grip, cut the onion in half through the center of the root. If you cut from the stem end, there is a chance that your knife will not travel through the center of the root, and there will be insufficient root remaining on one of the halves to hold it together during subsequent steps.

Peeling an Onion

Hold a half from the previous step firmly in your left hand and hold a sharp paring knife in your right hand, with your forefinger and middle finger wrapped around the blade. With the flat side of the onion toward your knife hand, slide the tip of the blade just under the skin at its edge. With your thumb, hold the skin firmly against the flat side of the blade, near the tip, and pull the skin down toward the root of the onion so it breaks off at the root. Discard the section of skin. Continue removing the skin in strips around the onion half, each time turning the onion toward the knife so a new section of skin is exposed.

CUTTING ONIONS (*right-hand version continued*)

Slicing Half an Onion into Half Rounds

Place a peeled onion half, cut side down, on the cutting board so that the root end is toward the left. Hold the onion with your left hand, with your fingertips pressing straight down toward the board. Position a chef's knife, held with a pinch grip, with the side of the blade against the flat side of the tip of your left forefinger. This way, your forefinger serves as a guide for the knife. Start each slice with the tip of the blade resting on, or near, the cutting board, with the handle angled up. As you bring the knife down, slide it forward through the onion to produce the slice. After each cut, shift your forefinger to the left a distance equal to the desired thickness of the next slice. It is important that the side of the blade always remain in contact with the flat surface of your forefinger.

In this way, onions can be sliced very quickly. There is, however, a better way to slice them if you want all the pieces to be similar in size. This first method produces half rings with blunt ends. With practice, the second method can produce a very nice result almost as quickly.

Slicing Half an Onion into Shreds

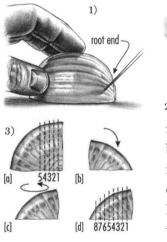

Place a peeled onion half on a cutting board with the cut side down and the root end toward your right. Hold the onion firmly with your left hand. Using a chef's knife held in a pinch grip, make a downward cut at a 45-degree angle to remove the root section; begin by cutting just above the edge of the root (1). Then turn the onion 90 degrees and cut the half into two quarters, from root to stem (2). Next, working with each quarter separately, place it on the board so one side is to your right. Make successive slices, as indicated by the numbers in (3a) in the illustration, until you have cut about half of the quarter. The number of cuts will vary depending on the size of the onion and the thickness of the slices. Next, lay the remaining portion of the quarter over on the board as indicated in (3b). Turn the onion around so that the other cut side is to your right, as indicated in (3c), and continue to slice until the onion is entirely cut, as in (3d).

Dicing an Onion, The Traditional Method

The following paragraphs describe three methods for dicing onions. The first is the most common method. It starts with making either a series of parallel, evenly spaced horizontal cuts, followed by a similar series of vertical cuts, as indicated in (1) in the illustration, or a series of parallel,

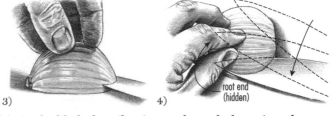

evenly spaced vertical cuts, followed by a similar series of horizontal cuts, as indicated in (2). The numbers represent the order of the cuts.

To make the horizontal cuts, place the onion half near the edge of the cutting board, with the root end toward your left, and press the fingertips of your left hand against the the top to hold it. Hold the chef's knife with a pinch grip in your right hand, with the blade parallel to the board, and draw the blade through the onion in

an arc toward you so the tip passes just short of the root (3). As the blade describes its arc through the onion, the handle stays in about the same position and only the blade tip moves (4). Repeat this process, moving through the onion, until you have made the desired number of horizontal slices.

Next, make the vertical cuts through the onion half. Keep the root toward your left hand, and hold the onion on both sides with that hand. Push the tip of the chef's knife down through the onion at a point just short of the root end and draw the blade out toward your knife hand. DO NOT cut through the root, which would cause the onion to fragment into pieces (5).

Finally, rotate the onion 90 degrees away from you with the root still to your left. Make successive vertical cuts across the cuts to create the individual cubes. Hold the onion firmly with your left hand, with your thumb and little or ring finger holding the sides and your middle fingers on the top of the onion, pressing straight down toward the cutting board. For each slice, rest the flat of the knife blade, held with a pinch grip, against the flat side of your forefinger. This way, your forefinger serves as a guide for

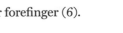

the knife. Start each slice with the tip of the blade in contact with, or near, the board, and the handle angled up. As you bring the knife down, also move it slightly forward so the edge of the blade moves easily through the onion as the slice is being made. After each cut, move your forefinger to the left a distance equal to the desired thickness of the next slice. It is important that the flat of the blade always remain in contact with the flat surface of your forefinger (6).

When there is too little onion left to slice, flip the piece over so the just-cut surface is against the cutting board, and trim the remainder into similar-size dice until only the root remains. This minimizes waste (7).

CUTTING ONIONS (*right-hand version continued*)

Dicing an Onion, The Fan Method

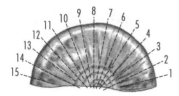

The second method of dicing the onion substitutes a fan-shape pattern of cuts for the initial horizontal and vertical cuts of the first method. Rather than making a series of horizontal cuts followed by a series of vertical cuts, you make one series of cuts by rotating the angle of the knife blade from almost parallel to the cutting board on one side (cut number 1 in the illustration) to almost parallel to the board on the other side (cut number 15). As you make the series of cuts, you alternate the depth of the cuts so some of them go all the way through the onion and some go only partway. The root end still should be toward your left hand, which holds the onion from the sides. Push the tip of the chef's knife through the onion near the root end and drawn it the blade straight out toward your knife hand. DO NOT cut through the root, which would cause the onion to fragment into pieces. After you've made all the cuts, rotate the onion 90 degrees, so the root is still to your left, and make successive crosswise cuts to separate the cubes, as in the first method.

Dicing Less Than Half an Onion

The third method is appropriate when you need to dice less than half an onion. It is also effective when a recipe calls for a very fine dice. Place an onion half on a cutting board cut side down and with the root end toward your left. Hold the onion firmly with your left hand, with your fingertips positioned straight down toward the cutting board. Position a chef's knife, held with a pinch grip, so the flat of the blade is against the flat side of the tip of your forefinger. This way, your forefinger serves as a guide for the knife. Start each slice with the tip of the blade in contact with, or near, the cutting board and the handle angled up. As you bring the knife down, also move it slightly forward so the edge of the blade moves easily through the onion as the slice is being made. It's important that the flat of the blade always remain in contact with the flat surface of your forefinger. When the knife is partway through the onion, move your forefinger over the spine of the knife to hold the newly cut slice in place. For this method to work well, it is important that the slices remain intact and in position. After each cut, move your forefinger to the left a distance equal to the desired thickness of the next slice. Cut only as many slices as you need (1).

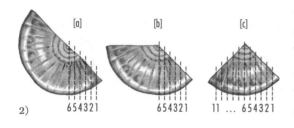

Carefully lay the slices flat on the cutting board, with the smaller slices on top of the larger ones and positioned as shown in (2a). Working from right to left, make successive parallel cuts with the chef's knife until you reach the center of the straight portion of the onion slices. Rotate the onion slices to the right and make another series of cuts from right to left (2b). Rotate the remaining onion slices again and make a final series of cuts (2c).

CUTTING ONIONS (*left-hand version*)

Trimming the Root

Hold the onion firmly in your right hand and a sharp paring knife in your left hand, with your forefinger wrapped around the blade. Support your knife hand by resting your left thumb firmly against the side of the onion (1). Cut the tendril-like portion of the root from the onion: using a slight sawing motion, make the cut at the juncture of the skin and the root so that the skin remains intact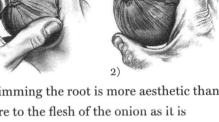

1)   2)

and the root is cut flush with the surface of the onion (2). The reason for trimming the root is more aesthetic than practical, but sometimes, if it is not trimmed, loose pieces of root will adhere to the flesh of the onion as it is being sliced or diced.

Trimming the Stem

In the same manner, slice off the stem end, removing only the tiniest amount of flesh so there is minimal waste.

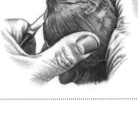

Splitting an Onion

If the onion is not going to be used whole, hold it firmly on a cutting board with the root end up. Using a chef's knife held with a pinch grip, cut the onion in half through the center of the root. If you cut from the stem end, there is a chance that your knife will not travel through the center of the root, and there will be insufficient root remaining on one of the halves to hold it together during subsequent steps.

Peeling an Onion

Hold a half from the previous step firmly in your right hand and hold a sharp paring knife in your left hand, with your forefinger and middle finger wrapped around the blade. With the flat side of the onion toward your knife hand, slide the tip of the blade just under the skin at its edge. With your thumb, hold the skin firmly against the flat side of the blade, near the tip, and pull the skin down toward the root of the onion so it breaks off at the root. Discard the section of skin. Continue removing the skin in strips around the onion half, each time turning the onion toward the knife so a new section of the skin is exposed.

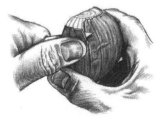

CUTTING ONIONS (*left-hand version continued*)

Slicing Half an Onion into Half Rounds

Place a peeled onion half, cut side down, on the cutting board so that the root end is toward the right. Hold the onion with your right hand, with your fingertips pressing straight down toward the board. Position a chef's knife, held with a pinch grip, with the side of the blade against the side of the tip of your right forefinger. This way, your forefinger serves as a guide for the knife. Start each slice with the tip of the blade resting on, or near, the cutting board, with the handle angled up. As you bring the knife down, slide it forward through the onion to produce the slice. After each cut, shift your forefinger to the right a distance equal to the desired thickness of the next slice. It is important that the side of the blade always remains in contact with the surface of your forefinger.

In this way, onions can be sliced very quickly. There is, however, a better way to slice them if you want all the pieces to be similar in size. This first method produces half rings with blunt ends. With practice, the second method can produce a very nice result almost as quickly.

Slicing Half an Onion into Shreds

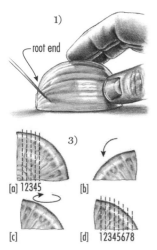

Place a peeled onion half on a cutting board with the cut side down and the root end toward your left. Hold the onion firmly with your right hand. Using a chef's knife held in a pinch grip, make a downward cut at a 45-degree angle to remove the root section; begin by cutting just above the edge of the root (1). Then turn the onion 90 degrees and cut the half into two quarters from root to stem (2). Next, working with each quarter separately, place it on the board so one cut side is to your left. Make successive slices, as indicated by the numbers in (3a) in the illustration, until you have cut about half of the quarter. The number of cuts will vary depending on to the size of the onion and the thickness of the slices. Next, lay the remaining portion of the quarter on the board as indicated in (3b). Turn the onion around so that the other cut side is to your left, as indicated in (3c), and continue to slice until the onion is entirely cut, as in (3d).

Dicing an Onion, The Traditional Method

The following paragraphs describe three methods for dicing onions. The first is the most common method. It starts with making either a series of parallel, evenly spaced horizontal cuts, followed by a similar series of vertical cuts, as indicated in (1) in the illustration, or a series of parallel, evenly spaced vertical cuts, followed by a similar series of horizontal cuts, as indicated by (2). The numbers represent the order of the cuts.

To make the horizontal cuts, place the onion half near the edge of the cutting board, with the root end toward your right, and press the fingertips of your right hand against the top to hold it. Hold the chef's knife with a pinch grip in your left hand, with the blade parallel to the board, and draw the blade

through the onion in an arc toward you so the tip passes just short of the root (3). As the blade describes its arc through the onion, the handle stays in about the same position and only the blade tip moves (4). Repeat this process, moving up through the onion, until you have made the desired number of horizontal slices.

Next, make the vertical cuts through the onion half. Keep the root toward your right hand, and hold the onion on both sides with that hand. Push the tip of the knife down through the onion at a point just short of the root end and draw the blade out toward your knife hand. DO NOT cut through the root, which would cause the onion to fragment into pieces (5).

Finally, rotate the onion 90 degrees away from you with the root still to your right. Make successive vertical cuts across the cuts just to create the individual cubes. Hold the onion firmly with your right hand, with your thumb and little or ring finger holding the sides and your middle fingers on the top of the onion pressing straight down toward the cutting board. For each slice, rest the flat of the knife blade, held with a pinch grip, against the flat side of your forefinger. This way, your forefinger serves as a guide for the

knife. Start each slice with the tip of the blade in contact with, or near, the board, with the handle angled up. As you bring the knife down, also move it slightly forward so the edge of the blade moves easily through the onion as the slice is being made. After each cut, move your forefinger to the right a distance equal to the desired thickness of the next slice. It is important that the flat of the blade always remain in contact with the flat surface of your forefinger (6).

When there is too little onion right to slice, flip the piece over so the just-cut surface is against the cutting board, and trim the remainder into similar-size dice until only the root remains. This minimizes waste (7).

CUTTING ONIONS (*left-hand version continued*)

Dicing an Onion, The Fan Method

The second method of dicing the onion substitutes a fan-shape pattern of cuts for the initial horizontal and vertical cuts of the first method. Rather than making a series of horizontal cuts followed by a series of vertical cuts, you make one series of cuts by rotating the angle of the knife blade from almost parallel to the cutting board on one side (cut number 1 in the illustration) to almost parallel to the board on the other side (cut number 15). As you make the series of cuts, you alternate the depth of the cuts so some of them go all the way through the onion and some go only partway. The root end should still be toward your right hand, which holds the onion from the sides. Push the tip of the chef's knife through the onion near the root end and draw the blade straight out toward your knife hand. DO NOT cut through the root, which would cause the onion to fragment into pieces. After you've made all the cuts, rotate the onion 90 degrees, so the root is still to your right, and make successive crosswise cuts to separate the cubes in the first method.

Dicing Less Than Half an Onion

The third method is appropriate when you need to dice less than half an onion. It is also effective when a recipe calls for a very fine dice. Place an onion half on a cutting board cut side down and with the root end toward your right. Hold the onion firmly with your right hand, with your fingertips positioned straight down toward the cutting board. Position a chef's knife, held with a pinch grip, so the flat of the blade is against the flat side of the tip of your forefinger. This way your forefinger serves as a guide for the knife.

1) Start each slice with the tip of the blade in contact with, or near, the cutting board, with the handle angled up. As you bring the knife down, also move it slightly forward so the edge of the blade moves easily through the onion as the slice is being made. It's important that the flat of the blade always remain in contact with the flat surface of your forefinger. When the knife is partway through the onion, move your forefinger over the spine of the knife to hold the newly cut slice in place. For this method to work well, it is important that the slices remain intact and in position. After each cut, move your forefinger to the right a distance equal to the desired thickness of the next slice. Cut only as many slices as you need (1).

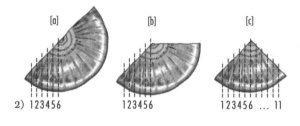

2) 123456   123456   123456 ... 11

Carefully lay the slices flat on the cutting board, with the smaller slices on top of the larger ones and positioned as shown in (2a). Working from left to right, make successive parallel cuts with the chef's knife until you reach the center of the straight portion of the onion slices. Rotate the onion slices to the left and make another series of cuts from left to right (2b). Rotate the remaining onion slices again and make a final series of cuts (2c).

CUTTING SHALLOTS

ALTHOUGH YOU MAY THINK OF A SHALLOT AS A SMALL ONION BECAUSE BOTH are members of the lily family, it is, in fact, a separate species. Shallots grow in clusters attached to a common root system. When you buy them, there is often a pair of shallots encased within a single skin. They're not identical twins though—one will be larger than the other.

Some shallots are quite round, like onions. Others have an elongated teardrop shape. Some have a heavy brown skin, others have a thin light-colored skin. Some are quite small, while others are a couple of inches across.

Shallots have a mild taste similar to that of an onion, with a hint of garlic. Because of their mild flavor, they are often used raw, and they often serve as the base for pan sauces.

Before using them, shallots should be trimmed, peeled, and thinly sliced or finely minced. A large shallot may have relatively thin layers compared to an onion of similar size. Because the layers tend to be thin, the spacing of the cuts has to be quite close together if the desired shape of a mince is a cube.

Although not as pungent as most onions, shallots can produce tears when cut. Slicing through a shallot with a sharp knife will release less of the enzyme that causes tearing than if the shallot is roughly and randomly chopped.

CUTTING SHALLOTS (*right-hand version*)

Trimming the Root

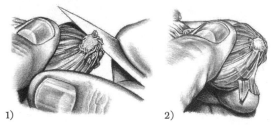

Within the skin of what looks like a single shallot is most often a pair of shallots, one slightly larger than the other, each with its own skin. Hold the shallot firmly in your left hand and a sharp paring knife in your right hand, with your forefinger and middle finger wrapped around the blade and the cutting edge toward your thumb. Support your knife hand by pressing your right thumb against the shallot (1). Cut about half of the root from the shallot. DO NOT cut off the entire root—just all of the loose portions (2). The reason for trimming the root is more aesthetic than practical, but sometimes, if it is not trimmed, loose pieces of root will adhere to the flesh of a shallot as it is sliced or diced.

Peeling a Shallot

Holding the knife the same way as above, remove the loose skin from the stem end of the shallot pair (1). Remove only the smallest amount of flesh so there is minimal waste. Often only the flesh of one of the two shallots in the pair will be exposed with this trimming (2). After the pair is separated, the smaller shallot can be further trimmed before peeling.

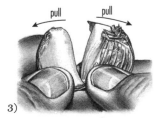

Make a small slit through the skin on one side of the shallot pair at the point where the two shallots appear to be joined. Gently separate the shallots by pulling them in opposite directions (3). (This step, of course, will not be necessary if you are working with only a single shallot.)

To peel the shallots, one at a time, hold each one firmly with the thumb and forefinger of your left hand and hold a sharp paring knife in your right, with your forefinger and middle finger wrapped around the blade. Slide the tip of the blade just under the skin at the cut edge. Press the skin against the flat side of the blade, near the tip, with your right thumb, then pull the skin down toward the root of the shallot so it breaks off at the root (4). Discard the piece of skin. Continue removing the skin in this fashion, each time turning the shallot toward the knife so new skin is exposed.

Slicing a Shallot

Cut the shallot lengthwise in half: hold it firmly with the thumb and forefinger of your left hand and a sharp paring knife in your right, with your forefinger and middle finger wrapped around the blade. Support your knife hand with your right thumb against the shallot; the knife blade should be at the root end of the shallot. Cut through the center of the root and continue cutting the full length of the shallot (1).

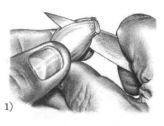

1)

To make simple slices, place a shallot half on the cutting board cut side down, with the root end toward the left. Hold the shallot firmly on both sides with the thumb and forefinger of your left hand and using a sharp knife held with a pinch grip in your right hand, make successive slices of the desired thickness. For each slice, place the tip of the knife on the cutting board beyond the shallot, with the knife handle angled upward, and draw the blade across the shallot to slice it (2).

2)

Dicing a Shallot

Place a peeled shallot half on the board cut side down, with the root end toward your left. With the thumb and forefinger of your left hand, hold the shallot firmly, with only minimal downward pressure. Hold a sharp paring knife with a pinch grip in your right hand so the blade is parallel with the cutting board and, using a slight sawing motion, make successive horizontal slices of the desired thickness, with the first cut at the bottom, nearest the cutting board and each successive cut above the previous one. DO NOT cut all the way through to the root with any of the cuts (1).

1)

Rotate the root end of the shallot half about 90 degrees away from you and adjust the grip of your left hand so your two fingers are near the cutting board and slightly compressing the shallot. Using the paring knife held with a pinch grip in your right hand with the blade perpendicular to the cutting board, make successive slices of the desired thickness. Start each cut by inserting the tip of the knife into the shallot, then draw the blade through the shallot to complete the cut. Begin on the right side of the shallot and make successive slices to the left. DO NOT cut all the way through to the root with any of the cuts (2).

2)

CUTTING SHALLOTS (*right-hand version continued*)

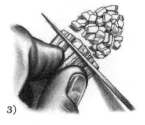

Finally, rotate the root end of the shallot about 90 degrees back toward you and make successive cuts crosswise to create tiny individual cubes. Grip the shallot with your thumb and forefinger to hold it together, and move your grip toward the root after you make each cut. Start each cut by placing the tip of the knife on the board beyond the shallot and with the handle angled upward, and draw the blade through the shallot to complete the cut (3).

3)

In the end, only a very small piece of the root should remain (4).

4)

CUTTING SHALLOTS *(left-hand version)*

Trimming the Root

Within the skin of what looks like a single shallot is most often a pair of shallots, one slightly larger than the other, each within its own skin. Hold the shallot firmly in your right hand and a sharp paring knife in your left hand, with your forefinger and middle finger wrapped around the blade and the cutting edge of the blade toward your thumb. Support your knife hand by pressing your left   thumb against the shallot (1). Cut about half of the root from the shallot. DO NOT cut off the entire root—just all of the loose portions (2). The reason for trimming the root is more aesthetic than practical, but sometimes, if it is not trimmed, loose pieces of root will adhere to the flesh of a shallot as it is sliced or diced.

Peeling a Shallot

Holding the knife the same way as above, remove the loose skin from the stem end of the shallot pair (1). Remove only the smallest amount of flesh so there is minimal waste. Often only the flesh of one of the two shallots in the pair will be exposed with this trimming (2). After the pair is separated, the smaller shallot can be further trimmed before peeling.

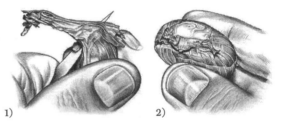

Make a small slit through the skin on one side of the shallot pair at the point where the two shallots appear to be joined. Gently separate the shallots by pulling them in opposite directions (3). (This step, of course, will not be necessary if you are working with only a single shallot.)

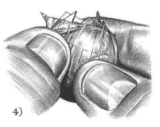

To peel the shallots, one at a time, hold each one firmly with the thumb and forefinger of your right hand and hold a sharp paring knife in your left, with your forefinger and middle finger wrapped around the blade. Slide the tip of the blade just under the skin at the cut edge. Press the skin against the flat side of the blade, near the tip, with your left thumb, then pull the skin down toward the root of the shallot so it breaks off at the root (4). Discard the piece of skin. Continue removing the skin in this fashion, each time turning the shallot toward the knife so new skin is exposed.

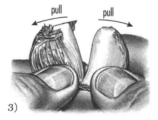

CUTTING SHALLOTS (*left-hand version continued*)

Slicing a Shallot

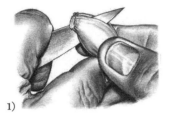

1)

Cut the shallot lengthwise in half: hold it firmly with the thumb and forefinger of your right hand and hold a sharp paring knife in your left, with your forefinger and middle finger wrapped around the blade. Support your knife hand with your left thumb against the shallot; the knife blade should be at the root end of the shallot. Cut through the center of the root and continue cutting the full length of the shallot (1).

2)

To make simple slices, place a shallot half on the cutting board cut side down, with the root end toward the right. Hold the shallot firmly on both sides with the thumb and forefinger of your right hand and, using a sharp paring knife held with a pinch grip in your left hand, make successive slices of the desired thickness. For each slice, place the tip of the knife onto the cutting board beyond the shallot, with the knife handle angled upward, and draw the blade across the shallot to slice it (2).

Dicing a Shallot

1)

Place a peeled shallot half on the board cut side down, with the root end toward your right. With the thumb and forefinger of your right hand, hold the shallot firmly, with only minimal downward pressure. Hold a sharp paring knife with a pinch grip in your left hand so the blade is parallel with the cutting board and, using a slight sawing motion, make successive horizontal slices of the desired thickness, with the first cut at the bottom, nearest the cutting board, and each successive cut above the previous one. DO NOT cut all the way through to the root with any of the cuts (1).

2)

Rotate the root end of the shallot half about 90 degrees away from you and adjust the grip of your right hand so your two fingers are near the cutting board and slightly compressing the shallot. Using the knife held with a pinch grip in your left hand with the blade perpendicular to the cutting board, make successive slices of the desired thickness. Start each cut by inserting the tip of the knife into the shallot, then draw the blade through the shallot to complete the cut. Begin on the left side of the shallot and make successive slices to the right. DO NOT cut all the way through to the root with any of the cuts (2).

Finally, rotate the root end of the shallot about 90 degrees back toward you and make successive cuts crosswise to create tiny individual cubes. Grip the shallot with your thumb and forefinger to hold it together, and move your grip toward the root after you make each cut. Start each cut by placing the tip of the knife on the board beyond the shallot and with the handle angled upward, and draw the blade through the shallot to complete the cut (3).

3)

In the end, only a very small piece of the root should remain (4).

4)

CUTTING GARLIC

GARLIC IS AN ESSENTIAL PART OF COOKING IN MOST CORNERS OF THE WORLD. Although garlic is mentioned in many of the oldest ancient texts, its country of origin is unknown.

Like shallots and onions, garlic is a member of the lily family. Unlike the other two, the layers of the garlic bulb do not separate into individual sections when it is cut.

What we call garlic cloves are, botanically speaking, bulbs. They are connected at a common root. The set of cloves is called a head. Each clove is covered by an individual skin, and the whole head is covered with a common skin. Garlic may have thick skin or very fine skin, depending on the time of year and source. The thick-skinned variety is much easier to peel. If the cloves are old, a sprout, called the germ, will be present in the center of each one. It should be removed, especially if it is green, because it can impart a bitter taste. (In some stores, peeled garlic is sold in jars. It has only about half the potency of fresh garlic. If you do buy it, trim the dark stem end before using.)

For cooking, garlic is used whole, sliced, minced, chopped, or pureed.

CUTTING GARLIC (*right-hand version*)

Trimming and Peeling a Garlic Clove

Separate an individual clove of garlic from the head. Hold the clove firmly between the thumb and forefinger of your left hand. Hold a sharp paring knife in your right, with your forefinger and middle finger wrapped around the blade and the cutting edge of the blade toward your thumb. Support your knife hand against the clove with your right thumb. Cut all the way through the root end of the clove. In the center of the clove, growing from the root, is the germ. The germ is almost the full width of the

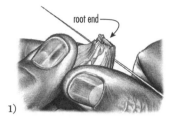

clove at the root end and tapers to a small point at the other end. The cut to remove the root should be made at the precise point where the germ narrows near the root end of the clove. Judging where this occurs is a combination of luck and experience. It is better to make multiple small cuts than to remove too much material on your first cut (1).

Holding the knife as in the previous step, hold the clove firmly between the thumb and forefinger of your left hand so the axis of the germ runs between your two fingers. Begin by cutting into the center of the germ as shown in (2a). Continue cutting as in (2b) until the clove is separated into two halves.

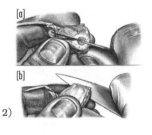

If the germ is green, sprouting, or well developed, remove it: hold a clove half as in the previous step, with the cut side facing you. Slide the tip of the knife blade between the skin of the germ, which appears as a half ring at the root end of the clove, and the flesh of the clove. Pry the germ out of its groove and discard (3).

With the thumb and forefinger of your left hand, hold the clove half firmly, with the skin side toward you. Hold a sharp paring knife in your right hand, with your forefinger and middle finger wrapped around the blade, and slide the tip of the blade just under the skin at the cut edge. With your right thumb, hold the skin firmly against the flat side of the blade, near the tip, then pull the skin off the clove and discard. Often the skin will release as a single piece; if not, remove the remainder in a similar manner (4).

CUTTING GARLIC (*right-hand version continued*)

Slicing a Garlic Clove

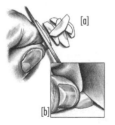

Place a peeled clove half cut side down on the cutting board, with the root end toward your right. Hold the clove firmly with the thumb and forefinger of your left hand, and using a sharp paring knife held with a pinch grip in your right hand, make successive slices of the desired thickness. For each slice, place the tip of the knife on the cutting board beyond the clove, with the knife handle angled upward, and draw the blade across the clove to slice it. In the illustration, [a] is the top view and [b] is the side view.

Dicing a Garlic Clove

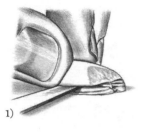

1)

Place a peeled clove half cut side down on the cutting board, with the root end toward your left. With the thumb and forefinger of your left hand, hold the clove with only minimal downward pressure. Hold a sharp paring knife in your right hand with a pinch grip so the blade is parallel with the cutting board, and using a slight sawing motion, make successive horizontal slices of the desired thickness. Start with the first cut closest to the cutting board, and make each successive cut above the previous one. DO NOT cut all the way through to the root with any of the cuts (1).

2)

Rotate the root end of the clove half about 90 degrees away from you and adjust the grip of your left hand so your two fingers are near the board and slightly compressing the clove. Using a sharp paring knife held with a pinch grip in your right hand so the blade is perpendicular to the cutting board, make vertical successive slices of the desired thickness. Start each cut by inserting the tip of the knife into the clove, and draw the blade through the clove to complete the cut. Begin on the right side of the clove and make successive slices to the left. DO NOT cut all the way through to the root (2).

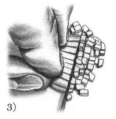

3)

Finally, rotate the root end of the clove about 90 degrees back toward you. Make successive crosswise cuts to separate the tiny individual pieces. As you do this, grip the clove with your thumb and forefinger to hold it together, and move your grip toward the root after each cut. Start each cut by placing the tip of the knife in contact with the board beyond the clove, with the handle angled upward, and draw the blade through the clove to complete the cut (3).

Pureeing a Garlic Clove

Place a peeled clove half cut side down on the board, close to the edge and with the root end toward your right. Hold the clove firmly with the thumb and forefinger of your left hand. Hold a chef's knife with the sharp edge up and use the spine to make successive "cuts" to smash a small portion of the clove at a time. After each one, move the blade half its thickness to the left to position it for the next cut. Be sure to bring the spine of the knife down all the way to the board on each "cut" to thoroughly smash the garlic clove. In the illustration, [a] is the side view and [b] is the top view. After the clove is totally smashed, move the garlic to the center of the cutting board with your knife edge, and use the sharp edge of the knife to mince any pieces that are still intact.

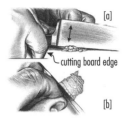

[a]

cutting board edge

[b]

CUTTING GARLIC (*left-hand version*)

Trimming and Peeling a Garlic Clove

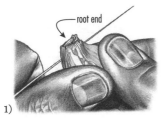

Separate an individual clove of garlic from the head. Hold the clove firmly between the thumb and forefinger of your right hand. Hold a sharp paring knife in your left, with your forefinger and middle finger wrapped around the blade, with the cutting edge of the blade towards your thumb. Support your knife hand against the clove with your left thumb. Cut all the way through the root end of the clove. In the center of the clove, growing from the root, is the germ. The germ is almost the full width of the clove at the root end and tapers to a small point of the other end. The cut to remove the root should be made at the precise point where the germ narrows near the root end of the clove. Judging where this occurs is a combination of luck and experience. It is better to make multiple small cuts than to remove too much material on your first cut (1).

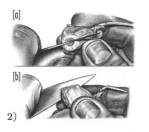

Holding the knife as in the previous step, hold the clove firmly between the thumb and forefinger of your right hand so the axis of the germ runs between your two fingers. Begin by cutting into the center of the germ as shown in (2a). Continue cutting as in (2b) until the clove is separated into two halves.

If the germ is green, sprouting, or well developed, remove it: hold a clove half as in the previous step, with the cut side facing you. Slide the tip of the knife blade between the skin of the germ, which appears as a half ring at the root end of the clove, and the flesh of the clove. Pry the germ out of its groove and discard (3).

With the thumb and forefinger of your right hand, hold the clove half firmly, with the skin side toward you. Hold a sharp paring knife in your left hand, with your forefinger and middle finger wrapped around the blade, and slide the tip of the blade just under the skin at the cut edge. With your left thumb, hold the skin firmly against the flat side of the blade, near the tip, then pull the skin off the clove and discard. Often the skin will release as a single piece; if not, remove the remainder in a similar manner (4).

Slicing a Garlic Clove

Place a clove half cut side down on the cutting board, with the root end toward your left. Hold the clove firmly with the thumb and forefinger of your right hand, and using a sharp paring knife held with a pinch grip in your left hand, make successive slices of the desired thickness. For each slice, place the tip of the knife on the cutting board beyond the clove, with the knife handle angled upward, and draw the blade across the clove to slice it. In the illustration, [a] is the top view and [b] is the side view.

Dicing a Garlic Clove

Place a peeled clove half cut side down on the cutting board, with the root end toward your right. With the thumb and forefinger of your right hand, hold the clove with only minimal downward pressure. Hold a sharp paring knife in your left hand with a pinch grip so the blade is parallel with the cutting board, and using a slight sawing motion, make successive horizontal slices of the desired thickness. Start with the first cut closest to the cutting board, and make each successive cut above the previous one. DO NOT cut all the way through to the root with any of the cuts (1).

1)

Rotate the root end of the clove half about 90 degrees away from you and adjust the grip of your right hand so your two fingers are down near the board and slightly compressing the clove. Using a sharp paring knife held with a pinch grip in your left hand so the blade is perpendicular to the cutting board, make vertical successive slices of the desired thickness. Start each cut by inserting the tip of the knife into the clove, and draw the blade through the clove to complete the cut. Begin on the left side of the clove and make successive slices to the right. DO NOT cut all the way through to the root (2).

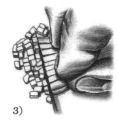

2)

Finally, rotate the root end of the clove about 90 degrees back toward you. Make successive crosswise cuts to separate the tiny individual pieces. As you do this, grip the clove with your thumb and forefinger to hold it together, and move your grip toward the root after each cut. Start each cut by placing the tip of the knife in contact with the board beyond the clove, with the handle angled upward, and draw the blade through the clove to complete the cut (3).

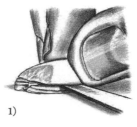

3)

CUTTING GARLIC (*left-hand version continued*)

Pureeing a Garlic Clove

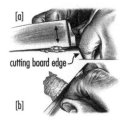

cutting board edge

[a]

[b]

Place a peeled clove half cut side down on the board, close to the edge and with the root end toward your left. Hold the clove firmly with the thumb and forefinger of your right hand. Hold a chef's knife with the sharp edge up and use the spine to make successive "cuts" to smash a small portion of the clove at a time. After each one, move the blade half its thickness to the right to position it for the next cut. Be sure to bring the spine of the knife down all the way to the board on each "cut" to thoroughly smash the garlic clove. In the illustration, [a] is the side view and [b] is the top view. After the clove is totally smashed, move the garlic to the center of the cutting board with your knife edge, and use the sharp edge of the knife to mince any pieces that are still intact.

CUTTING CARROTS AND OTHER CONICAL VEGETABLES

CUTTING CARROTS, PARSNIPS, AND OTHER CONICAL VEGETABLES CAN PRESENT A problem if you desire uniformly shaped pieces. Uniform pieces cook at the same rate, and they make a dish visually appealing.

Plastic mandolines that can rapidly slice a carrot into thin rounds or shreds are available, and sometimes their use may be appropriate, but it is important to know how to achieve the same results manually. (The only exception is grated carrots, something impossible to achieve with a knife.)

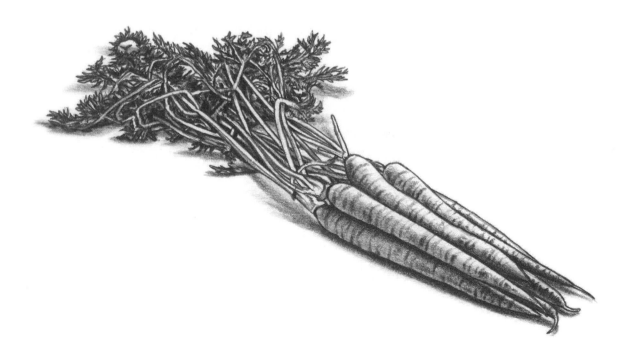

CUTTING CARROTS AND OTHER CONICAL VEGETABLES *(right-hand version)*

Peeling a Carrot

1)

Nowadays, the carrots sold in stores are well washed prior to sale, and therefore their skin, which is full of nutrients, doesn't absolutely require removal. Some people scrape off the skin with the blade of a knife. This method can make a mess of your work area and leave the surface of the carrot quite rough. If you wish to remove the skin, use a peeler. A yoke-type peeler, shown in the illustration, is my preferred tool for this. To peel a carrot, hold it in your left hand and the peeler in your right. Peel the carrot from the narrow end to the wide end. After each strip of skin is removed, rotate the carrot to expose a new section of skin (1).

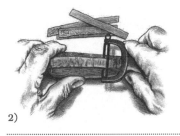

2)

As an alternate method, lay the carrot on a cutting board, and support the wide end of the carrot with your left hand. With the peeler, remove the skin in strokes from the wide end to the narrow end. After each strip of skin is removed, rotate the carrot to expose a new unpeeled section (2).

Slicing a Carrot

Lay a peeled carrot on the cutting board with the narrow end toward your left. With your left hand, hold the carrot firmly, with your fingertips pressing straight down on top of the carrot. Position a sharp chef's knife held with a pinch grip so the flat of the blade rests against the flat side of the tip of your forefinger. This way, your forefinger serves as a guide for the knife. If making simple rounds, position the knife at a right angle to the carrot. If the slices are intended for julienne or dice, place the knife diagonal to the carrot so you will produce slices about 2 inches long. Start each slice with the tip of the blade in contact with, or near, the cutting board, with the handle angled up. As you bring the knife down, slide it forward so the edge of the blade is moving through the carrot as you produce the slice. After each cut, move your forefinger to the left a distance equal to the desired thickness of the next slice. It is important that the flat of the blade always remain in contact with the flat surface of your forefinger.

Julienning a Carrot

Stack three or four carrot slices at a time on the cutting board. Hold the stack firmly in place with your left hand by pressing down on top of it with your fingertips in a vertical position. Position the chef's knife, held with a pinch grip, so the flat of the blade rests against the flat side of the tip of your forefinger. This way, your forefinger serves as a guide for the knife. Start each cut with the tip of the blade in contact with, or near, the cutting board, with the handle angled up. As you bring the knife down, slide it forward  so the edge of the blade is moving through the carrot as you produce the julienne. After each cut, move your forefinger to the left a distance equal to the desired width of the next cut. Ideally, the width of this cut should be the same as the thickness of the slice, so the resulting strips have a perfectly square cross section. As you do this, it is important that the flat of the blade always remain in contact with the flat surface of your forefinger.

Dicing a Carrot

Gather the julienned strips from the previous step together into a stack, with all the strips parallel to one another. With the fingertips of your left hand in a vertical position, hold the stack firmly in place. Position the chef's knife, held with a pinch grip, so the flat of the blade rests against the flat side of the tip of your forefinger. This way, your forefinger serves as a guide for the knife. Start each cut with the tip of the blade in contact with, or  near, the cutting board, with the handle angled up. As you bring the knife down, slide it forward so the edge of the blade is moving through the carrot as you produce the cubes. After each cut, slide your forefinger to the left a distance equal to the desired width of the next cut. Ideally, the width of this cut will be equal to the thickness of the strips, so the resulting dice will be perfect cubes. It is important that the flat of the blade always remain in contact with the flat surface of your forefinger.

Roll Cutting a Carrot

For stewing and roasting, the carrots can be cut into irregular shapes of approximately the same size using the roll-cut technique. Hold a peeled carrot firmly on the cutting board with your left hand. Hold a chef's knife with a pinch grip at about a 45-degree angle to the carrot. Start each cut with the tip of the blade in contact with, or near, the cutting board, with the handle angled up. As you bring the knife down, slide the blade forward through the carrot  to produce the cut pieces. After each cut, roll the carrot 90 degrees to the left. The width of each cut should be constant, even as the portion of carrot being cut becomes wider.

CUTTING CARROTS AND OTHER CONICAL VEGETABLES *(left-hand version)*

Peeling a Carrot

1)

Nowadays, the carrots sold in stores are well washed prior to sale. And therefore their skin, which is full of nutrients, doesn't absolutely require removal. Some people scrape off the skin with the blade of a knife. This method can make a mess of your work area and leave the surface of the carrot quite rough. If you wish to remove the skin, use a peeler. A yoke-type peeler, shown in the illustration, is my preferred tool for this. To peel a carrot, hold it in your right hand and the peeler in your left. Peel the carrot from the narrow end to the wide end. After each strip of skin is removed, rotate the carrot to expose a new section of skin (1).

2)

As an alternate method, lay the carrot on a cutting board, and support the wide end of the carrot with your right hand. With the peeler, remove the skin in strokes from the wide end to the narrow end. After each strip of skin is removed, rotate the carrot to expose a new unpeeled section (2).

Slicing a Carrot

Lay a peeled carrot on the cutting board with the narrow end toward your right. With your right hand, hold the carrot firmly, with your fingertips pressing straight down on top of the carrot. Position a sharp chef's knife held with a pinch grip so the flat of the blade rests against the flat side of the tip of your forefinger. This way, your forefinger serves as a guide for the knife. If making simple rounds, position the knife at a right angle to the carrot. If the slices are intended for a julienne or dice, place the knife diagonal to the carrot so you produce slices about 2 inches long. Start each slice with the tip of the blade in contact with, or near, the cutting board, with the handle angled up. As you bring the knife down, slide it forward so the edge of the blade is moving through the carrot as you produce the slice. After each cut, move your forefinger to the right a distance equal to the desired thickness of the next slice. It is important that the flat of the blade always remain in contact with the flat surface of your forefinger.

Julienning a Carrot

Stack three or four carrot slices at a time on the cutting board. Hold the stack firmly in place with your right hand by pressing down on top of it with your fingertips in a vertical position. Position the chef's knife, held with a pinch grip, so the flat of the blade rests against the flat side of the tip of your forefinger. This way, your forefinger serves as a guide for the knife. Start each cut with the tip of the blade in contact with, or near, the cutting board, with the handle angled up. As you bring the knife down, slide it forward  so the edge of the blade is moving through the carrot as you produce the julienne. After each cut, move your forefinger to the right a distance equal to the desired width of the next cut. Ideally, the width of this cut should be the same as the thickness of the slice, so the resulting strips have a perfectly square cross section. As you do this, it is important that the flat of the blade always remain in contact with the flat surface of your forefinger.

Dicing a Carrot

Gather the julienned strips from the previous step together into a stack, with all the strips parallel to one another. With the fingertips of your right hand in a vertical position, hold the stack firmly in place. Position the chef's knife, held with a pinch grip, so the flat of the blade rests against the flat side of the tip of your forefinger. This way, your forefinger serves as a guide for the knife. Start each cut with the tip of the blade in contact with, or near, the cutting board, with the handle angled up. As you bring the knife down, slide it  forward so the edge of the blade is moving through the carrot as you produce the cubes. After each cut, slide your forefinger to the right a distance equal to the desired width of the next cut. Ideally, the width of this cut will be equal to the thickness of the strips, so the resulting dice will be perfect cubes. It is important that the flat of the blade always remain in contact with the flat surface of your forefinger.

Roll Cutting a Carrot

For stewing and roasting, the carrot can be cut into irregular shapes of approximately the same size using the roll-cut technique. Hold a peeled carrot firmly on the cutting board with your right hand. Hold a chef's knife with a pinch grip at about a 45-degree angle to the carrot. Start each cut with the tip of the blade in contact with, or near, the cutting board, and the handle angled up. As you bring the knife down, slide the blade forward through the carrot to produce the cut pieces. After each cut, roll the carrot 90 degrees to the right. The width of each cut should be constant, even as the portion of carrot being cut becomes wider.

CUTTING ZUCCHINI AND OTHER CYLINDRICAL VEGETABLES

THE FAMILIAR DARK GREEN ZUCCHINI IS A TYPE OF SUMMER SQUASH AVAILABLE IN a multitude of shapes. When small, they tend to be straight and cylindrical; as they grow larger, they can become a bit curved or crooked—but the principles of cutting all zucchini remain the same. These techniques also work for other similarly shaped vegetables, such as other summer squashes and even cucumbers (although these sometimes need to be seeded before use). Eggplants that are more cylindrical than spherical can be cut with the same techniques.

CUTTING ZUCCHINI AND OTHER CYLINDRICAL VEGETABLES *(right-hand version)*

Slicing a Zucchini

Place a zucchini on a cutting board with the narrow end, if there is one, toward your left. With the fingertips of your left hand positioned on the top of the zucchini and pointing straight downward, hold the zucchini firmly in place. Position a sharp chef's knife, held with a pinch grip, so the flat of the blade rests against the flat side of the tip of your forefinger. This way, your forefinger serves as a guide for the knife. If making simple rounds, position the knife at a right angle to the zucchini. If making the slices as a preparation for julienne or dice, position the knife diagonal to the zucchini so you will produce slice about 1½ to 2 inches long. Start each slice with the tip of the blade on, or near, the cutting board, with the handle angled up. As you bring the knife down, slide it forward through the zucchini to produce the slice. After each cut, move your forefinger to the left a distance equal to the desired thickness of the next slice. It is important that the flat of the blade always remain in contact with the flat surface of your forefinger.

Julienning a Zucchini

Stack three or four zucchini slices from the previous step at a time on the cutting board. Hold the stack firmly in place with your left hand, pressing down on top of it with your fingertips in a vertical position. Position a sharp chef's knife, held with a pinch grip, so the flat of the blade rests against the side of the tip of your forefinger. This way, your forefinger serves as a guide for the knife. Start each cut with the tip of the blade in contact with, or near, the cutting board, with the handle angled up. As you bring the knife down, slide the blade forward so that it moves through the zucchini as you produce the strips. After each cut, move your forefinger to the left a distance equal to the desired width of the next cut. Ideally, the width of this cut should be the same as the thickness of the slice, so the resulting strips have a perfectly square cross section. As you do this, it is important that the flat of the blade always remain in contact with the flat surface of your forefinger.

CUTTING ZUCCHINI AND OTHER CYLINDRICAL VEGETABLES (*right-hand version continued*)

Dicing a Zucchini

Gather the julienned strips from the previous step together into a stack, with all the strips parallel to one another. Hold the stack firmly in place with your left hand, pressing down on top of it with your fingertips in a vertical position. Position a sharp knife, held with a pinch grip, so the flat of the blade rests against the flat side of the tip of your forefinger. This way your forefinger serves as a guide for the knife. Start each cut with the tip of the blade in contact with, or near, the cutting board, with the handle angled up. As you bring the knife down, slide the blade forward so that it moves through the zucchini as you produce the cubes. After each cut, move your forefinger to the left a distance equal to the desired width of the next cut. Ideally, the width of this cut should be the same as the thickness of the slice, so the resulting dice are perfect cubes. As you do this, it is important that the flat of the blade always remain in contact with the flat surface of your forefinger.

CUTTING ZUCCHINI AND OTHER CYLINDRICAL VEGETABLES *(left-hand version)*

Slicing a Zucchini

Place a zucchini on a cutting board with the narrow end, if there is one, toward your right. With the fingertips of your right hand positioned on the top of the zucchini and pointing straight downward, hold the zucchini firmly in place. Position a sharp chef's knife, held with a pinch grip, so the flat of the blade rests against the flat side of the tip of your forefinger. This way, your forefinger serves as a guide for the knife. If making simple rounds, position the knife at a right angle to the zucchini. If making the slices as  a preparation for a julienne or dice, position the knife diagonal to the zucchini to so you will produce slices about 1½ to 2 inches long. Begin each slice with the tip of the blade on, or near, the cutting board, with the handle angled up. As you bring the knife down, slide it forward through the zucchini to produce the slice. After each cut, move your forefinger to the right a distance equal to the desired thickness of the next slice. It is important that the flat of the blade always remain in contact with the flat surface of your forefinger.

Julienning a Zucchini

Stack three or four zucchini slices from the previous step at a time on the cutting board. Hold the stack firmly in place with your right hand, pressing down on top of it with your fingertips in a vertical position. Position a sharp chef's knife, held with a pinch grip, so the flat of the blade rests against the flat side of the tip of your forefinger. This way, your forefinger serves as a guide for the knife. Start each cut with the tip of the blade in  contact with, or near, the cutting board, with the handle angled up. As you bring the knife down, slide the blade forward so that it moves through the zucchini as you produce the strips. After each cut, move your forefinger to the right a distance equal to the desired width of the next cut. Ideally, the width of this cut should be the same as the thickness of the slice, so the resulting strips have a perfectly square cross section. As you do this, it is important that the flat of the blade always remain in contact with the flat surface of your forefinger.

CUTTING ZUCCHINI AND OTHER CYLINDRICAL VEGETABLES (*left-hand version continued*)

Dicing a Zucchini

Gather the julienned strips from the previous step together into a stack, with all the strips parallel to one another. Hold the stack firmly in place with your right hand, pressing down on top of it with your fingertips in a vertical position. Position a sharp chef's knife, held with a pinch grip, so the flat of the blade rests against the flat side of the tip of your forefinger. This way, your forefinger serves as a guide for the knife. Start each cut with the tip of the blade in contact with, or near, the cutting board, with the handle angled up. As you bring the knife down, slide the blade forward so that it moves through the zucchini as you produce the cubes. After each cut, move your forefinger to the right a distance equal to the desired width of the next cut. Ideally, the width of this cut should be the same as the thickness of the slice, so the resulting dice are perfect cubes. As you do this, it is important that the flat of the blade always remain in contact with the flat surface of your forefinger.

CUTTING TURNIPS AND OTHER SMOOTH-SKINNED SPHERICAL VEGETABLES

TURNIPS COME IN A WIDE VARIETY OF SHAPES. IN THE FIRST CENTURY A.D., PLINY described long, flat, and round turnips. For this set of cutting techniques, the round turnip stands for all vegetables with smooth skin, a somewhat spherical shape, and a consistent texture. That would include the rounder eggplants as well as rutabagas and beets. (Cylindrical eggplants should be cut in a manner similar to zucchini.) Potatoes are handled separately in the following section.

Some of these vegetables can be quite large, but with a little care and patience and a large sharp knife, they can be cut into very thin slices, strips, or cubes. I find it very satisfying to turn a good-sized turnip into an attractive pile of ⅛-inch cubes. But if you are aiming to make a turnip puree, ½-inch cubes are small enough and will be faster to turn out.

CUTTING TURNIPS AND OTHER SMOOTH-SKINNED SPHERICAL VEGETABLES *(right-hand version)*

Peeling a Turnip

First use a sharp chef's knife to trim both the root and stem ends flat from a turnip. Hold it firmly in your left hand and the peeler in your right. Support your right hand against the turnip with your thumb. Peel the turnip from top to bottom. A yoke-type peeler, shown in the illustration, does the job best. After you have peeled each strip of skin, rotate the turnip toward you to expose a new section of skin.

Slicing a Turnip

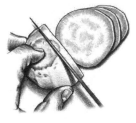

Place a peeled turnip on the cutting board on one of the cut ends. With your forefinger pointing straight down toward the cutting board, hold the turnip firmly in place with your left hand. Hold the chef's knife, with a pinch grip, with your right hand. Because of the thickness of the turnip, the edge of the blade will be approximately parallel to the cutting board. Saw the knife forward and backward through the turnip for each slice. After cutting each slice, move your forefinger to the left a distance equal to the desired thickness of the next slice.

Julienning a Turnip

Stack two or three turnip slices at a time on the cutting board. Hold the stack firmly in place with your left hand, pressing down on top of it with your fingertips. Position the chef's knife, held with a pinch grip in your right hand, so the flat of the blade rests against the flat side of the tip of your forefinger. This way, your forefinger serves as a guide for the knife. Start each cut with the tip of the blade in contact with, or near, the cutting board, with the handle angled up. As you bring the knife down, slide the blade forward so that it moves through the turnip as you produce the strips. After each cut, move your forefinger to the left a distance equal to the desired width of the next cut. Ideally, the width of this cut should be the same as the thickness of the slice, so the resulting strips have a perfectly square cross section. As you do this, it is important that the flat of the blade always remain in contact with the flat surface of your forefinger.

Dicing a Turnip

Gather the julienned strips from the previous step together into a stack, with all the strips parallel to one another. Hold the stack firmly in place with your left hand, pressing down on top of it with your fingertips in a vertical position. Position the chef's knife, held with a pinch grip in your right hand, so the flat of the blade rests against the flat side of the tip of your forefinger. This way, your forefinger serves as a guide for the knife. Start each cut with the tip of the blade in contact with, or near, the cutting board, with the handle angled  up. As you bring the knife down, slide the blade forward so that it moves through the turnip as you produce the cubes. After each cut, move your forefinger to the left a distance equal to the desired width of the next cut. Ideally, the width of this cut should be the same as the width of the strips, so the resulting dice are perfect cubes. As you do this, it is important that the flat of the blade always remain in contact with the flat surface of your forefinger.

CUTTING TURNIPS AND OTHER SMOOTH-SKINNED SPHERICAL VEGETABLES (*left-hand version*)

Peeling a Turnip

First use a sharp chef's knife to trim both the root and stem ends flat from a turnip. Hold it firmly in your right hand and the peeler in your left. Support your left hand against the turnip with your thumb. Peel the turnip from top to bottom. A yoke-type peeler, shown in the illustration, does the job best. After you have peeled each strip of skin, rotate the turnip toward you to expose a new section of skin.

Slicing a Turnip

Place a peeled turnip on the cutting board on one of the cut ends. With your forefinger pointing straight down toward the cutting board, hold the turnip firmly in place with your right hand. Hold the chef's knife, with a pinch grip, with your left hand. Because of the thickness of the turnip, the edge of the blade will be approximately parallel to the cutting board. Saw the knife forward and backward through the turnip for each slice. After cutting each slice, move your forefinger to the right a distance equal to the desired thickness of the next slice.

Julienning a Turnip

Stack two or three turnip slices at a time on the cutting board. Hold the stack firmly in place with your right hand, pressing down on top of it with your fingertips. Position the chef's knife, held with a pinch grip, in your left hand, so the flat of the blade rests against the flat side of the tip of your forefinger. This way, your forefinger serves as a guide for the knife. Start each cut with the tip of the blade in contact with, or near, the cutting board, with the handle angled up. As you bring the knife down, slide the blade forward so that it moves through the turnip as you produce the strips. After each cut, move your forefinger to the right a distance equal to the desired width of the next cut. Ideally, the width of this cut should be the same as the thickness of the slice, so the resulting strips have a perfectly square cross section. As you do this, it is important that the flat of the blade always remain in contact with the flat surface of your forefinger.

Dicing a Turnip

Gather the julienned strips from the previous step together into a stack, with all the strips parallel to one another. Hold the stack firmly in place with your right hand, pressing down on top of it with your fingertips in a vertical position. Position the chef's knife, held with a pinch grip in your left hand, so the flat of the blade rests against the flat side of the tip of your forefinger. This way, your forefinger serves as a guide for the knife. Start each cut with the tip of the blade in contact with, or near, the cutting board, with  the handle angled up. As you bring the knife down, slide the blade forward so that it moves through the turnip as you produce the cubes. After each cut, move your forefinger to the right a distance equal to the desired width of the next cut. Ideally, the width of this cut should be the same as the width of the strips so the resulting dice are perfect cubes. As you do this, it is important that the flat of the blade always remain in contact with the flat surface of your forefinger.

CUTTING POTATOES

POTATOES COME IN A VARIETY OF SHAPES AND COLORS. THE COLOR, OF COURSE, doesn't affect how the potato is cut, but the shape, can, as can the water content, starch content, and age of the potato. All of these may vary from potato to potato, though luckily not enough to seriously change the cutting methods used.

Potatoes with a higher water content are harder to slice than those with a lower content. The moisture causes the side of the knife to "bind" to the potato, and this slows down the cutting process, since it can require a separate effort to release the potato from the blade. Using a knife with grantons reduces this effect; see page 18.

When you cut starchy potatoes, starch will collect on the knife blade and become sticky, slowing down the cutting. When this happens, rinse the blade in cold water and dry it before proceeding.

For most recipes, potatoes are sliced or julienned. Small cubes are a nice addition to vegetable soups and cook very fast. They are also great fried in goose fat and a splendid substitute for French fries. For a fancier version, use a baller, as described in the last technique, to create potato balls. These too are excellent fried or cooked in cream.

If you need a large quantity of very thinly sliced potatoes, a Japanese mandoline can produce quick, consistent results much faster than a knife.

CUTTING POTATOES (*right-hand version*)

Peeling a Potato

Hold a potato firmly in your left hand and the peeler in your right. A yoke-type peeler, shown in the illustration, does the job best. Support your right hand against the potato with your thumb. Peel the potato from top to bottom. After you peel each strip of skin, rotate the potato toward you to expose a new section of skin.

Slicing a Potato

Use a sharp chef's knife to trim a thin slice from one side of the potato to create a flat surface. Rest the potato on this side for the next step so it won't roll on the cutting board (1).

1)

To slice the potato, place it on the cutting board on the flat side. With your forefinger pointing straight down toward the cutting board, hold the potato firmly in place with your left hand. Hold the chef's knife, with a pinch grip, in your right hand. Because of the thickness of the potato, the edge of the blade will be approximately parallel to the cutting board. Saw the knife forward and backward through the potato for each slice. After cutting each slice, move your forefinger to the left a distance equal to the desired thickness of the next slice (2).

2)

Julienning a Potato

Stack two or three potato slices at a time on the cutting board. Hold the stack firmly in place with your left hand, pressing down on top of it with your fingertips. Position the chef's knife, held with a pinch grip, so the flat of the blade rests against the flat side of the tip of your forefinger. This way, your forefinger serves as a guide for the knife. Start each cut with the tip of the blade in contact with, or near, the cutting board, with the handle angled up. As you bring the knife down, slide the blade forward so that it moves through the potato as you produce the strips. After each cut, move your forefinger to the left a distance equal to the desired width of the next cut. Ideally, the width of this cut should be the same as the thickness of the slice, so the resulting strips have a perfectly square cross section. As you do this, it is important that the flat of the blade always remain in contact with the flat surface of your forefinger.

CUTTING POTATOES (*right-hand version continued*)

Dicing a Potato

Gather the julienned strips from the previous step together into a stack, with all the strips parallel to one another. Hold the stack firmly in place with your left hand, pressing down on top of it with your fingertips in a vertical position. Position the chef's knife, held with a pinch grip, so the flat of the blade rests against the flat side of the tip of your forefinger. This way, your forefinger serves as a guide for the knife. Start each cut with the tip of the blade in contact with, or near, the cutting board, with the handle angled up. As you bring the knife down, slide the blade forward so that it moves through the potato as you produce the cubes. After each cut, move your forefinger to the left a distance equal to the desired width of the next cut. Ideally, the width of this cut should be the same as the width of the strips, so the resulting dice are perfect cubes. As you do this, it is important that the flat of the blade always remain in contact with the flat surface of your forefinger.

Making Potato Balls

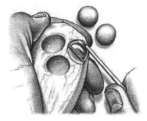

For a more decorative cut, use a baller that's about three-eighths to half an inch across to cut spherical shapes from the potato. Hold the potato firmly in your left hand and the baller in your right. Press the baller into the surface of the potato, moving the handle around in a circular motion to cut out a rounded potato ball. This method produces a lot of waste potato, which can be cooked and used for purees.

CUTTING POTATOES (*left-hand version*)

Peeling a Potato

Hold a potato firmly in your right hand and the peeler in your left. A yoke-type peeler, shown in the illustration, does the job best. Support your left hand against the potato with your thumb. Peel the potato from top to bottom. After you peel each strip of skin, rotate the potato toward you to expose a new section of skin.

Slicing a Potato

Use a sharp chef's knife to trim a thin slice from one side of the potato to create a flat surface. Rest the potato on this side for the next step so it won't roll on the cutting board (1).

1)

To slice the potato, place it on the cutting board on the flat side. With your forefinger pointing straight down toward the cutting board, hold the potato firmly in place with your right hand. Hold the chef's knife, with a pinch grip, in your left hand. Because of the thickness of the potato, the edge of the blade will be approximately parallel to the cutting board. Saw the knife forward and backward through the potato for each slice. After cutting each slice, move your forefinger to the right a distance equal to the desired thickness of the next slice (2).

2)

Julienning a Potato

Stack two or three potato slices at a time on the cutting board. Hold the stack firmly in place with your right hand, pressing down on top of it with your fingertips. Position the chef's knife, held with a pinch grip, so the flat of the blade rests against the flat side of the tip of your forefinger. This way, your forefinger serves as a guide for the knife. Start each cut with the tip of the blade in contact with, or near, the cutting board, with the handle angled up. As you bring the knife down, slide the blade forward so that it moves through the potato as you produce the strips. After each cut,

move your forefinger to the right a distance equal to the desired width of the next cut. Ideally, the width of this cut should be the same as the thickness of the slice, so the resulting strips have a perfectly square cross section. As you do this, it is important that the flat of the blade always remain in contact with the flat surface of your forefinger.

CUTTING POTATOES (*left-hand version continued*)

Dicing a Potato

Gather the julienned strips from the previous step together into a stack, with all the strips parallel to one another. Hold the stack firmly in place with your right hand, pressing down on top of it with your fingertips in a vertical position. Position the chef's knife, held with a pinch grip, so the flat of the blade rests against the flat side of the tip of your forefinger. This way, your forefinger serves as a guide for the knife. Start each cut with the tip of the blade in contact with, or near, the cutting board, with the handle angled up. As you bring the knife down, slide the blade forward so that it moves through the potato as you produce the cubes. After each cut, move your forefinger to the right a distance equal to the desired width of the next cut. Ideally, the width of this cut should be the same as the width of the strips, so the resulting dice are perfect cubes. As you do this, it is important that the flat of the blade always remain in contact with the flat surface of your forefinger.

Making Potato Balls

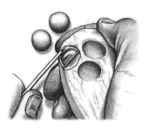

For a more decorative cut, use a baller that's about three-eighths to half an inch across to cut spherical shapes from the potato. Hold the potato firmly in your right hand and the baller in your left. Press the baller into the surface of the potato, moving the handle around in a circular motion to cut out a rounded ball. This method produces a lot of waste potato, which can be cooked and used for purees.

CUTTING CELERY ROOT AND OTHER ROUGH-SKINNED SPHERICAL VEGETABLES

THE GROUP OF ROUGH-SKINNED SPHERICAL VEGETABLES, REPRESENTED HERE BY celery root (celeriac), is handled similarly to its smooth-skinned cousins, turnips and potatoes, except for peeling. Because of the convolutions in the surface of these vegetables, using a simple vegetable peeler is difficult, if not impossible. Employing the method described below requires care to remove all the skin while not removing, and thus wasting, much of the underlying flesh.

CUTTING CELERY ROOT AND OTHER ROUGH-SKINNED SPHERICAL VEGETABLES (*right-hand version*)

Peeling Celery Root

If necessary, use a sharp chef's knife to trim the stem end flush with the body of the celery root. Place the root on the cutting board so you can plan how you will peel it. The peel should be cut from the root as indicated by the dotted line in the illustration (1).

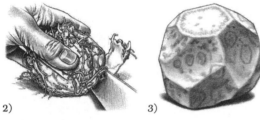

To peel the celery root, hold it firmly in your left hand and hold a sharp chef's knife in your right hand with a pinch grip. Use a sawing motion with the knife. It is important to start the cut with the blade parallel to the surface of the celery root and then to turn it while making the cut so it remains parallel to the surface. Peel the celery root from the top to bottom (2). After peeling each strip of skin, rotate the celery root toward you to expose a new section of skin. The peeled celery root will have a rounded but irregular shape (3).

Slicing Celery Root

Place a peeled celery root on the cutting board on the cut end. Hold the root firmly in place with your left hand, pressing down on top of it with your fingertips. Hold the chef's knife in your right hand with a pinch grip. Because of the thickness of the celery root, the edge of the blade is held approximately parallel to the cutting board. Saw the knife forward and backward through the celery root for each slice.

Julienning Celery Root

Stack two or three celery root slices at a time on the cutting board. Hold the stack firmly in place with your left hand, pressing down on top of it with your fingertips. Hold the knife in your right hand with a pinch grip. Because of the thickness of the celery root, the edge of the blade is held approximately parallel to the cutting board. Saw the knife forward and backward through the celery root as you produce the strips.

Dicing Celery Root

Gather the julienned strips from the previous step together into a stack, with all the strips parallel to one another. Hold the stack firmly in place with your left hand, pressing down on top of it with your fingertips. Hold the chef's knife in your right hand with a pinch grip. Because of the thickness of the celery root, the edge of the blade is held approximately parallel to the cutting board. Saw the knife forward and backward through the celery root as you produce the cubes.

CUTTING CELERY ROOT AND OTHER ROUGH-SKINNED SPHERICAL VEGETABLES (*left-hand version*)

Peeling Celery Root

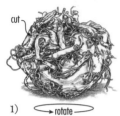

1) →rotate→

If necessary, use a sharp chef's knife to trim the stem end flush with the body of the celery root. Place the root on the cutting board so you can plan how you will peel it. The peel should be cut from the root as indicated by the dotted line in the illustration (1).

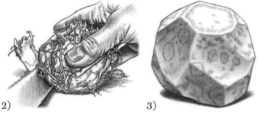

2)   3)

To peel the celery root, hold it firmly in your right hand and hold a sharp chef's knife in your left hand with a pinch grip. Use a sawing motion with the knife. It is important to start the cut with the blade parallel to the surface of the celery root and then to turn it while making the cut so it remains parallel to the surface. Peel the celery root from the top to bottom (2). After peeling each strip of skin, rotate the celery root toward you to expose a new section of skin. The peeled celery root will have a rounded but irregular shape (3).

Slicing Celery Root

Place a celery root on the cutting board on the cut end. Hold the root firmly in place with your right hand, pressing down on top of it with your fingertips. Hold the chef's knife in your left hand with a pinch grip. Because of the thickness of the celery root, the edge of the blade is held approximately parallel to the cutting board. Saw the knife forward and backward through the celery root for each slice.

Julienning Celery Root

Stack two or three celery root slices at a time on the cutting board. Hold the stack firmly in place with your right hand, pressing down on top of it with your fingertips. Hold the chef's knife in your left hand with a pinch grip. Because of the thickness of the celery root, the edge of the blade is held approximately parallel to the cutting board. Saw the knife forward and backward through the celery root as you produce the strips.

Dicing Celery Root

Gather the julienned strips from the previous step together into a stack, with all the strips parallel to one another. Hold the stack firmly in place with your right hand, pressing down on top of it with your fingertips. Hold the chef's knife in your left hand with a pinch grip. Because of the thickness of the celery root, the edge of the blade is held approximately parallel to the cutting board. Saw the knife forward and backward through the celery root as you produce the cubes.

CUTTING LEEKS

THE LEEK IS ONE OF THE OLDEST CULTIVATED VEGETABLES AND IS MENTIONED IN the Bible. In nineteenth-century France, leeks were called "poor man's asparagus." I guess times have changed since leeks cost more per pound than asparagus in my market!

Because the stalk is hidden from the sun during growth, it is white. If a grower exposes the stalk to light, it will form chlorophyll and turn green like the upper part of the plant. So, as the stalk grows, the grower needs to pile dirt against it to keep it white. The process is called blanching. Done properly, blanching can produce a white stalk a foot or more in length. Most recipes call for only the white part of the leek.

Because of the blanching process, the first step in preparing a leek is to thoroughly clean all the dirt that clings to it, especially at the base of the leaves. Some leeks are filthy, while others can be quite clean.

CUTTING LEEKS (*right-hand version*)

Trimming a Leek

Hold the leek firmly in your left hand and hold a sharp chef's knife in your right hand with a pinch grip. Cut just the tendril-like portion of the root from the leek, making a straight cut slightly above the juncture of the skin and root so a small portion of the root section remains intact (1). The reason for trimming root is more aesthetic than practical, but sometimes, if it is not trimmed, pieces of root will become loose and adhere to the flesh of the leek as it is sliced or diced (2).

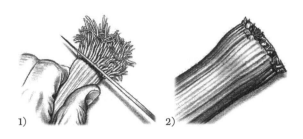

The thick dark green portions of the leek leaves are usually discarded. As you move from the outer layers inward, the tender portion of each layer becomes longer. When removing the thick dark green leaves, remove one layer at a time. Hold the leek against the board with your left hand. Using a chef's knife held in your right hand in a pinch grip, trim the thick green portion of the layer almost tangentially with the stalk of the leek. Flip the leek over and trim the next layer on the other side in a similar manner (3). Continue until only the tender, light-green portions of the leek remain (4).

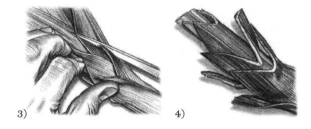

Cleaning a Leek

To remove the dirt commonly found between the layers at the point where each leaf turns from white to light green, place the trimmed leek on the cutting board with the root end to your left. Hold the leek firmly with your left hand. Holding the chef's knife in your right hand with a pinch grip, insert the tip of the knife into the leek to slit it down the middle to the ends of the leaves: start the cut at the point where the dirt shows through the white portion of the outermost layer (1). After making the cut, gently spread the layers out under running water to wash out the dirt (2). When done, be sure to shake out any water, and re-form the leek into its natural shape.

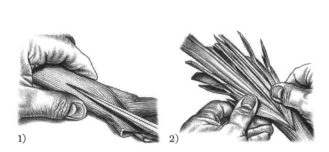

CUTTING LEEKS (*right-hand version continued*)

Slicing a Leek

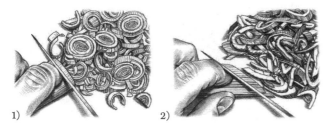

1) 2)

Leeks are often cut into rounds (1) or diagonal slices (2). Diagonal slices separate more easily and are more attractive than rounds. Other than the angle of the cut, the technique for cutting either is the same. Place the leek on the cutting board so the root end is toward the left. With your fingertips positioned straight down toward the board, hold the leek firmly with your left hand. Position a sharp chef's knife, held with a pinch grip, so the flat of the blade rests against the flat side of the tip of your forefinger. This way, your forefinger serves as a guide for the knife. Start each cut with the tip of the blade in contact with, or near, the cutting board, with the handle angled up. As you bring the knife down, slide the blade forward so that it moves through the leek as you produce the slices. After each cut, move your forefinger to the left a distance equal to the desired thickness of the next cut. Ideally, the thickness of this cut should be the same as the thickness of the previous slice, so the resulting rounds have a uniform thickness. As you do this, it is important that the flat of the blade always remain in contact with the flat surface of your forefinger.

Mincing a Leek

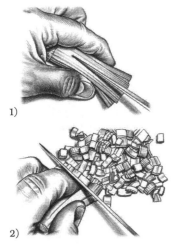

1)

2)

Place the trimmed and washed leek on the cutting board with the root end to the left. Hold the leek firmly with your left hand. Holding the chef's knife in your right hand with a pinch grip, insert the tip of the knife into the leek near the root and slit it down the middle for its entire length (1). Turn the leek 90 degrees, keeping the root end to the left, and make a second lengthwise slit. Make further slits between the first two, but this time do not cut all the way to the center of the leek. Cut only through as many layers as is necessary to divide the layers into strips of about the same width. After all the slits are made, rotate the root end 90 degrees toward you. With your fingertips positioned straight down toward the board, hold the leek firmly with your left hand. Position the chef's knife held with a pinch grip, so the flat of the blade rests against the flat side of the tip of your forefinger. This way, your forefinger serves as a guide for the knife. Start each cut with the tip of the blade in contact with, or near, the cutting board, with the handle angled up. As you bring the knife down, slide the blade forward so that it moves through the leek as you produce the slices. After each cut, move your forefinger to the left a distance equal to the desired thickness of the next cut. Ideally, the thickness of this cut should be the same as the previous one, so the results appear uniform. As you do this, it is important that the flat of the blade always remain in contact with the flat surface of your forefinger (2).

Making Leek Strings

Use medium to large, cleaned leeks, thicker than 1½ inches across. The leeks should also have at least 6 inches of white before the green portion starts. Carefully remove the outer layers one at a time by making a slit, to the depth of two or three layers, with the tip of a sharp paring knife down the length of the leek. Stack one or two layers flat on the cutting board and begin to tightly roll them up from the root end (1). When you reach the point where the layers starting to turn green—a little light green is okay—trim off the green part of leek with the tip of a sharp chef's knife held with a pinch grip. Without allowing the leek roll to loosen, turn it in your left hand so it is positioned for crosscutting, holding it with your fingertips pointing straight down toward the board. Position the chef's knife, held in a pinch grip, so the flat of the blade rests against the flat side of the tip of your forefinger. This way, your forefinger serves as a guide for the knife (2). The width of the slices should be the same as the thickness of the individual layer, so that when the cut "strings" are unwound, they are as wide as they are thick. Start each cut with the tip of the blade in contact with, or near, the cutting board, with the handle angled up. As you bring the knife down, slide the blade forward so that it moves through the leek as you produce the slices. After each cut, move your forefinger to the left a distance equal to the desired width of the next cut. As you do this, it is important that the flat of the blade always remain in contact with the flat surface of your forefinger. Continue shredding layers from the leek until the portion remaining is too narrow, about half an inch wide (3).

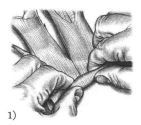

1)

2)

3)

CUTTING LEEKS (*left-hand version*)

Trimming a Leek

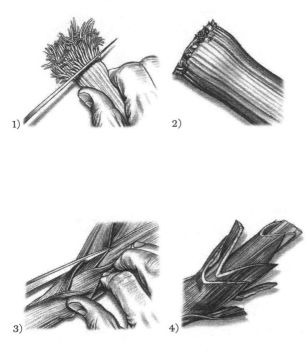

Hold the leek firmly in your right hand and hold a sharp chef's knife in your left hand with a pinch grip. Cut just the tendril-like portion of the root from the leek, making a straight cut slightly above the juncture of the skin and root so a small portion of the root section remains intact (1). The reason for trimming the root is more aesthetic than practical, but sometimes, if it is not trimmed, pieces of root will become loose and adhere to the flesh of the leek as it is sliced or diced (2).

The thick dark green portions of the leek leaves are usually discarded. As you move from the outer layers inward, the tender portion of each layer becomes longer. When removing the thick dark green leaves, remove one layer at a time. Hold the leek against the board with your right hand. Using a chef's knife held in your left hand in a pinch grip, trim the thick green portion of the layer almost tangentially with the stalk of the leek. Flip the leek over and trim the next layer on the other side in a similar manner (3). Continue until only the tender, light-green portions of the leek remain (4).

Cleaning a Leek

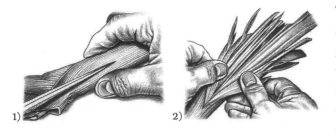

To remove the dirt commonly found between the layers at the point where each leaf turns from white to light green, place the trimmed leek on the cutting board with the root end to your right. Hold the leek firmly with your right hand. Holding the chef's knife in your left hand with a pinch grip, insert the tip of the knife into the leek to slit it down the middle to the ends of the leaves: start the cut where the dirt shows through the white portion of the outermost layer (1). After making the cut, gently spread out the layers under running water to wash out the dirt. When done, be sure to shake out any water, and re-form the leek into its natural shape (2).

Slicing a Leek

Leeks are often cut into rounds (1) or diagonal slices (2).
Diagonal slices separate more easily and are more
attractive than rounds. Other than the angle of the cut,
the technique for cutting either is the same. Place the
leek on the cutting board so the root end is toward the
right. With your fingertips positioned straight down

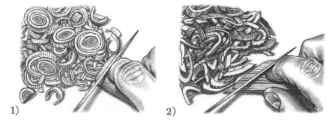

1) 2)

toward the board, hold the leek firmly with your right hand. Position a sharp chef's knife, held with a pinch grip, so
the flat of the blade rests against the flat side of the tip of your forefinger. This way, your forefinger serves as a guide
for the knife. Start each cut with the tip of the blade in contact with, or near, the cutting board, with the handle
angled up. As you bring the knife down, slide the blade forward so that it moves through the leek as you produce the
slices. After each cut, move your forefinger to the right a distance equal to the desired thickness of the next cut.
Ideally, the thickness of this cut should be the same as the thickness of the previous slice, so the resulting rounds
have a uniform thickness. As you do this, it is important that the flat of the blade always remain in contact with the
flat surface of your forefinger.

Mincing a Leek

Place the trimmed and washed leek on the cutting board with the root end to the right.
Hold the leek firmly with your right hand. Holding the chef's knife in your left hand with
a pinch grip, insert the tip of the knife into the leek near the root and slit it down the
middle for its entire length (1). Turn the leek 90 degrees, keeping the root end to the left,
and make a second lengthwise slit. Make further slits between the first two, but this time
do not cut all the way to the center of the leek. Cut only through as many layers as is
necessary to divide the layers into strips of about the same width. After all the slits are
made, rotate the root end 90 degrees toward you. With your fingertips positioned
straight down toward the board, hold the leek firmly with your right hand. Position
the chef's knife, held with a pinch grip, so the flat of the blade rests against the flat
side of the tip of your forefinger. This way, your forefinger serves as a guide for the
knife. Start each cut with the tip of the blade in contact with, or near, the cutting

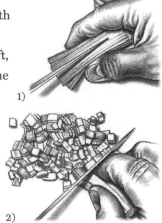

1) 2)

board, with the handle angled up. As you bring the knife down, slide the blade forward so that it moves through the
leek as you produce the slices. After each cut, move your forefinger to the right a distance equal to the desired
thickness of the next cut. Ideally, the thickness of this cut should be the same as the previous one, so the results
appear uniform. As you do this, it is important that the flat of the blade always remain in contact with the flat
surface of your forefinger (2).

CUTTING LEEKS (*left-hand version continued*)

Making Leek Strings

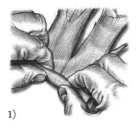

1)

2)

3)

To make leek strings, use medium to large, cleaned leeks, thicker than 1½ inches across. The leeks should also have at least 6 inches of white before the green portion starts. Carefully remove the outer layers one at a time by making a slit, to the depth of two or three layers, with the tip of a sharp paring knife down the length of the leek. Stack one or two layers flat on the cutting board and begin to tightly roll them up from the root end (1). When you reach the point where the layers are starting to turn green—a little light green is okay—trim off the green part of the leek with the tip of a sharp chef's knife held with a pinch grip. Without allowing the leek roll to loosen, turn it in your right hand so it is positioned for crosscutting, holding it with your fingertips pointing straight down toward the board. Position the chef's knife, held in a pinch grip, so the flat of the blade rests against the flat side of the tip of your forefinger. This way, your forefinger serves as a guide for the knife (2). The width of the slices should be the same as the thickness of the individual layer, so that when the cut "strings" are unwound, they are as wide as they are thick. Start each cut with the tip of the blade in contact with, or near, the cutting board, with the handle angled up. As you bring the knife down, slide the blade forward so that it moves through the leek as you produce the slices. After each cut, move your forefinger to the right a distance equal to the desired width of the next cut. As you do this, it is important that the flat of the blade always remain in contact with the flat surface of your forefinger. Continue shredding layers from the leek until the portion remaining is too narrow, about half an inch wide (3).

CUTTING GREEN ONIONS

GREEN ONIONS ARE SELDOM THE STAR OF THE SHOW BUT OFTEN PART OF THE chorus. In the 1950s in California, it was common to serve a plate of raw green onions, carrots, celery, and black olives at the start of a meal— something to eat with your cocktail. But today, home cooks and chefs have embraced their flavor and texture, and serve them cooked as appetizers or side dishes.

There's a bit of confusion as to what to call green onions. To some people they are scallions. To others they might even be called spring onions, though true spring onions have a bulbous white portion instead of the straight one found on green onions.

Green onions are an inexpensive garnish. Generally, they are sold with much of their greenery trimmed off and wrapped tightly with a couple of rubber bands. They will last longer in the refrigerator if the rubber bands are removed and they are stored loosely in an open plastic bag. If the market sprayed the onions with water to keep them fresh looking, they should be dried before storing.

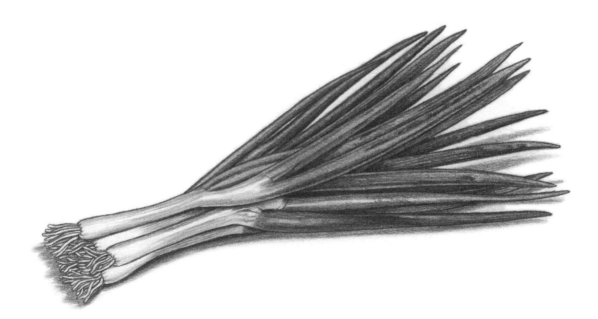

CUTTING GREEN ONIONS (*right-hand version*)

Trimming a Green Onion

Hold the green onion firmly in your left hand and a sharp chef's knife in your right with a pinch grip. Cut the roots from the onion, making a straight cut slightly above the juncture of the skin and the roots so all the roots are removed.

Shredding a Green Onion

1)

In preparation for mincing a green onion or to produce shreds, lay the onion on the cutting board with the white portion to your right. With your left hand, hold the onion firmly, leaving the white portion exposed. Curl your fingertips upward so they are not in the same plane as the knife blade. Holding a chef's knife in your right hand with a pinch grip and with the side of the blade parallel to the cutting board, make one or more cuts the entire length of the white portion; the number of cuts depends on the thickness of the onion. This is one cut that cannot be made with a sawing motion. Instead, jiggle the blade forward and back slightly as you push it through the onion (1).

2)

For a really fine shred or mince, make one last cut into the top of the onion with the tip of the chef's knife. Holding the knife with a pinch grip, insert the tip into the top of the white portion and draw the knife to the right. Note that the onion is not moved from its original position for this last cut, which must go all the way through the onion (2).

3)

If you are using the green portion of the onion as well as the white, turn the onion around so that the green portion is to your right. Slit each green stalk at least once; for wide stalks, make multiple slits: hold the stalks against the cutting board with your left thumb and forefinger. Using the chef's knife held with a pinch grip, slit each stalk with the tip of your knife, piercing the stalk with the tip and then drawing the knife to the right through the end of the onion (3).

For shreds, hold the green onion strips together in a stack with their ends aligned. Using the chef's knife held with a pinch grip, cut the onions to the desired lengths. If the onions are to be minced, it usually saves time to cut them into shorter lengths first. The pieces can then be stacked in greater quantity so that more can be minced at one time (4).

4)

Mincing a Green Onion

Hold the green onion strips from the previous step with your left hand with your fingertips positioned straight down toward the cutting board. Position the chef's knife, held with a pinch grip, so the flat of the blade rests against the flat side of the tip of your forefinger. This way, your forefinger serves as a guide for the knife. Start each cut with the tip of the blade in contact with, or near, the cutting board, with the handle angled up. As you bring the knife down, slide the blade forward so that it moves through the green onions as you produce the mince. After each cut, move your forefinger to the left a distance equal to the desired width of the next cut. Ideally, the width of this cut should be the same as the previous one, so the results appear uniform. As you do this, it is important that the flat of the blade always remain in contact with the flat surface of your forefinger.

Slicing a Green Onion

Green onions are often cut into rounds or diagonal slices. Diagonal slices separate more easily and are more attractive than rounds. Other than the angle of the cut, the technique for cutting either is the same. Place the onion on the cutting board so the root end is toward the left. With your fingertips positioned straight down toward the board, hold the onion firmly with your left hand. Position a sharp chef's knife, held with a pinch grip, so the flat of the blade rests against the flat side of the tip of your

forefinger. This way, your forefinger serves as a guide for the knife. Start each cut with the tip of the blade in contact with, or near, the cutting board, with the handle angled up. As you bring the knife down, slide the blade forward so that it moves through the green onion as you produce the slices. After each cut, move your forefinger to the left a distance equal to the desired width of the next cut. Ideally, the width of this cut should be the same as the width of the previous one so the resulting rounds are uniform. As you do this, it is important that the flat of the blade always remain in contact with the flat surface of your forefinger.

CUTTING GREEN ONIONS (*left-hand version*)

Trimming a Green Onion

Hold the green onion firmly in your right hand and a sharp chef's knife in your left with a pinch grip. Cut the roots from the onion, making a straight cut slightly above the juncture of the skin and the roots so all the roots are removed.

Shredding a Green Onion

1)

In preparation for mincing a green onion or to produce shreds, lay the onion on the cutting board with the white portion to your left. With your right hand, hold the onion firmly, leaving the white portion exposed. Curl your fingertips upward so they are not in the same plane as the knife blade. Holding a chef's knife in your left hand with a pinch grip and with the side of the blade parallel to the cutting board, make one or more cuts the entire length of the white portion; the number of cuts depends on the thickness of the green onion. This is one cut that cannot be made with a sawing motion. Instead, jiggle the blade forward and back slightly as you push it through the onion (1).

2)

For a really fine shred or mince, make one last cut into the top of the onion with the tip of the chef's knife. Holding the knife with a pinch grip, insert the tip into the top of the white portion and draw the knife to the left. Note that the onion is not moved from its original position for this last cut, which must go all the way through the onion (2).

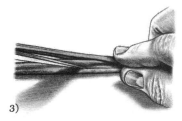

3)

If you are using the green portion of the onion as well as the white, turn the onion around so that the green portion is to your left. Slit each green stalk at least once; for wide stalks, make multiple slits: hold the stalks against the cutting board with your right thumb and forefinger. Using the chef's knife held with a pinch grip, slit each stalk with the tip of your knife, piercing the stalk with the tip and then drawing the knife to the left through the end of the onion (3).

For shreds, hold the green onion strips together in a stack with their ends aligned. Using the chef's knife held with a pinch grip, cut the onions to the desired lengths. If the onions are to be minced, it usually saves time to cut the onions into shorter lengths first. The pieces can then be stacked in greater quantity so that more can be minced at one time (4).

4)

Mincing a Green Onion

Hold the green onion strips from the previous step with your right hand with your fingertips positioned straight down towards the cutting board. Position the chef's knife, held with a pinch grip, so the flat of the blade rests against the flat side of the tip of your forefinger. This way, your forefinger serves as a guide for the knife. Start each cut with the tip of the blade in contact with, or near, the cutting board, with the handle angled up. As you bring the knife down, slide the blade forward so that it moves through the green onions  as you produce the mince. After each cut, move your forefinger to the right a distance equal to the desired width of the next cut. Ideally, the width of this cut should be the same as the previous one, so the results appear uniform. As you do this, it is important that the flat of the blade always remain in contact with the flat surface of your forefinger.

Slicing a Green Onion

Green onions are often cut into rounds or diagonal slices. Diagonal slices separate more easily and are more attractive than rounds. Other than the angle of the cut, the technique for cutting either is the same. Place the onion on the cutting board so the root end is toward the right. With your fingertips positioned straight down toward the board, hold the onion firmly with your right hand. Position a sharp chef's knife, held with a pinch grip, so the flat of the blade rests against the flat side of the tip of your forefinger.  This way, your forefinger serves as a guide for the knife. Start each cut with the tip of the blade in contact with, or near, the cutting board, with the handle angled up. As you bring the knife down, slide the blade forward so that it moves through the green onion as you produce the slices. After each cut, move your forefinger to the right a distance equal to the desired width of the next cut. Ideally, the width of this cut should be the same as the width of the previous one, so the resulting rounds are uniform. As you do this, it is important that the flat of the blade always remain in contact with the flat surface of your forefinger.

CUTTING CELERY

OPEN A BUNCH OF CELERY BY SEPARATING ALL THE STALKS. LAY THE STALKS OUT on the counter. What do you notice about them? Each is a different size and thickness. This can pose a challenge if your goal is to dice the celery uniformly. Cutting a uniform dice requires a bit of planning on the part of the cook. Look at each stalk before starting to cut it. In the end, perfect uniformity is impossible, but it is possible to have all the pieces more or less the same size. Think averages.

Even when a recipe calls for simply cutting the celery into 2-inch lengths, some will need to be slit lengthwise two or three times if you'd like all the pieces to be of similar size. The more uniform the pieces, the more evenly they will cook.

I believe that when you serve celery there should be "no strings attached." Although most recipes don't call for celery to be peeled, the results are often nicer if the strings are removed. Consequently, I always peel the celery first unless the strings will be strained out later during the cooking process. Removing the strings is easy and doesn't take much time.

Most contemporary recipes use celery raw. This is unfortunate, since celery makes a great cooked vegetable and a luscious soup. The classic celery Victor is essentially just celery blanched in broth, allowed to cool, and served in a vinaigrette flavored with herbs.

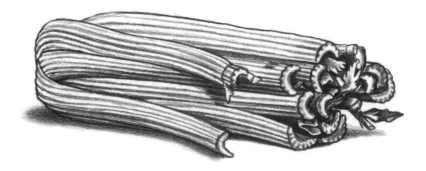

CUTTING CELERY (*right-hand version*)

Peeling Celery

A yoke-type peeler, shown in the illustration, is my preferred tool for peeling celery. To peel a stalk of celery, hold the stalk vertical in your left hand and the peeler in your right. Peel the stalk from the narrow end to the wide end. After each strip is removed, rotate the stalk toward you to expose a new strip. Continue until all the strings are removed.

Slicing Celery

Celery can be sliced crosswise, but a diagonal cut makes better-looking slices. To slice celery, place the stalk on the cutting board with the wide end toward your left. Hold the stalk firmly with your left hand with the fingertips positioned straight down toward the cutting board. Position a sharp chef's knife, held with a pinch grip, so the flat of the blade rests against the flat side of the tip of your forefinger. This way, your forefinger serves as a guide for the knife. To make simple slices, position the knife

perpendicular to the stalk. For diagonal slices, angle the knife as shown in the illustration. Start each cut with the tip of the blade in contact with, or near, the cutting board, with the handle angled up. As you bring the knife down, slide the blade forward so that it moves through the celery as you produce the slices. After each cut, move your forefinger to the left a distance equal to the desired thickness of the next cut. Ideally, the thickness of this cut should be the same as the previous one, so the results appear uniform. As you do this, it is important that the flat of the blade always remain in contact with the flat surface of your forefinger.

Julienning Celery

Place a peeled celery stalk round side down on the cutting board. Hold the stalk with your left hand. Using a sharp paring knife held in your right hand with a pinch grip, make successive cuts down the entire length of the stalk (1). The number of cuts and the order in which they are made will depend on the size of the stalk, as shown in the illustration (2). Stalks that vary drastically in width may require more cuts at the wide end than at the narrow end. Sometimes the julienne process is easier if the stalk is first cut in half or into thirds.

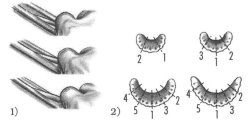

CUTTING CELERY (*right-hand version continued*)

Dicing Celery

Gather the julienned strips from the previous step together into a stack, with all the strips parallel to one another. Hold the stack firmly in place with your left hand, pressing down on top of it with your fingertips in a vertical position. Position the chef's knife, held with a pinch grip, so the flat of the blade rests against the flat side of the tip of your forefinger. This way, your forefinger serves as a guide for the knife. Start each cut with the tip of the blade in contact with, or near, the cutting board, with the handle angled up. As you bring the knife down, slide the blade forward so that it moves through the celery as you produce the dice. After each cut, move your forefinger to the left a distance equal to the desired width of the next cut. Ideally, the width of this cut should be the same as the thickness of the slice, so the resulting dice are cubes. As you do this, it is important that the flat of the blade always remain in contact with the flat surface of your forefinger.

CUTTING CELERY (*left-hand version*)

Peeling Celery

A yoke-type peeler, as shown in the illustration, is my preferred tool for peeling celery. To peel a stalk of celery, hold the stalk vertical in your right hand and the peeler in your left. Peel the stalk from the narrow end to the wide end. After each strip is removed, rotate the stalk toward you to expose a new strip. Continue until all the strings are removed.

Slicing Celery

Celery can be sliced crosswise, but a diagonal cut makes better-looking slices. To slice celery, place the stalk on the cutting board with the wide end toward your right. Hold the stalk firmly with your right hand with the fingertips positioned straight down toward the cutting board. Position a sharp chef's knife, held with a pinch grip, so the flat of the blade rests against the flat side of the tip of your forefinger. This way, your forefinger serves as a guide for the knife. To make simple slices, position the knife

perpendicular to the stalk. For diagonal slices, angle the knife as shown in the illustration. Start each cut with the tip of the blade in contact with, or near, the cutting board, with the handle angled up. As you bring the knife down, slide the blade forward so that it moves through the celery as you produce the slices. After each cut, move your forefinger to the right a distance equal to the desired thickness of the next cut. Ideally, the thickness of this cut should be the same as the previous one, so the results appear uniform. As you do this, it is important that the flat of the blade always remain in contact with the flat surface of your forefinger.

Julienning Celery

Place a peeled celery stalk round side down on the cutting board. Hold the stalk with your right hand. Using a sharp paring knife held in your left hand with a pinch grip, make successive cuts down the entire length of the stalk (1). The number of cuts and the order in which they are made will depend on the size of the stalk, as shown in the illustration (2). Stalks that vary drastically in width may require more cuts at the wide end than at the narrow end. Sometimes the julienne process is easier if the stalk is first cut in half or into thirds.

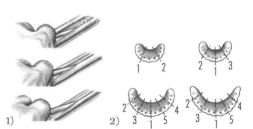

CUTTING CELERY *(left-hand version continued)*

Dicing Celery

Gather the julienned strips from the previous step together into a stack, with all the strips parallel to one another. Hold the stack firmly in place with your right hand, pressing down on top of it with your fingertips in a vertical position. Position the chef's knife, held with a pinch grip, so the flat of the blade rests against the flat side of the tip of your forefinger. This way, your forefinger serves as a guide for the knife. Start each cut with the tip of the blade in contact with, or near, the cutting board, with the handle angled up. As you bring the knife down, slide the blade forward so that it moves through the celery as you produce the dice. After each cut, move your forefinger to the right a distance equal to the desired width of the next cut. Ideally, the width of this cut should be the same as the thickness of the slice, so the resulting dice are cubes. As you do this, it is important that the flat of the blade always remain in contact with the flat surface of your forefinger.

CUTTING FENNEL

FENNEL IS A VERSATILE PLANT. THE SEEDS, STEMS, AND LEAVES ARE ALL USED IN cooking. (The parts of the bulbous portion of fennel that look like layers are actually leaves.) Although the seeds are most commonly used to flavor foods, the dried stems can be used in braised dishes. The fennel leaves served as a vegetable are from a variety that produces the thickened bulb that we see in the market. Fennel is sometimes labeled anise or *finocchio,* the Italian name. Both cooked and raw, the leaves have a delightful anise-like flavor. Shaved very thin, raw fennel is often used in a salad. When cooked, it can be served crunchy or until it starts to melt.

The technique described in this section is for shaving fennel with a knife. Once the bulbs are split and cored, though, this can also be done very quickly with a Japanese mandoline.

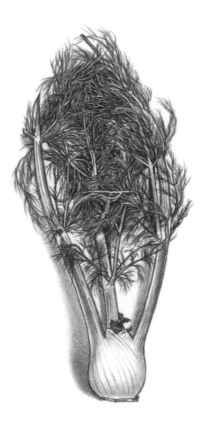

CUTTING FENNEL (*right-hand version*)

Trimming Fennel

Fennel is sold either thoroughly trimmed or with a substantial portion of the stalks, stems, and fine green fern still attached to the bulb-like section. If they are attached, remove the stalks before using the fennel. (The stems can be dried to use as a flavoring in sauces and stocks.) To trim the bulb, hold it firmly against the cutting board with your left hand, with the stalks to your right. Holding a sharp chef's knife in a pinch grip in your right hand, use the tip of the knife to cut off the stalks where they exit the bulb. If the base of the bulb has not been trimmed flat, square it off with the chef's knife.

Coring Fennel

1)

Stand the fennel bulb on its base and hold it firmly in place against the cutting board with your left hand. With the chef's knife held in a pinch grip, cut through the center of the bulb to create two equal halves. Start near the tip of the knife and advance the cutting edge toward the heel as you push the blade through the bulb. The bulb should split easily, without having to saw with the blade (1).

2)

As you look at the two cut halves of the fennel bulb, you will notice a solid core at their base. The core can be quite tough and most of it should be removed. To remove it, hold a fennel half firmly in your left hand, with the cut section facing you. Use a sharp paring knife held in your right hand, with your forefinger and middle finger wrapped around the blade. Support your right hand against the fennel with your thumb. Remove the core by cutting away a conical portion of it, leaving only a minimal amount of core, but do not cut as far as the leaves, or the bulb will fall apart (2).

Shaving Fennel

Fennel can be shaved or finely sliced either across the bulb (1) or lengthwise (2). This is simply a matter of personal preference and/or what is specified in the recipe. In either case, with your left hand, hold a fennel half firmly against the cutting board, cut side down, with your fingertips positioned straight down toward the board. Position the chef's knife, held 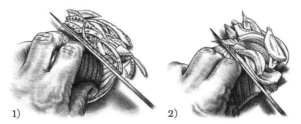 with a pinch grip, so the flat of the blade rests against the flat side of the tip of your forefinger. This way, your forefinger serves as a guide for the knife. Start each cut with the tip of the blade in contact with, or near, the cutting board, with the handle angled up. As you bring the knife down, slide the blade forward so that it moves through the fennel as you produce the slices. After each cut, move your forefinger to the left a distance equal to the desired thickness of the next cut. Ideally, the thickness of this cut should be the same as the previous one, so the results are uniform. As you do this, it is important that the flat of the blade always remain in contact with the flat surface of your forefinger.

CUTTING FENNEL (*left-hand version*)

Trimming Fennel

Fennel is sold either thoroughly trimmed or with a substantial portion of the stalks, stems, and fine green fern still attached to the bulb-like section. If they are attached, remove the stalks before using the fennel. (The stems can be dried to use as a flavoring in sauces and stocks.) To trim the bulb, hold it firmly against the cutting board with your right hand, with the stalks to your left. Holding a sharp chef's knife in a pinch grip in your left hand, use the tip of the knife to cut off the stalks where they exit the bulb. If the base of the bulb has not been trimmed flat, square it off with the chef's knife.

Coring Fennel

1)

Stand the fennel bulb on its base and hold it firmly in place against the cutting board with your right hand. With the chef's knife held in a pinch grip, cut through the center of the bulb to create two equal halves. Start near the tip of the knife and advance the cutting edge toward the heel as you push the blade through the bulb. The bulb should split easily, without having to saw with the blade (1).

2)

As you look at the two cut halves of the fennel bulb, you will notice a solid core at their base. The core can be quite tough and most of it should be removed. To remove it, hold a fennel half firmly in your right hand, with the cut section facing you. Use a sharp paring knife held in your left hand, with your forefinger and middle finger wrapped around the blade. Support your left hand against the fennel with your thumb. Remove the core by cutting away a conical portion of it, leaving only a minimal amount of core, but do not cut as far as the leaves, or the bulb will fall apart (2).

Shaving Fennel

Fennel can be shaved or finely sliced either across the bulb (1) or lengthwise (2). This is simply a matter of personal preference and/or what is specified in the recipe. In either case, with your right hand, hold a fennel half firmly against the cutting board, cut side down, with your fingertips positioned straight down toward the board. Position the

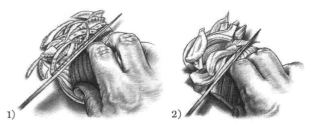

1)   2)

chef's knife, held with a pinch grip, so the flat of the blade rests against the flat side of the tip of your forefinger. This way, your forefinger serves as a guide for the knife. Start each cut with the tip of the blade in contact with, or near, the cutting board, with the handle angled up. As you bring the knife down, slide the blade forward so that it moves through the fennel as you produce the slices. After each cut, move your forefinger to the right a distance equal to the desired thickness of the next cut. Ideally, the thickness of this cut should be the same as the previous one, so the results are uniform. As you do this, it is important that the flat of the blade always remain in contact with the flat surface of your forefinger.

CUTTING ASPARAGUS

ASPARAGUS, A GENUS OF *LILIACEAE* (THE LILY FAMILY INCLUDING LEEKS AND onions), includes more than one hundred species found in the warm and temperate regions of America and Europe. Both the Greeks and Romans are known to have eaten asparagus. The Egyptians even shared them with their gods. It is thought that the Arabs introduced asparagus into Spain and from there it spread to France. Early colonists to North America planted asparagus.

Until modern times, asparagus remained a food for the privileged. In 1843, asparagus and beef were priced similarly in France, at about half a franc per pound. In earlier times, one to one and a half pounds of asparagus were allotted per diner. Nowadays, six to eight ounces per person is considered generous. Perhaps it was the vegetable's reputation as an aphrodisiac that accounts for the larger portions of the past?

If left alone, the asparagus stalks that we eat would grow into a lacy fern. At the end of the season, asparagus farmers allow the last stalks to grow into ferns so the roots, which live many seasons, receive nourishment for the remainder of the year. An asparagus field in the summer is quite a sight.

Many people, unfortunately, follow the bad advice they've received about removing the ends of the asparagus stalks by snapping them off. This method usually wastes a great deal of the edible portion of the stalk. I've seen people discard over half of every stalk because of the snapping technique. You'll find the method for trimming asparagus presented in this section is far less wasteful.

CUTTING ASPARAGUS (*right-hand version*)

Trimming Asparagus

To avoid trimming too much off the root ends of the stalks when prepping asparagus, place two or three stalks at a time on a cutting board with the bottom ends evened up. Hold them firmly in place with your left hand. Using a sharp chef's knife held with a pinch grip, cut off a small portion of the bottom of each stalk. A piece that is no longer than it is wide will usually be sufficient to remove any area that has dried out since the asparagus was harvested. As you make the cut, notice whether the stalk slices smoothly or feels tough and fibrous. If the cut was smooth, it is not necessary to remove any more of the stalk. If the cut felt tough, trim off a little more off the stalk until you reach the tender area. In my experience, fewer than one in twenty stalks requires more than an initial trimming.

Peeling Fat Asparagus

Most recipes don't specifically call for asparagus to be peeled, but it is preferable when you desire sweeter, less stringy asparagus. There are two basic methods that can be used; the first works better with fat asparagus. A yoke-type peeler, shown in the illustration, is the ideal tool. To peel the stalk of asparagus, hold it in your left hand and the peeler in your right. Peel from the stalk from ½ inch or so below the developed part of the tip to the cut end. After each strip of skin is removed, rotate the stalk toward you to expose a new section of skin.

Peeling Slender Asparagus

The second method employs a combination of trimming and peeling. It is usually used for slimmer asparagus stalks. First remove the small "leaves" along the length of the stalk: hold the stalk in your left hand and a small paring knife in your right, with your forefinger and middle finger wrapped around the blade. Slide the tip of the blade just under the leaf. With

1) 2)

your thumb, hold the leaf firmly against the flat side of the blade near the tip, snap the leaf off, and discard (1). When all the leaves are removed, place the stalk on the cutting board and peel the last 2 inches or so with a yoke-type peeler as described in the first method (2).

CUTTING ASPARAGUS *(left-hand version)*

Trimming Asparagus

To avoid trimming too much off the root ends of the stalks when prepping asparagus place two or three stalks at a time on a cutting board with the bottom ends evened up. Hold them firmly in place with your right hand. Using a sharp chef's knife held with a pinch grip, cut off a small portion of the bottom of each stalk. A piece that is no longer than it is wide will usually be sufficient to remove any area that has dried out since the asparagus was harvested. As you make the cut, notice whether the stalk slices smoothly or feels tough and fibrous. If the cut was smooth, it is not necessary to remove any more of the stalk. If the cut felt tough, trim off a little more off the stalk until you reach the tender area. In my experience, fewer than one in twenty stalks requires more than an initial trimming.

Peeling Fat Asparagus

Most recipes don't specifically call for asparagus to be peeled, but it is preferable when you desire sweeter, less stringy asparagus. There are two basic methods that can be used; the first works better with fat asparagus. A yoke-type peeler, shown in the illustration, is the ideal tool. To peel the stalk of asparagus, hold it in your right hand and the peeler in your left. Peel from the stalk from ½ inch or so below the developed part of the tip to the cut end. After each strip of skin is removed, rotate the stalk toward you to expose a new section of skin.

Peeling Slender Asparagus

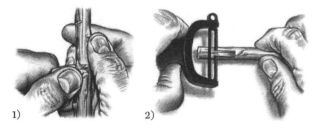

1)   2)

The second method employs a combination of trimming and peeling. It is usually used for slimmer asparagus stalks. First remove the small "leaves" along the length of the stalk: hold the stalk in your right hand and a small paring knife in your left, with your forefinger and middle finger wrapped around the blade. Slide the tip of the blade just under the leaf. With your thumb, hold the leaf firmly against the flat side of the blade near the tip, snap the leaf off, and discard (1). When all the leaves are removed, place the stalk on the cutting board and peel the last 2 inches or so with a yoke-type peeler as described in the first method (2).

CUTTING ARTICHOKES

PEOPLE EITHER LOVE ARTICHOKES OR HATE THEM. SOME LIKE THEM BUT DON'T like the way the kitchen smells when they are cooking. Some don't know how to eat an artichoke.

The artichoke is really an edible thistle. The raw thistle is trimmed and then boiled or steamed until the heart is tender. In many families, the only way to eat an artichoke is with one's fingers. Each diner then pulls the leaves off one at a time and eats the soft portion, where it was attached to the base, after first dipping it in a sauce, typically melted butter or mayonnaise. When I was growing up, we would speculate that you could tell a lot about a person based on the way he or she did or didn't organize the discarded leaves.

In the United States, most artichokes are of the green globe variety. In southern Europe, it is common to find artichokes of other shapes and colors. Whatever their shape or color, the cut or torn surfaces of any artichoke will rapidly darken when exposed to the air. To prevent this, the artichokes should be placed in acidulated water immediately after they are cut. Acidulated water is made by adding an acid to water. Common acids are white vinegar, which should be added at a ratio of 1½ tablespoons per quart of cold water, or lemon juice, added at a ratio of 3 tablespoons per quart of cold water.

CUTTING ARTICHOKES (*right-hand version*)

Trimming and Peeling an Artichoke

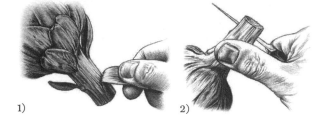

1)

2)

If the artichoke still has its stem attached, remove any leaves attached to the stem by pulling them toward the cut end (1). Trim the end of the stem with a paring knife held in your right hand and the artichoke held in your left. Support the stem with your thumb positioned in opposition to the blade but offset, so it's not directly in front of the cutting edge (2).

3)

To peel the stem, hold the artichoke in your left hand and a sharp paring knife in your right hand, with your forefinger wrapped around the blade. Support the stem with your thumb positioned against the cut end of the stem. Start each pass of the knife at the base of the artichoke, and use just the tip of the knife to peel the stem. Remove only a thin piece of skin with each pass of the knife, and rotate the artichoke toward your right hand after each pass to expose new skin. Be careful not to whittle the stem (3).

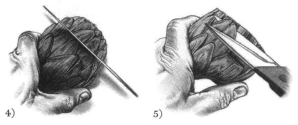

4)

5)

To prepare the artichoke for cooking whole, lay it on a cutting board and firmly grasp the bottom portion between the thumb and forefinger of your left hand. Using a large knife with a serrated blade or a sharp chef's knife held in a pinch grip in your right hand, cut off the top quarter of the artichoke using a sawing motion (4). Then, using a pair of heavy-duty scissors, cut the thorn and a bit of the top from each remaining leaf. Rotate the artichoke toward you as you trim the leaves one after another (5). The artichoke is now ready for cooking.

Preparing an Artichoke Heart

1)

If only the heart of the artichoke is to be used in the recipe, cut off the top of the artichoke as described above, but remove about half of the artichoke. By hand, snap off the coarse, darker green leaves surrounding the heart until the lighter, softer inner leaves are exposed (1). Some recipes call for the heart alone, without the stem. In this case, hold the heart firmly against a cutting board with your left hand, with the stem to your right, and cut off the stem flush with the artichoke's base using a chef's knife.

To get to the artichoke's heart, grasp the remaining artichoke with your left hand. Hold a paring knife in your right hand, with your forefinger wrapped around the blade, and rotate the artichoke into the blade with your left hand while sawing back and forth with the knife; support the artichoke with the thumb of your right hand. Cut through the top of the artichoke at about a 45-degree angle, then continue to cut through the leaves until you reach the heart, being careful not to cut into it (2). Ignore the fuzzy choke for the moment. After removing the leaves, turn the artichoke heart in your left hand so the bottom can be trimmed and, holding your knife once more at about a 45-degree angle, remove the stringy portion of each leaf remnant on the base (3).

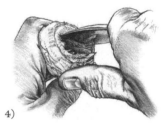

2)

3)

Use a dessert spoon to scrape the choke from the heart. Hold the spoon in your right hand so only the bowl of the spoon is exposed, and scrape with the edge of the spoon. Remove only the fuzzy portion of the choke (4).

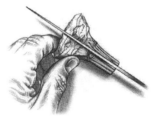

4)

Cutting an Artichoke Heart

Depending on the recipe and the size of the artichoke, you may need to cut the heart into halves, quarters, or eighths. Hold the artichoke heart firmly against a cutting board with your left hand. With a chef's knife held in a pinch grip in your right hand, first cut the heart in half. Start the cut with the tip of the knife and proceed by pushing the knife forward and downward to complete the cut. Then cut the heart into as many wedges as required.

CUTTING ARTICHOKES (*left-hand version*)

Trimming and Peeling an Artichoke

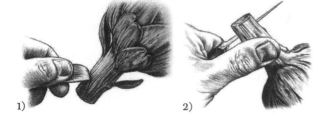

1)
2)

If the artichoke still has its stem attached, remove any leaves attached to the stem by pulling them toward the cut end (1). Trim the end of the stem with a paring knife held in your left hand and the artichoke held in your right. Support the stem with your thumb positioned in opposition to the blade but offset so it's not directly in front of the cutting edge (2).

3)

To peel the stem, hold the artichoke in your right hand and a sharp paring knife in your left hand, with your forefinger wrapped around the blade. Support the stem with your thumb positioned against the cut end of the stem. Start each pass of the knife at the base of the artichoke, and use just the tip of the knife to peel the stem. Remove only a thin piece of skin with each pass of the knife, and rotate the artichoke toward your left hand after each pass to expose new skin. Be careful not to whittle the stem (3).

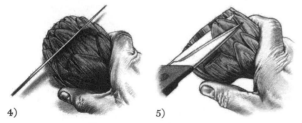

4)
5)

To prepare the artichoke for cooking whole, lay it on a cutting board and firmly grasp the bottom portion between the thumb and forefinger of your right hand. Using a large knife with a serrated blade or a sharp chef's knife held in a pinch grip in your left hand, cut off the top quarter of the artichoke using a sawing motion (4). Then, using a pair of heavy-duty scissors, cut the thorn and a bit of the top from each remaining leaf. Rotate the artichoke toward you as you trim the leaves one after another (5). The artichoke is now ready for cooking.

Preparing an Artichoke Heart

1)

If only the heart of the artichoke is to be used in the recipe, cut off the top of the artichoke as described above, but remove about half of the artichoke. By hand, snap off the coarse, darker green leaves surrounding the heart until the lighter, softer inner leaves are exposed (1). Some recipes call for the heart alone, without the stem. In this case, hold the heart firmly against a cutting board with your right hand, with the stem to your left, and cut off the stems flush with the artichoke's base using a chef's knife.

To get to the artichoke's heart, grasp the remaining artichoke with your right hand. Hold a paring knife in your left hand, with your forefinger wrapped around the blade, and rotate the artichoke into the blade with your right hand while sawing back and forth with the knife; support the artichoke with the thumb of your left hand. 2)

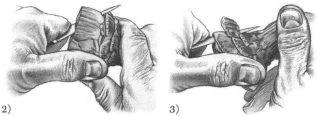

3)

Cut through the top of the artichoke at about a 45-degree angle, then continue to cut through the leaves until you reach the heart, being careful not to cut into it (2). Ignore the fuzzy choke for the moment. After removing the leaves, turn the artichoke heart in your right hand so the bottom can be trimmed and, holding your knife once more at about a 45-degree angle, remove the stringy portion of each leaf remnant on the base (3).

Use a dessert spoon to scrape the choke from the heart. Hold the spoon in your left hand so only the bowl of the spoon is exposed, and scrape with the edge of the spoon. Remove only the fuzzy portion of the choke (4).

4)

Cutting an Artichoke Heart

Depending on the recipe and the size of the artichoke, you may need to cut the heart into halves, quarters, or eighths. Hold the artichoke heart firmly against a cutting board with your right hand. With a chef's knife held in a pinch grip with your left hand, first cut the heart in half. Start the cut with the tip of the knife and proceed by pushing the knife forward and downward to complete the cut. Then cut the heart into as many wedges as required.

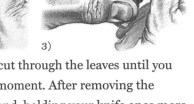

CUTTING CABBAGE

THERE ARE MANY VEGETABLES IN THE CABBAGE FAMILY, SUCH AS BRUSSELS SPROUTS and bok choy, along with many with cabbage in their name. In this section, we are concerned with the firm spherical heads of green or red cabbage. Sometimes the leaves are smooth and sometimes they are crinkly, as in the case of Savoy cabbage.

When purchasing head cabbage, look for ones that feel dense. The heads should be rock hard and not the least bit spongy.

If you often prepare recipes that call for shredding a large quantity of cabbage, such as sauerkraut, consider investing in a kraut board. This is a tool designed specifically for shredding cabbage, a job it does very well and very fast.

CUTTING CABBAGE (*right-hand version*)

Coring Cabbage

Place the head on the cutting board with the core pointing down and to your right. Support the head with your left hand. Cut through the center of the head with a large chef's knife held with a pinch grip in your right hand. It is important to cut through the very center of the core so that each half will hold together after cutting (1). Once you have cut the head in half, cut each half in two: place each half cut side down on the cutting board with the core to your right. Support the half with your left hand. Cut through the center of the core with the chef's knife held with a pinch grip in your right hand. Finally, remove any dirty or damaged leaves from the outside of each quarter.

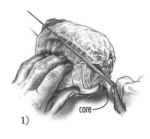

1)

Working separately with each quarter, place it with one cut side down flat on the cutting board and the second cut surface facing toward your right. The core should point to your left. Support the quarter with your left hand. Using the tip of the chef's knife held with a pinch grip in your right hand, remove the core by cutting out a wedge-shaped piece. Start at the top of the core and cut toward the base. The wedge should be pointed at the top and wide at the base. Try to remove only the core and the minimum amount of leaves connected to it (2).

2)

Shredding Cabbage

Using your left hand, flop the quarter toward you so that it rests on the surface just created by cutting out the wedge of core. Hold the quarter firmly in place with your left hand with your fingertips positioned straight down toward the cutting board. Position the chef's knife, held with a pinch grip, so the flat of the blade rests against the flat side of the tip of your forefinger. This way, your forefinger serves as a guide for the knife. Start each cut with the tip of the blade in contact with, or near, the cutting

board, with the handle angled up. As you bring the knife down, slide the blade forward so that it moves through the cabbage as you produce the shreds. Make the slices very narrow for shredded cabbage or wider for larger pieces. After each cut, move your forefinger to the left a distance equal to the desired thickness of the next cut. Ideally, the thickness of this cut should be the same as the previous one, so the results appear uniform. As you do this, it is important that the flat of the blade always remain in contact with the flat surface of your forefinger. When you are about three-quarters of the way through the quarter, turn it 90 degrees and continue cutting. This helps to produce slices of equal width all the way to the end of the quarter.

CUTTING CABBAGE (*left-hand version*)

Coring Cabbage

1)

Place the head on the cutting board with the core pointing down and to your left. Support the head with your right hand. Cut through the center of the head with a large chef's knife held with a pinch grip in your left hand. It is important to cut through the very center of the core so that each half will hold together after cutting (1). Once you have cut the head in half, cut each half in two: place each half cut side down on the cutting board with the core to your left. Support the half with your right hand. Cut through the center of the core with the chef's knife held with a pinch grip in your left hand. Finally, remove any dirty or damaged leaves from the outside of each quarter.

2)

Working separately with each quarter, place it with one cut side down flat on the cutting board and the second cut surface facing toward your left. The core should point to your right. Support the quarter with your right hand. Using the tip of the chef's knife held with a pinch grip in your left hand, remove the core by cutting out a wedge-shaped piece. Start at the top of the core and cut toward the base. The wedge should be pointed at the top and wide at the base. Try to remove only the core and the minimum amount of leaves connected to it (2).

Shredding Cabbage

Using your right hand, flop the quarter toward you so that it rests on the surface just created by cutting out the wedge of core. Hold the quarter firmly in place with your right hand with your fingertips positioned straight down toward the cutting board. Position the chef's knife, held with a pinch grip, so the flat of the blade rests against the flat side of the tip of your forefinger. This way, your forefinger serves as a guide for the knife. Start each cut with the tip of the blade in contact with, or near, the cutting board, with the handle angled up. As you bring the knife down, slide the blade forward so that it moves through the cabbage as you produce the shreds. Make the slices very narrow for shredded cabbage or wider for larger pieces. After each cut, move your forefinger to the right a distance equal to the desired thickness of the next cut. Ideally, the thickness of this cut should be the same as the previous one, so the results appear uniform. As you do this, it is important that the flat of the blade always remain in contact with the flat surface of your forefinger. When you are about three-quarters of the way through the quarter, turn it 90 degrees and continue cutting. This helps to produce slices of equal width all the way to the end of the quarter.

CUTTING CHARD, KALE, AND OTHER LEAFY GREENS

MANY LEAFY GREEN VEGETABLES ARE EXCELLENT SOURCES OF VITAMINS A AND C and contribute calcium, iron, fiber, and other nutrients. Supposedly foods rich in vitamins A and C are associated with the reduced risk of certain cancers. Greens are also very low in calories and sodium. All greens are fat and cholesterol free.

Spinach is generally tender enough to eat raw and requires only a minimal amount of preparation for cooking. If the stems are to be removed from the leaves, they can be pinched off with your fingers. But chard, beet greens, kale, mustard, and collards are best cooked. Usually the stems are discarded before cooking, but in some cases, as with chard and beet greens, the stems can be cooked separately or partially precooked and finished with the leaves.

It is usually easier to wash greens after they have been cut for cooking. The leafy portions can be immersed in a basin of cold water and agitated to remove any dirt. The stems, after they are cut to size, can be placed in a strainer and washed in the same water. It is usually not necessary to thoroughly dry greens before cooking, but this depends on the recipe.

In the following instructions, I have used chard to represent all leafy greens.

CUTTING CHARD, KALE, AND OTHER LEAFY GREENS (*right-hand version*)

Trimming Chard

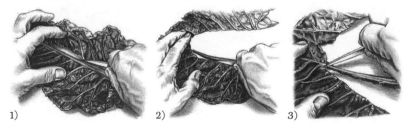

1) 2) 3)

To remove the stem from an individual chard leaf, lay the leaf rib side up on a cutting board. Hold the leaf flat with your left hand. Use a sharp paring knife held with a pinch grip in your right hand. Start at a point where the stem is very narrow, and cut the stem away from the leaf in two passes, one on each side of the stem, cutting as close to the stem as you can without cutting into it (1, 2). Finally, cut the tip of the stem away from the leaf (3). Depending on how you are going to use them, you may need to reserve the leaves and stems separately.

4)

Alternatively, fold the leaf over so that the stem is at the fold. Hold the folded leaf flat with your left hand, with the fold away from you and the tip of the leaf to your left. Using a sharp paring knife held with a pinch grip in your right hand, cut the stem away from the leaf, cutting as close to the stem as you can. Cut from left to right, and cut the stem away from the leaf in a single pass (4). Depending on how you are going to use them, you may need to reserve the leaves and stems separately.

Slicing Chard Leaves

Lay several trimmed chard leaves at a time on top of each other and, starting from a long side, roll them into a tight cylinder. Then hold the cylinder against the cutting board with your left hand and slice the cylinder crosswise with a sharp chef's knife held with a pinch grip in your right hand. Start each cut with the tip of the blade in contact with, or near, the cutting board, with the handle angled up. As you bring the knife down, slide the blade forward so that it moves through the greens as you produce the slices. After each cut, move your forefinger to the left a distance equal to the desired thickness of the next cut. Ideally, the thickness of this cut should be the same as the previous one, so the results appear uniform.

Slicing Chard Stems

To prepare the stems for cooking, stack them together so that their dried-out ends are lined up more or less evenly. Hold the stack of stems firmly against the cutting board with your left hand, and trim off the dried-out portions with the chef's knife held with a pinch grip in your right hand (1).

1)

For many recipes, the stems are cut into shorter lengths. Hold the stack of stems firmly against the cutting board with your left hand. Holding the chef's knife with a pinch grip in your right hand, cut across the stems. Start each cut with the tip of the blade in contact with, or near, the cutting board, with the handle angled up. As you bring the knife down, slide the blade forward so that it moves through the stems as you complete the cut (2).

2)

Julienning Chard Stems

Place each chard stem, concave side down, on the cutting board. Hold it in place with your left hand. Using a sharp paring knife held with a pinch grip in your right hand, make successive cuts through the entire length of the stem by drawing your knife to the right. The number of cuts will depend on the width of the stem—stems that vary drastically in width may require more cuts at the wide end than at the narrow end.

Dicing Chard Stems

Gather the julienned strips from the previous step together into a stack. Hold the stack firmly with your left hand, with your fingertips positioned straight down toward the cutting board. Position the chef's knife, held in a pinch grip, so the flat of the blade rests against the flat side of the tip of your forefinger. This way, your forefinger serves as a guide for the knife. Start each cut with the tip of the blade in contact with, or near, the cutting board, with the handle angled up. As you bring the knife down, slide the blade forward so that it moves through the stems as you produce the dice. After each cut, move your forefinger to the left a distance equal to the desired thickness of the next cut. Ideally, the thickness of this cut should be the same as the previous one, so the results appear uniform. As you do this, it is important that the flat of the blade always remain in contact with the flat surface of your forefinger.

CUTTING CHARD, KALE, AND OTHER LEAFY GREENS *(left-hand version)*

Trimming Chard

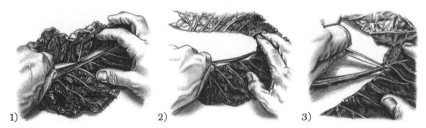

1) 2) 3)

To remove the stem from an individual chard leaf, lay the leaf rib side up on a cutting board. Hold the leaf flat with your right hand. Use a sharp paring knife held with a pinch grip in your left hand. Start at a point where the stem is very narrow, and cut the stem away from the leaf in two passes, one on each side of the stem, cutting as close to the stem as you can without cutting into it (1, 2). Finally, cut the tip of the stem away from the leaf (3). Depending on how you are going to use them, you may need to reserve the leaves and stems separately.

4)

Alternatively, fold the leaf over so that the stem is at the fold. Hold the folded leaf flat with your right hand, with the fold away from you and the tip of the leaf to your right. Using a sharp paring knife held with a pinch grip in your left hand, cut the stem away from the leaf, cutting as close to the stem as you can. Cut from right to left, and cut the stem away from the leaf in a single pass (4). Depending on how you are going to use them, you may need to reserve the leaves and stems separately.

Slicing Chard Leaves

Lay several trimmed chard leaves at a time on top of each other and, starting from a long side, roll them into a tight cylinder. Then hold the cylinder against the cutting board with your right hand and slice the cylinder crosswise with a sharp chef's knife held with a pinch grip in your left hand. Start each cut with the tip of the blade in contact with, or near, the cutting board, with the handle angled up. As you bring the knife down, slide the blade forward so that it moves through the greens as you produce the slices. After each cut, move your forefinger to the right a distance equal to the desired thickness of the next cut. Ideally, the thickness of this cut should be the same as the previous one, so the results appear uniform.

Slicing Chard Stems

To prepare the stems for cooking, stack them together so that their dried-out ends are lined up more or less evenly. Hold the stack of stems firmly against the cutting board with your right hand, and trim off the dried-out portions with the chef's knife held with a pinch grip in your left hand (1).

1)

For many recipes, the stems are cut into shorter lengths. Hold the stack of stems firmly against the cutting board with your right hand. Holding the chef's knife with a pinch grip in your left hand, cut across the stems. Start each cut with the tip of the blade in contact with, or near, the cutting board, with the handle angled up. As you bring the knife down, slide the blade forward so that it moves through the stems as you complete the cut (2).

2)

Julienning Chard Stems

Place each chard stem, concave side down, on the cutting board. Hold it in place with your right hand. Using a sharp paring knife held with a pinch grip in your left hand, make successive cuts through the entire length of the stem by drawing your knife to the left. The number of cuts will depend on the width of the stem—stems that vary drastically in width may require more cuts at the wide end than at the narrow end.

Dicing Chard Stems

Gather the julienned strips from the previous step together into a stack. Hold the stack firmly with your right hand, with your fingertips positioned straight down toward the cutting board. Position the chef's knife, held in a pinch grip, so the flat of the blade rests against the flat side of the tip of your forefinger. This way, your forefinger serves as a guide for the knife. Start each cut with the tip of the blade in contact with, or near, the cutting board, with the handle angled up. As you bring the knife down, slide the blade forward so

that it moves through the stems as you produce the dice. After each cut, move your forefinger to the right a distance equal to the desired thickness of the next cut. Ideally, the thickness of this cut should be the same as the previous one, so the results appear uniform. As you do this, it is important that the flat of the blade always remain in contact with the flat surface of your forefinger.

CUTTING HERBS

THERE SEEMS TO BE A PERSONAL ASPECT TO CUTTING HERBS. EVERYONE HAS A unique way of doing it and firmly believes his or her method is best. Some people use a mezzaluna and a special cutting board or wooden bowl. (That's what my mother used.) Others place the herbs in a jar and snip them with scissors, or put them in a blender or food processor, or use a handheld device, marketed as an herb mill, that mechanically tears the herbs asunder. I use a knife.

A knife cuts the herbs rather than tears them. It's faster and requires less cleanup, it can be used equally well for small and large amounts, and there's less waste.

It is usually best to cut an herb immediately before using it. Herbs such as basil will discolor if cut too long before use. But a few, such as parsley, can be cut well in advance. Herbs that can't be cut in advance can be washed, dried, and the leaves removed ahead of time and then cut at the last minute.

CUTTING HERBS (*right-hand version*)

Mincing Herbs

Mound the herbs in the center of the cutting board. Hold the handle of a sharp chef's knife with a pinch grip in your right hand, and hold the tip of the blade loosely between the thumb and forefinger of your left hand. Use your left hand as sort of a pivot point, keeping the tip of the blade more or less in the same place. Starting at the far side of

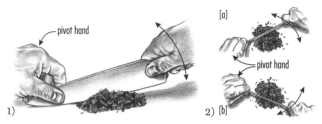

the mound, slowly bring your right hand toward you while rapidly chopping up and down (1). Once you have reached the near side of the mound, move your right hand away from you, continuing the same rapid motion. Start this process with your pivot hand nearer you, as in (2a) in the illustration, and repeat the chopping process several times; then move your pivot further from you, as in (2b), and repeat the chopping process several times. As you proceed, the chopping will cause the mound to spread: use your knife to gather the herbs into a mound once more. Then scrape any herbs stuck to the sides of the blade back into the mound with your forefinger, and repeat the chopping process until the herbs are minced as fine as needed.

Shredding Herbs (Chiffonade)

Large leaf herbs, such as basil, are often cut into thin strips rather than minced. The result is called a chiffonade. Stack four or five leaves at a time on the cutting board, placing smaller leaves on top of larger ones,

with their tips to your left and their stems ends to your right (1). Tightly roll up the stack at an angle that is more or less diagonal to the center line of the leaves (2). If you roll them this way, you can hold the roll tight by pinching it near its left end. Keep the roll tight (3).

To complete the chiffonade, hold the roll firmly on the cutting board with your left hand, with your fingertips positioned straight down toward the board. Position the chef's knife, held in a pinch grip, so the flat of the blade rests against the flat side of the tip of your forefinger. This way, your forefinger serves as a guide for the knife. Position the knife perpendicular to the roll and cut square across it each time. Start each cut with the tip of the blade in contact with, or near, the cutting board, with the handle angled up. As you bring the knife down, slide the

blade forward so that it moves through the herbs as you produce the thin strips. After each cut, move your forefinger to the left a distance equal to the desired width of the next slice, which should be as thin as possible. As you do this, it is important that the flat of the blade always remain in contact with the flat surface of your forefinger (4).

CUTTING HERBS (*left-hand version*)

Mincing Herbs

1)   2)

Mound the herbs in the center of the cutting board. Hold the handle of a sharp chef's knife with a pinch grip in your left hand, and hold the tip of the blade loosely between the thumb and forefinger of your right hand. Use your right hand as sort of a pivot point, keeping the tip of the blade more or less in the same place. Starting at the far side of the mound, slowly bring your left hand toward you while rapidly chopping up and down (1). Once you have reached the near side of the mound, move your left hand away from you, continuing the same rapid motion. Start this process with your pivot hand nearer you, as in (2a) in the illustration, and repeat the chopping process several times; then move your pivot further from you, as in (2b), and repeat the chopping process several times. As you proceed, the chopping will cause the mound to spread: use your knife to gather the herbs into a mound once more. Then scrape any herbs stuck to the sides of the blade back into the mound with your forefinger, and repeat the chopping process until the herbs are minced as finely as needed.

Shredding Herbs (Chiffonade)

1) direction of roll   2)   3)

Large leaf herbs, such as basil, are often cut into thin strips rather than minced. The result is called a chiffonade. Stack four or five leaves at a time on the cutting board, placing smaller leaves on top of larger ones, with their tips to your right and their stems ends to your left (1). Tightly roll up the stack at an angle that is more or less diagonal to the center line of the leaves (2). If you roll them this way, you can hold the roll tight by pinching it near its right end. Keep the roll tight (3).

4)

To complete the chiffonade, hold the roll firmly on the cutting board with your right hand, with your fingertips positioned straight down toward the board. Position the chef's knife, held in a pinch grip, so the flat of the blade rests against the flat side of the tip of your forefinger. This way, your forefinger serves as a guide for the knife. Position the knife perpendicular to the roll and cut square across it each time. Start each cut with the tip of the blade in contact with, or near, the cutting board, with the handle angled up. As you bring the knife down, slide the blade forward so that it moves through the herbs as you produce the thin strips. After each cut, move your forefinger to the right a distance equal to the desired width of the next slice, which should be as thin as possible. As you do this, it is important that the flat of the blade always remain in contact with the flat surface of your forefinger (4).

CUTTING GINGER

GINGER, THOUGH OFTEN CALLED GINGERROOT, IS NOT A ROOT AT ALL, BUT A rhizome, an underground stem. Ginger originated in southern China but is now grown throughout the tropical regions of the world. Young ginger has an almost transparent skin of very light yellow. However, the ginger most often available in the local grocery store is older, with a heavy, tan-colored skin.

When buying ginger, look for a piece with a smooth skin. Ginger is usually displayed on the shelf as a gnarly mass with an appearance somewhat like a stag's horn, but most markets allow you to break off a section rather than having to buy the whole mass. The broken end should appear moist, not dried out.

Store ginger in the refrigerator. It will keep for a while, especially if well wrapped. To store peeled portions, wrap tightly in plastic wrap and twist the ends of the plastic to remove all the air.

Chefs have differing opinions on how to peel ginger. The following techniques describe three methods.

CUTTING GINGER (*right-hand version*)

Trimming Ginger

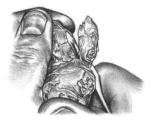

It is not uncommon for a piece of ginger to have several irregular areas where other pieces of the rhizome were once attached. These should be trimmed flush with the surface of the ginger. To do this, hold the ginger firmly in your left hand and hold a sharp paring knife in your right, with your forefinger wrapped around the blade. Support your knife hand against the ginger with your right thumb, and trim the ginger as needed.

Peeling Ginger

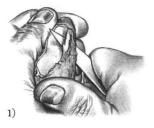

1)

To peel ginger with a knife, hold the piece of ginger firmly in your left hand and hold a sharp paring knife in your right, with your forefinger wrapped around the blade. Support your knife hand against the ginger with your right thumb. Peel the entire surface of the piece, but be careful to remove the peel and only the minimum of underlying flesh. As each piece of skin is removed, rotate the piece of ginger to your left to expose a new area of skin (1).

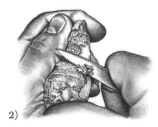

2)

Some cooks prefer scraping the skin rather than peeling it. Depending on the age of the ginger and how it has been stored, this is more or less easily done. Hold the edge of the blade perpendicular to the skin and move it down the ginger the same way as if you were peeling the skin. The scraping method can be messier than the peeling method, as it has a tendency to spray a small amount of ginger juice onto your work area (2). (In another common method, a spoon is used to scrape the skin off the ginger. Since I usually have a sharp paring knife already at hand, I prefer to use it rather than dirty a spoon.)

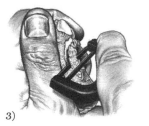

3)

The skin of ginger can also be removed with a peeler. A yoke-type peeler, shown in the illustration, is my preferred type. Hold the ginger firmly in your left hand and the peeler in your right. Support your right hand against your left with your thumb, and peel the piece of ginger from top to bottom. After each strip of skin is peeled, rotate the ginger to your left you to expose a new section of skin (3).

Slicing Ginger

Use a sharp chef's knife to trim a thin slice from one side of the piece of ginger to create a flat surface (1). Rest the ginger on this side for slicing so it won't roll on the cutting board.

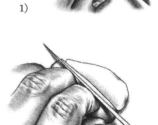

1)

Hold the ginger firmly with your left hand, with your fingertips positioned straight down toward the board. Position the chef's knife, held with a pinch grip, so the flat of the blade rests against the flat side of the tip of your forefinger. This way, your forefinger serves as a guide for the knife. Start each cut with the tip of the blade in contact with, or near, the cutting board, with the handle angled up. As you bring the knife down, slide the blade forward and back with a sawing motion to produce the slices (2). After each cut, move your forefinger to the left a distance equal to the desired thickness of the next cut. Ideally, the thickness of this cut should be the same as the previous one, so the results appear uniform. As you do this, it is important that the flat of the blade always remain in contact with the flat surface of your forefinger. Make each slice as thin as possible, because even a small amount of fresh ginger can impart a powerful flavor.

2)

Julienning Ginger

Stack three or four ginger slices together at a time on the cutting board. Hold the stack firmly with your left hand, with your fingertips positioned straight down toward the board. Position the chef's knife, held with a pinch grip, so the flat of the blade rests against the flat side of the tip of your forefinger. This way, your forefinger serves as a guide for the knife. Start each cut with the tip of the blade in contact with, or near, the cutting board, with the handle angled up. As you bring the knife down, slide the blade forward and back with a sawing motion as you produce the strips. After each cut, move your forefinger to the left a distance equal to the desired thickness of the next cut. Ideally, the thickness of this cut should be the same as the thickness of the slices, so the resulting strips have a square cross section. As you do this, it is important that the flat of the blade always remain in contact with the flat surface of your forefinger.

CUTTING GINGER (*right-hand version continued*)

Dicing Ginger

Gather the julienned strips from the previous step into a stack. Hold the stack firmly in place with your left hand, with your fingertips positioned straight down toward the board. Position the chef's knife, held with a pinch grip, so the flat of the blade rests against the flat side of the tip of your forefinger. This way, your forefinger serves as a guide for the knife. Start each cut with the tip of the blade in contact with, or near, the cutting board, with the handle angled up. As you bring the knife down, slide the blade forward and back with a sawing motion as you produce the dice. After each cut, move your forefinger to the left, a distance equal to the desired thickness of the next cut. Ideally, the thickness of this cut should be the same as the previous one, so the resulting dice are perfect cubes. As you do this, it is important that the flat of the blade always remain in contact with the flat surface of your forefinger.

CUTTING GINGER (*left-hand version*)

Trimming Ginger

It is not uncommon for a piece of ginger to have several irregular areas where other pieces of the rhizome were once attached. These should be trimmed flush with the surface of the ginger. To do this, hold the ginger firmly in your right hand and hold a sharp paring knife in your left, with your forefinger wrapped around the blade. Support your knife hand against the ginger with your left thumb, and trim the ginger as needed.

Peeling Ginger

To peel ginger with a knife, hold the piece of ginger firmly in your right hand and hold a sharp paring knife in your left, with your forefinger wrapped around the blade. Support your knife hand against the ginger with your left thumb. Peel the entire surface of the piece, but be careful to remove the peel and only the minimum of underlying flesh. As each piece of skin is removed, rotate the piece of ginger to your right to expose a new area of skin (1).

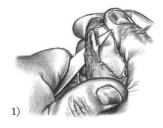
1)

Some cooks prefer scraping the skin rather than peeling it. Depending on the age of the ginger and how it has been stored, this is more or less easily done. Hold the edge of the blade perpendicular to the skin and move it down the ginger the same way as if you were peeling the skin. The scraping method can be messier than the peeling method, as it has a tendency to spray a small amount of ginger juice onto your work area (2). (In another common method, a spoon is used to scrape the skin off the ginger. Since I usually have a sharp paring knife already at hand, I prefer to use it rather than dirty a spoon.)

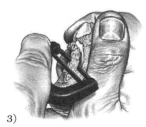
2)

The skin of ginger can also be removed with a peeler. A yoke-type peeler, shown in the illustration, is my preferred type. Hold the ginger firmly in your right hand and the peeler in your left. Support your left hand against your right with your thumb, and peel the piece of ginger from top to bottom. After each strip of skin is peeled, rotate the ginger to your right to expose a new section of skin (3).

3)

CUTTING GINGER (*left-hand version continued*)

Slicing Ginger

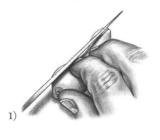

1)

Use a sharp chef's knife to trim a thin slice from one side of the piece of ginger to create a flat surface (1). Rest the ginger on this side for slicing so it won't roll on the cutting board.

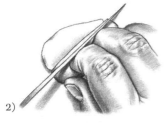

2)

Hold the ginger firmly with your right hand, with your fingertips positioned straight down toward the board. Position the chef's knife, held with a pinch grip, so the flat of the blade rests against the flat side of the tip of your forefinger. This way, your forefinger serves as a guide for the knife. Start each cut with the tip of the blade in contact with, or near, the cutting board, with the handle angled up. As you bring the knife down, slide the blade forward and back with a sawing motion to produce the slices (2). After each cut, move your forefinger to the right a distance equal to the desired thickness of the next cut. Ideally, the thickness of this cut should be the same as the previous one, so the results appear uniform. As you do this, it is important that the flat of the blade always remain in contact with the flat surface of your forefinger. Make each slice as thin as possible, because even a small amount of fresh ginger can impart a powerful flavor.

Julienning Ginger

Stack three or four ginger slices together at a time on the cutting board. Hold the stack firmly with your right hand, with your fingertips positioned straight down toward the board. Position the chef's knife, held with a pinch grip, so the flat of the blade rests against the flat side of the tip of your forefinger. This way, your forefinger serves as a guide for the knife. Start each cut with the tip of the blade in contact with, or near, the cutting board, with the handle angled up. As you bring the knife down, slide the blade forward and back with a sawing motion to produce the strips. After each cut, move your forefinger to the right a distance equal to the desired thickness of the next cut. Ideally, the thickness of this cut should be the same as the thickness of the slices, so the resulting strips have a square cross section. As you do this, it is important that the flat of the blade always remain in contact with the flat surface of your forefinger.

Dicing Ginger

Gather the julienned strips from the previous step into a stack. Hold the stack firmly in place with your right hand, with your fingertips positioned straight down toward the board. Position the chef's knife, held with a pinch grip, so the flat of the blade rests against the flat side of the tip of your forefinger. This way, your forefinger serves as a guide for the knife. Start each cut with the tip of the blade in contact with, or near, the cutting board, with the handle angled up. As you bring the knife down, slide the blade forward and back with a sawing motion to produce the dice. After each cut, move your forefinger to the right a distance equal to the desired thickness of the next cut. Ideally, the thickness of this cut should be the same as the previous one, so the resulting dice are perfect cubes. As you do this, it is important that the flat of the blade always remain in contact with the flat surface of your forefinger.

CUTTING CAULIFLOWER AND BROCCOLI

CAULIFLOWER AND BROCCOLI ARE BOTH MEMBERS OF THE CABBAGE FAMILY. Their physical structures are similar enough that the techniques used for cutting them can be described the same way. The only significant difference is that the florets of broccoli separate from the bunch much more easily than those of cauliflower.

When purchasing cauliflower, look for firm, unbroken heads with an unblemished, white surface. The stalk should appear moist and solid, not hollow and dried out. Look for cauliflower with some of the green leaves still attached to the base, to protect the white head.

When purchasing broccoli, look for bright green heads with short stalks. None of the florets should be brown or yellow. If the broccoli has a long stalk, trim it from the crown and use separately. These large stalks can be peeled and then cut like other cylindrical vegetables.

CUTTING CAULIFLOWER AND BROCCOLI (*right-hand version*)

Trimming Cauliflower

Hold the cauliflower firmly in your left hand with the stalk (core) toward you. Hold a sharp paring knife in your right, with your forefinger wrapped around the blade, and support your knife hand against the stalk of the cauliflower with your right thumb. Starting at the base of the leaves, cut them away from the stalk. Even after an individual leaf is cut, you may need to pull it away from the cauliflower to remove it. Work your way around the entire base of cauliflower until all the leaves are removed. Try to make the cuts circular around the stalk.

Separating Cauliflower into Florets

Hold the paring knife in your right hand, with your forefinger wrapped around the blade. Cut through the base of each floret where it meets the stalk (1). As you cut each floret from the stalk, gently rotate it outward to separate it completely from the stalk (2). If not using the whole head, remove only as many florets as needed for

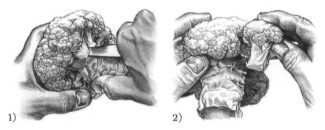

1)   2)

your recipe. If the already trimmed stalk gets in your way as you move along it, cut it away. (Though not suitable for most dishes, the stalk can be used in purees.) As you proceed from the base to the top of the head, the size of the florets will become smaller. Larger florets may need to be halved or quartered. Cut from the base toward the top so the halves or quarters are about the same size.

CUTTING CAULIFLOWER AND BROCCOLI (*left-hand version*)

Trimming Cauliflower

Hold the cauliflower firmly in your right hand with the stalk (core) toward you. Hold a sharp paring knife in your left, with your forefinger wrapped around the blade, and support your knife hand against the stalk of the cauliflower with your left thumb. Starting at the base of the leaves, cut them away from the stalk. Even after an individual leaf is cut, you may need to pull it away from the cauliflower to remove it. Work your way around the entire base of cauliflower until all the leaves are removed. Try to make the cuts circular around the stalk.

Separating Cauliflower into Florets

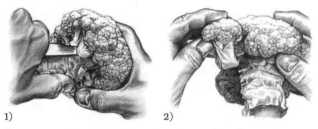

1)   2)

Hold the paring knife in your left hand, with your forefinger wrapped around the blade. Cut through the base of each floret where it meets the stalk (1). As you cut each floret from the stalk, gently rotate it outward to separate it completely from the stalk (2). If not using the whole head, remove only as many florets as needed for your recipe. If the already trimmed stalk gets in your way as you move along it, cut it away. (Though not suitable for most dishes, the stalk can be used in purees.) As you proceed from the base to the top of the head, the size of the florets will become smaller. Larger florets may need to be halved or quartered. Cut from the base toward the top so the halves or quarters are about the same size.

CUTTING PEPPERS

PEPPERS COME IN MYRIAD SHAPES, COLORS, AND FLAVORS. FROM THE STANDPOINT of cutting, shape is the most important. That is, unless you rub your eyes while cutting a hot pepper—then you won't care about shape at all. People with sensitive skin should wear protective gloves when handling hot peppers. But even with gloves, you still don't want to rub your eyes.

All peppers, whether elongated and cylindrical, boxy, or convoluted and twisted, have a similar structure. All have one-sixteenth- to one-quarter-inch thick flesh covered by a thin, tough skin. The surface of the pepper is supported by two to five internal ribs that hold them together. In hot peppers, the ribs, with their light-colored pith, are the hottest portion. Inside any pepper, a concentrated cluster of seeds is connected to the stem. After the pith, these are the next hottest part of a pepper. In the cutting methods explained and illustrated here, both the seeds and the pith are discarded.

CUTTING PEPPERS (*right-hand version*)

Trimming a Pepper

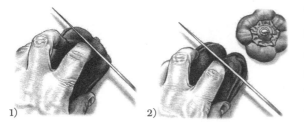

1)
2)

To make the cutting process easier, choose peppers with symmetrical shapes if possible. Those with convoluted bodies are interesting to look at but more difficult to cut into usable shapes. Place the pepper on the cutting board with the stem to the right. Hold the pepper firmly with your left hand, with the tip of your forefinger pointing straight down toward the cutting board. Position a sharp chef's knife, held with a pinch grip, so the flat of the blade rests against the flat side of the tip of your forefinger. This way, your forefinger serves as a guide for the knife. Use a sawing motion to cut straight through the pepper: the cut should be made just where the stem meets the body (1). Turn the pepper and trim off the bottom. This cut should be made at the level of the little tip in the center of the base of the pepper (2). Both of the pieces cut from the pepper can be julienned or diced using the methods described below for the body of the pepper.

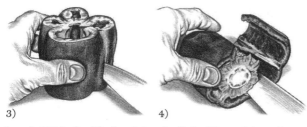

3)
4)

Stand the trimmed pepper upright on the cutting board, and grip it lightly with your left hand. Using the chef's knife held with a pinch grip in your right hand, make a vertical cut all the way through the flesh down one side of the pepper, just to the right of a rib (3). Lay the pepper on its side on the cutting board, and hold it with your left hand. With the blade of the chef's knife positioned parallel to the cutting board, cut through each of the ribs to slice them off as you "unroll" the pepper (4). Discard the seeds and core.

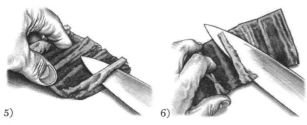

5)
6)

Now, trim any remaining portions of ribs still attached to the wall of the pepper: place the pepper skin side down on the cutting board, and support it in place with your left hand. Using the chef's knife held with a pinch grip in your right hand, with the blade parallel to the cutting board and flush with the inner surface of the pepper, trim away the remaining portions of ribs (5). The harder you push the blade flat against the pepper, which also will help to flatten it, the more the ribs will be trimmed and the cleaner the result (6).

Julienning a Pepper

Turn the pepper "sheet" from the previous step flesh side down on the cutting board. (Some chefs recommend placing peppers skin side down because the softer flesh is easier to cut through, but with a sharp knife, I have found that I can produce a finer julienne with the skin side up.) Hold the pepper firmly in place with your left hand, with your fingertips positioned straight down toward the cutting board. Position the chef's knife, held with a pinch grip, so the flat of the blade rests against the flat side of the tip of your  forefinger. This way, your forefinger becomes a guide for the knife. Start each cut with the tip of the blade in contact with, or near, the cutting board, with the handle angled up. As you bring the knife down, slide it forward so the edge of the blade is moving left through the pepper as you produce the julienne. After each cut, move your forefinger to the left a distance equal to the desired thickness of the next cut. Ideally, the thickness of this cut should be the same as the thickness of the previous strips. As you do this, it is important that the flat of the blade always remain in contact with the flat surface of your forefinger.

Dicing a Pepper

Gather the julienned strips from the previous step together into a stack. Hold the stack firmly with your left hand, with your fingertips positioned straight down toward the cutting board. Position the chef's knife, held in a pinch grip, so the flat of the blade rests against the flat side of the tip of your forefinger. This way, your forefinger becomes a guide for the knife. Start each cut with the tip of the blade in contact with, or near, the cutting board, with the handle angled up. As you bring the knife down, slide it forward so the  edge of the blade is moving left through the pepper as you produce the dice. After each cut, move your forefinger to the left a distance equal to the desired thickness of the next cut. Ideally, the thickness of this cut should be the same as the thickness of the previous cuts so the resulting dice are uniform. As you do this, it is important that the flat of the blade always remain in contact with the flat surface of your forefinger.

CUTTING PEPPERS (*right-hand version continued*)

Finely Julienning or Dicing a Pepper

1)

A recipe may call for a julienne or dice that is finer than what is determined by the natural thickness of the pepper's wall. To make these finer pieces uniform, the "sheet" of pepper must be thinned. Lay the pepper skin side down on the cutting board. Hold it absolutely flat with the slightly spread fingers of your left hand. Using the chef's knife held with a pinch grip in your right hand, with the blade positioned parallel to the cutting board and with nothing but the skin between it and the board, saw back and forth to separate the pepper flesh from the skin. The blade must be held flat against the skin throughout the entire process (1). If all the skin is not removed on the first pass, which is often the case, carefully repeat the process in the areas where any skin remains.

2)

If you need an even thinner sheet, the pepper just skinned can be cut in half. Hold it against the board with your left hand splayed out flat. Curl your fingertips slightly upward to keep them out of harm's way. Using the chef's knife held with a pinch grip in your right hand, with the blade positioned parallel to the board and up from the board a distance equal to half the thickness of the pepper flesh, saw back and forth to slice the sheet into two thinner sheets. The blade must remain parallel to the cutting board throughout the entire cut (2).

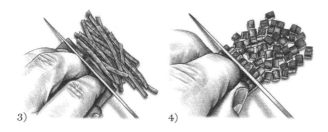

3)   4)

To julienne (3) or dice (4) these thinner sheets of pepper, proceed as described above.

CUTTING PEPPERS (*left-hand version*)

Trimming a Pepper

To make the cutting process easier, choose peppers with symmetrical shapes if possible. Those with convoluted bodies are interesting to look at but more difficult to cut into usable shapes. Place the pepper on the cutting board with the stem to the left. Hold the pepper firmly with your right hand, with the tip of your forefinger pointing straight down toward the 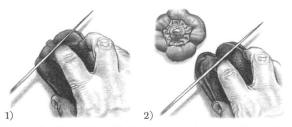 cutting board. Position a sharp chef's knife, held with a pinch grip, so the flat of the blade rests against the flat side of the tip of your forefinger. This way, your forefinger serves as a guide for the knife. Use a sawing motion to cut straight through the pepper: the cut should be made just where the stem meets the body (1). Turn the pepper and trim off the bottom. This cut should be made at the level of the little tip in the center of the base of the pepper (2). Both of the pieces cut from the pepper can be julienned or diced using the methods described below for the body of the pepper.

Stand the trimmed pepper upright on the cutting board, and grip it lightly with your right hand. Using the chef's knife held with a pinch grip in your left hand, make a vertical cut all the way through the flesh down one side of the pepper, just to the left of a rib (3). Lay the pepper on its side on the cutting board and hold it with your 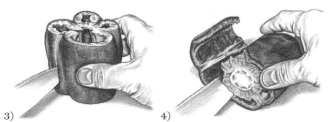 right hand. With the blade of the chef's knife positioned parallel to the cutting board, cut through each of the ribs to slice them off as you "unroll" the pepper (4). Discard the seeds and core.

Now, trim any remaining portions of ribs still attached to the wall of the pepper. Place the pepper skin side down on the cutting board, and support it in place with your right hand. Using the chef's knife held with a pinch grip in your left hand, with the blade parallel to the cutting board and flush with the inner surface of the pepper, trim away the 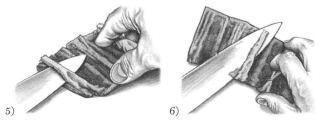 remaining portions of ribs (5). The harder you push the blade flat against the pepper, which also will help to flatten it, the more the ribs will be trimmed and the cleaner the result (6).

CUTTING PEPPERS (*left-hand version continued*)

Julienning a Pepper

Turn the pepper "sheet" from the previous step flesh side down on the cutting board. (Some chefs recommend placing peppers skin side down because the softer flesh is easier to cut through, but with a sharp knife, I have found that I can produce a finer julienne with the skin side up.) Hold the pepper firmly in place with your right hand, with your fingertips positioned straight down toward the cutting board. Position the chef's knife, held with a pinch grip, so the flat of the blade rests against the flat side of the tip of your forefinger. This way, your forefinger becomes a guide for the knife. Start each cut with the tip of the blade in contact with, or near, the cutting board, with the handle angled up. As you bring the knife down, slide it forward so the edge of the blade is moving right through the pepper as you produce the julienne. After each cut, move your forefinger to the right a distance equal to the desired thickness of the next cut. Ideally, the thickness of this cut should be the same as the thickness of the previous strip. As you do this, it is important that the flat of the blade always remain in contact with the flat surface of your forefinger.

Dicing a Pepper

Gather the julienned strips from the previous step together into a stack. Hold the stack firmly with your right hand, with your fingertips positioned straight down toward the cutting board. Position the chef's knife, held in a pinch grip, so the flat of the blade rests against the flat side of the tip of your forefinger. This way, your forefinger becomes a guide for the knife. Start each cut with the tip of the blade in contact with, or near, the cutting board, with the handle angled up. As you bring the knife down, slide it forward so the edge of the blade is moving right through the pepper as you produce the dice. After each cut, move your forefinger to the right a distance equal to the desired thickness of the next cut. Ideally, the thickness of this cut should be the same as the thickness of the previous cuts, so the resulting dice are uniform. As you do this, it is important that the flat of the blade always remain in contact with the flat surface of your forefinger.

Finely Julienning or Dicing a Pepper

A recipe may call for a julienne or dice that is finer than what is determined by the natural thickness of the pepper's wall. To make these finer pieces uniform, the "sheet" of pepper must be thinned. Lay the pepper skin side down on the cutting board. Hold it absolutely flat with the slightly spread fingers of your right hand. Using the chef's knife held with a pinch grip in your left hand, with the blade positioned parallel to the cutting board and with nothing but the skin between it and the board, saw back and forth to separate the pepper flesh from the skin. The blade must be held flat against the skin throughout the entire process (1). If all the skin is not removed on the first pass, which is often the case, carefully repeat the process in the areas where any skin remains.

1)

If you need an even thinner sheet, the pepper just skinned can be cut in half. Hold it against the board with your right hand splayed out flat. Curl your fingertips slightly upward to keep them out of harm's way. Using the chef's knife held with a pinch grip in your left hand with the blade positioned parallel to the board and up from the board a distance equal to half the thickness of the pepper flesh, saw back and forth to slice the sheet into two thinner sheets. The blade must remain parallel to the cutting board throughout the entire cut (2).

2)

To julienne (3) or dice (4) these thinner sheets of pepper, proceed as described above.

3)   4)

CUTTING MUSHROOMS

ALTHOUGH WILD MUSHROOMS ARE MORE COMMONLY AVAILABLE IN MARKETS today than in the past, most of mushrooms that find their way into our shopping bags are still the domesticated common mushroom with a white or brown skin. Their size may vary from small to large to the super-giant portobello, which is just a common brown mushroom on steroids. No matter their size, they can all be cut the same way. (Wild mushrooms, however, require their own "personal" ways of preparation. Some are simply trimmed and sliced, whereas others may require removing the gills or scraping their stems. These types of mushrooms are not covered in this set of techniques.)

When purchasing common mushrooms, look for ones with closed caps and short stems. There should be no cuts on the cap, and the mushroom should feel firm and dry to the touch. Once you bring the mushrooms home from the market, store them in an open bag or bowl so that moisture cannot accumulate inside the package. Since mushrooms act like miniature sponges, it is best not to wash them until just prior to use.

CUTTING MUSHROOMS (*right-hand version*)

Trimming a Mushroom

Depending on how you are going to use them, you may or may not need to trim the stems of mushrooms significantly. If they are to be used whole, you need only trim the stems to a more or less even length. If the mushrooms are to be sliced, the stems are often trimmed flush with the cap. If they are to be julienned or diced, the stems must be trimmed flush with the caps. To trim the stem of a mushroom, hold the mushroom cap firmly between the thumb, forefinger, and middle finger of

your left hand with the stem up. Hold a sharp paring knife in your right hand, with your forefinger and middle finger wrapped around the blade and the cutting edge of the blade toward your thumb. Support your right hand against the mushroom cap with your right thumb, and cut all the way through the stem with a slight sawing motion. Discard the cut stems or save for use in stocks.

Peeling a Mushroom

As an alternative to washing common mushrooms, the caps can be peeled, especially if the mushrooms are a bit old or soft. Hold a mushroom, trimmed stem side up, firmly between the thumb, forefinger, and middle finger of your left hand. Hold the paring knife in your right hand, with your forefinger and middle finger wrapped around the blade and the blade parallel to your thumb. Gently scrape across the bottom edge of the cap to raise up a thin piece of skin. On a mature mushroom, the

tip of the knife can be inserted between the cap and the stem to grasp a piece of skin. Hold the skin against the flat side of the blade near the tip with your thumb and gently pull the skin off the cap, rotating the cap up and away from you as you pull off the skin. Rotate the mushroom to the right in your hand and remove the next piece of skin. Continue until all the skin is removed around the edge of the cap. Usually there will be a little skin remaining in the center of the cap; this can sometimes be gently scraped away. Discard the peelings or save for use in stocks.

CUTTING MUSHROOMS (*right-hand version continued*)

Slicing a Mushroom

To slice a mushroom vertically, place it on the cutting board trimmed stem side down. Hold the mushroom firmly with your left hand, with your fingertips positioned straight down toward the cutting board. Position a sharp chef's knife, held with a pinch grip, so the flat of the blade rests against the flat side of the tip of your forefinger. This way, your forefinger serves as a guide for the knife. Start each cut with the tip of the blade in contact with, or near, the cutting board, with the handle angled up. As you bring the knife down, slide it forward so the edge of the blade is moving left through the mushroom as you produce the slice. After each cut, move your forefinger to the left a distance equal to the desired thickness of the next cut. Ideally, the thickness of this cut should be the same as the thickness of the previous slice, so the resulting pieces are uniform. As you do this, it is important that the flat of the blade always remain in contact with the flat surface of your forefinger.

Julienning a Mushroom

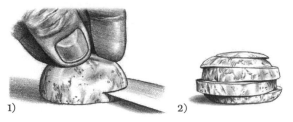

1)   2)

To dice a mushroom, you must first cut it into horizontal slices and then julienne it. Place a mushroom trimmed stem side down on the cutting board. Hold it with the fingertips of your left hand placed loosely on top of the mushroom. Position a sharp chef's knife, held with a pinch grip, so the blade is parallel to and just above the cutting board. Carefully, using a sawing motion, make the first slice (1). (Since mushrooms shrink when they are cooked, the slices should not be too thin.) Move the first slice to the right and use it as a gauge for the next slice. When all the slices are completed, stack them up for the following step (2).

3)

To complete the julienne, hold the stacked mushroom slices together on the cutting board between the thumb and fingers of your left hand. Holding the chef's knife with a pinch grip, working from right to left, make successive cuts through the mushroom slices. The thickness of each cut should be about the same as the thickness of the slices. Try to hold all the strips of mushroom together throughout the cutting process (3). Julienned mushroom strips are usually produced as a step in dicing, not used as is.

Dicing a Mushroom

Gather the julienned strips from the previous step together into a stack. Hold the stack firmly with your left hand, with your fingertips positioned straight down toward the board. Position the chef's knife, held with a pinch grip, so the flat of the blade rests against the flat side of the tip of your forefinger. This way, your forefinger serves as a guide for the knife. Start each cut with the tip of the blade in contact with, or near, the cutting board, with the handle angled up. As you bring the knife down, slide it forward so the edge of the blade is  moving left through the mushroom as you produce the dice. After each cut, move your forefinger to the left a distance equal to the desired thickness of the next cut. Ideally, the thickness of this cut should be the same as the thickness of the previous cuts so the resulting dice are uniform. As you do this, it is important that the flat of the blade always remain in contact with the side of your forefinger.

CUTTING MUSHROOMS *(left-hand version)*

Trimming a Mushroom

Depending on how you are going to use them, you may or may not need to trim the stems of mushrooms significantly. If they are to used whole, you need only trim the stems to a more or less even length. If the mushrooms are to be sliced, the stems are often trimmed flush with the cap. If they are to be julienned or diced, the stems must be trimmed flush with the caps. To trim the stem of a mushroom, hold the mushroom cap firmly between the thumb, forefinger, and middle finger of your right hand with the stem up. Hold a sharp paring knife in your left hand, with your forefinger and middle finger wrapped around the blade and the cutting edge of the blade toward your thumb. Support your left hand against the mushroom cap with your left thumb, and cut all the way through the stem with a slight sawing motion. Discard the cut stems or save for use in stocks.

Peeling a Mushroom

As an alternative to washing common mushrooms, the caps can be peeled, especially if the mushrooms are a bit old or soft. Hold a mushroom, trimmed stem side up, firmly between the thumb, forefinger, and middle finger of your right hand. Hold the paring knife in your left hand, with your forefinger and middle finger wrapped around the blade and the blade parallel to your thumb. Gently scrape across the bottom edge of the cap to raise up a thin piece of skin. On a mature mushroom, the tip of the knife can be inserted between the cap and the stem to grasp a piece of skin. Hold the skin against the flat side of the blade near the tip with your thumb and gently pull the skin off the cap, rotating the cap up and away from you as you pull off the skin. Rotate the mushroom to the left in your hand and remove the next piece of skin. Continue until all the skin is removed around the edge of the cap. Usually there will be a little skin remaining in the center of the cap; this can sometimes be gently scraped away. Discard the peelings or save for use in stocks.

Slicing a Mushroom

To slice a mushroom vertically, place it on the cutting board trimmed stem side down. Hold the mushroom firmly with your right hand, with your fingertips positioned straight down toward the cutting board. Position a sharp chef's knife, held with a pinch grip, so the flat of the blade rests against the flat side of the tip of your forefinger. This way, your forefinger serves as a guide for the knife. Start each cut with the tip of the blade in contact with, or near, the cutting board, with the handle angled up. As you bring the knife down, slide it forward so the edge of the blade is moving right through the mushroom as you produce the slice. After each cut, move your forefinger to the right a distance equal to the desired thickness of the next cut. Ideally, the thickness of this cut should be the same as the thickness of the previous slice, so the resulting pieces are uniform. As you do this, it is important that the flat of the blade always remain in contact with the flat surface of your forefinger.

Julienning a Mushroom

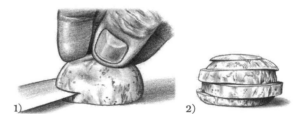

To dice a mushroom, you must first cut it into horizontal slices and then julienne it. Place a mushroom trimmed stem side down on the cutting board. Hold it with the fingertips of your right hand placed loosely on top of the mushroom. Position a sharp chef's knife, held with a pinch grip, so the blade is parallel to and just above the cutting board. Carefully, using a sawing motion, make the first slice (1). (Since mushrooms shrink when they are cooked, the slices should not be too thin.) Move the first slice slightly to the left and use it as a gauge for the next slice. When all the slices are completed, stack them up for the following step (2).

To complete the julienne, hold the stacked mushroom slices together on the cutting board between the thumb and fingers of your right hand. Holding the chef's knife with a pinch grip, working from left to right, make successive cuts through the mushroom slices. The thickness of each cut should be about the same as the thickness of the slices. Try to hold all the strips of mushroom together throughout the cutting process (3). Julienned mushroom strips are usually produced as a step in dicing, not used as is.

CUTTING MUSHROOMS *(left-hand version continued)*

Dicing a Mushroom

Gather the julienned strips from the previous step together into a stack. Hold the stack firmly with your right hand, with your fingertips positioned straight down toward the board. Position the chef's knife, held with a pinch grip, so the flat of the blade rests against the flat side of the tip of your forefinger. This way, your forefinger serves as a guide for the knife. Start each cut with the tip of the blade in contact with, or near, the cutting board, with the handle angled up. As you bring the knife down, slide it forward so the edge of the blade is moving right through the mushroom as you produce the dice. After each cut, move your forefinger to the right a distance equal to the desired thickness of the next cut. Ideally, the thickness of this cut should be the same as the thickness of the previous cut, so the resulting dice are perfect cubes. As you do this, it is important that the flat of the blade always remain in contact with the flat surface of your forefinger.

CUTTING TOMATOES

ALTHOUGH TOMATOES BOTANICALLY ARE A FRUIT, IN 1893, IN *NIX V. HEDDEN*, the U.S. Supreme Court determined that tomatoes were a vegetable so that a ten-percent tariff could be placed on their import. At the time, fruit could be imported duty-free, but vegetables were subject to a tariff. Today we still think of tomatoes as a vegetable because we tend to prepare them as vegetables. When was the last time you chomped on a tomato as you would an apple?

Tomatoes are available in a number of varieties. The smaller ones, such as the many variations of cherry and grape tomatoes, are often eaten whole or simply cut in half. The larger ones, such as the round salad tomato and the plum-shaped Roma tomato, are generally cut up whether eaten raw or cooked.

CUTTING TOMATOES (*right-hand version*)

Coring a Tomato

Most tomato preparations begin with removing the core. Hold the tomato firmly in your left hand and hold a sharp paring knife in a pinch grip in your right. Support your knife hand against the tomato with your middle finger, and pierce the tomato just a bit away from the core with the tip of the blade extending to the center of the tomato at about a 45-degree angle. While moving the knife in and out with a sawing motion, rotate the tomato into the edge of the knife to carve out a conical-shaped piece around the core. Remove and discard the core.

Peeling a Tomato with a Knife

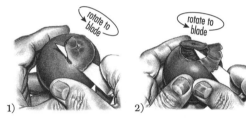

1) 2) 3)

Some recipes call for peeled tomatoes. To peel a tomato with a knife, hold the tomato loosely in the fingers of your left hand, with the stem end toward your fingers. Hold a sharp paring knife in your right hand, with your forefinger wrapped around the blade. Support your knife hand against the tomato with your right thumb, and cut a disk from the blossom end of the tomato, leaving it attached by about a ½-inch strip of skin. Make this first cut as shallow as possible (1). Then proceed to peel the tomato by rotating it into the knife blade to remove a long ½-inch-wide ribbon of skin. As you do this, gently saw back and forth with the blade (2). Work your way in a continuous spiral all the way around and down the tomato until the entire skin is removed (3). Try to remove as little of the flesh as possible. Discard the skin (or save it for making decorative tomato roses).

Peeling a Tomato by Blanching

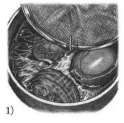

1)

If you have more than a few tomatoes to peel, the previous method may be too time-consuming. As an alternative, bring a pot of water to a rolling boil. While the water is heating, core the tomatoes and then cut an X in the skin of the opposite end (1). Prepare an ice bath by filling a large bowl with cold water and some ice cubes. Carefully place a few tomatoes at a time in the boiling water, and leave them just until their skins split. The time this takes depends on the type of tomato and how ripe it is. In any case, never blanch a tomato for more than a minute. As soon as the tomato skin splits or a minute is up, transfer the tomatoes to the ice bath with a skimmer. (You can also use the skimmer to rotate the tomatoes in the boiling water to find splits that are out of view.)

Once each tomato is cold, hold it in the fingers of your left hand and hold a paring knife in your right, with your forefinger and middle finger wrapped around the blade. Slide the tip of the blade just under a loose piece of skin, hold the skin firmly against the flat side of the blade, near the tip, with your thumb, and pull the skin down toward the core end of the tomato to remove it (2). Discard the skin. Continue removing the skin, rotating the tomato toward the knife so new skin is exposed, until all the skin has been removed.

2)

Slicing a Tomato

For simple slices, a tomato can be cut vertically or horizontally. The vertical method works better for firm tomatoes and the horizontal for soft tomatoes, especially if they have been peeled. For the vertical method, place a tomato on a cutting board with the stem end toward the right. Hold the tomato firmly with your left hand, with your fingertips positioned straight down toward the board. Position a sharp chef's knife, held with a pinch grip, so the flat of the blade rests against the flat side of the tip of your forefinger.

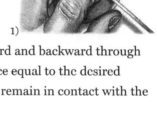

1)

This way, your forefinger serves as a guide for the knife. As you cut, slide the blade forward and backward through the tomato to produce the slices. After each cut, move your forefinger to the left a distance equal to the desired thickness of the next slice. As you do this, it is important that the flat of the blade always remain in contact with the flat surface of your forefinger (1).

For the horizontal method, place the tomato stem end down on the cutting board. Hold the tomato loosely with the fingertips of your left hand. Position a chef's knife, held with a pinch grip, so the blade is parallel to the board. Carefully, using a sawing motion, make the first slice at the bottom of the tomato. Move this slice to the right and use it as a gauge for the next slice (2).

2)

Coarsely Chopping a Tomato

Place a peeled tomato on the cutting board with the stem end to the right. Hold the tomato with the fingertips of your left hand. Hold a sharp chef's knife with a pinch grip in your right hand, and make a single cut right through the center of the tomato (1). Gently squeeze each half to expel the juice and seeds (2). Any reluctant seeds can be removed with your fingertips or with the edge of a teaspoon.

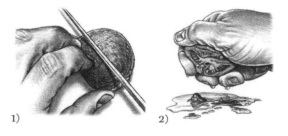

1)   2)

CUTTING TOMATOES (*right-hand version continued*)

3)

Hold a tomato half, cut side down, on the cutting board with your left hand, with your fingertips positioned straight down toward the cutting board. Position a sharp chef's knife, held with a pinch grip, so the flat of the blade rests against the flat side of the tip of your forefinger. This way, your forefinger serves as a guide for the knife. Start each cut with the tip of the blade in contact with, or near, the cutting board, with the handle angled up. As you bring the knife down, slide it forward so the edge of the blade is moving left through the tomato as you produce the slice. After each cut, move your forefinger to the left a distance equal to the desired thickness of the next cut. As you do this, it is important that the flat of the blade always remain in contact with the flat surface of your forefinger (3).

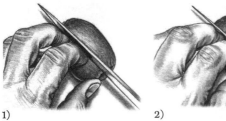

4)

Stack the strips of tomato and rotate 90 degrees. Hold the stack with your left hand, with your fingertips positioned straight down toward the board. Once again, position a sharp chef's knife, held with a pinch grip, so the flat of the blade rests against the flat side of the tip of your forefinger. Start each cut with the tip of the blade in contact with, or near, the cutting board, with the handle angled up. As you bring the knife down, slide it forward so the edge of the blade is moving through the tomato as you produce the dice. After each cut, move your forefinger to the left a distance equal to the desired thickness of the next cut. As you do this, it is important that the flat of the blade always remain in contact with the flat surface of your forefinger (4). This method is generally used for quickly and coarsely chopping tomatoes and the result is sometimes referred to as a *concassé*. The dicing method below is used for a more uniform cut.

Seeding a Tomato

1)

2)

Place a whole, peeled tomato on the cutting board, and hold it with the fingertips of your left hand. Hold the chef's knife with a pinch grip in your right hand, and make a cut through the axis of the tomato to split it into two halves (1). Repeat this operation on each of the halves to make four wedges. (If the tomato is quite large, cut it into six or eight wedges.) Be sure to place each half cut side down when splitting it (2).

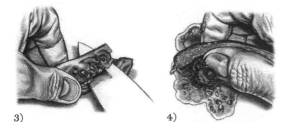

3)

4)

Work with each wedge separately. Lay the wedge cut side up on the cutting board. Hold the tomato with the thumb and forefinger of your left hand. Using the chef's knife held with a pinch grip in your right hand, with the blade almost parallel to the cutting board, cut out the seeds and the core (3). In some tomatoes, these will come out cleanly. In others, it will be necessary to use your right thumb to strip any tenacious seeds from the tomato (4).

Shredding a Tomato

Place a cleaned tomato wedge on the cutting board.
Hold it firmly with your left hand, with your fingertips
positioned straight down toward the board. Position a
sharp chef's knife, held with a pinch grip, so the flat of
the blade rests against the flat side of the tip of your
forefinger. This way, your forefinger serves as a guide

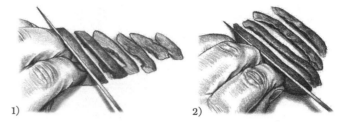

1)
2)

for the knife. The cuts should be made at about a 45-degree angle if the strips are to be the final result (1). If they are
to be diced, the cuts should be parallel to the long axis of the tomato wedge. Start each cut with the tip of the blade
in contact with, or near, the cutting board, with the handle angled up. As you bring the knife down, slide it forward
so the edge of the blade is moving left through the tomato as you produce a slice. After each cut, move your
forefinger to the left a distance equal to the desired thickness of the next cut. Ideally, the thickness of this cut should
be equal to the thickness of the tomato flesh, so the resulting strips have a square cross section. It is important that
the flat of the blade always remain in contact with the flat surface of your forefinger (2).

Dicing a Tomato

Gather the tomato strips from the previous step together into a stack on the cutting
board. Hold the stack firmly with your left hand, with your fingertips positioned straight
down toward the cutting board. Position the chef's knife, held with a pinch grip, so the
flat of the blade rests against the flat side of the tip of your forefinger. This way, your
forefinger serves as a guide for the knife. Start each cut with the tip of the blade in contact
with, or near, the cutting board, with the handle angled up. As you bring the knife down,

slide it forward so the edge of the blade is moving through the tomato as you produce the dice. After each cut, move
your forefinger to the left a distance equal to the desired thickness of the next cut. Ideally, the thickness of this cut
should be equal to the thickness of the strips, so the resulting dice will be uniform. As you do this, it is important
that the flat of the blade always remain in contact with the flat surface of your forefinger.

CUTTING TOMATOES (*left-hand version*)

Coring a Tomato

Most tomato preparations begin with removing the core. Hold the tomato firmly in your right hand and hold a sharp paring knife in a pinch grip in your left. Support your knife hand against the tomato with your middle finger, and pierce the tomato just a bit away from the core with the tip of the blade extending to the center of the tomato at about a 45-degree angle. While moving the knife in and out with a sawing motion, rotate the tomato into the edge of the knife to carve out a conical-shaped piece around the core. Remove and discard the core.

Peeling a Tomato with a Knife

1) 2) 3)

Some recipes call for peeled tomatoes. To peel a tomato with a knife, hold the tomato loosely in the fingers of your right hand, with the stem end toward your fingers. Hold a sharp paring knife in your left hand, with your forefinger wrapped around the blade. Support your knife hand against the tomato with your left thumb, and cut a disk from the blossom end of the tomato, leaving it attached by about a ½-inch strip of skin. Make this first cut as shallow as possible (1). Then proceed to peel the tomato by rotating it into the knife blade to remove a long ½-inch-wide ribbon of skin. As you do this, gently saw back and forth with the blade (2). Work your way in a continuous spiral all the way around and down the tomato until the entire skin is removed (3). Try to remove as little of the flesh as possible. Discard the skin (or save it for making decorative tomato roses).

Peeling a Tomato by Blanching

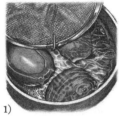

1)

If you have more than a few tomatoes to peel, the previous method may be too time-consuming. As an alternative, bring a pot of water to a rolling boil. While the water is heating, core the tomatoes and then cut an X in the skin of the opposite end (1). Prepare an ice bath by filling a large bowl with cold water and some ice cubes. Carefully place a few tomatoes at a time into the boiling water and leave them just until their skins split. The time this takes depends on the type of tomato and how ripe it is. In any case, never blanch a tomato for more than a minute. As soon as the tomato skin splits or a minute is up, transfer the tomatoes to the ice bath with a skimmer. (You can also use the skimmer to rotate the tomatoes in the boiling water to find splits that are out of view.)

Once each tomato is cold, hold it in the fingers of your right hand and hold a paring knife in your left, with your forefinger and middle finger wrapped around the blade. Slide the tip of the blade just under a loose piece of skin, hold the skin firmly against the flat side of the blade, near the tip, with your thumb, and pull the skin down toward the core end of the tomato to remove it (2). Discard the skin. Continue removing the skin, rotating the tomato toward the knife so new skin is exposed, until all the skin has been removed.

2)

Slicing a Tomato

For simple slices, a tomato can cut vertically or horizontally. The vertical method works better for firm tomatoes and the horizontal for soft tomatoes, especially if they have been peeled. For the vertical method, place a tomato on a cutting board with the stem end toward the left. Hold the tomato firmly with your right hand, with your fingertips positioned straight down toward the board. Position a sharp chef's knife, held with a pinch grip, so the flat of the blade rests against the flat side of the tip of your forefinger.

1)

This way, your forefinger serves as a guide for the knife. As you cut, slide the blade forward and backward through the tomato to produce the slices. After each cut, move your forefinger to the right a distance equal to the desired thickness of the next slice. As you do this, it is important that the flat of the blade always remain in contact with the flat surface of your forefinger (1).

For the horizontal method, place the tomato stem end down on the cutting board. Hold the tomato loosely with the fingertips of your right hand. Position a chef's knife, held with a pinch grip, so the blade is parallel to the board. Carefully, using a sawing motion, make the first slice at the bottom of the tomato. Move this slice to the left and use it as a gauge for the next slice (2).

2)

Coarsely Chopping a Tomato

Place a peeled tomato on the cutting board with the stem end to the left. Hold the tomato with the fingertips of your right hand. Hold a sharp chef's knife with a pinch grip in your left hand, and make a single cut right through the center of the tomato (1). Gently squeeze each half to expel the juice and seeds (2). Any reluctant seeds can be removed with your fingertips or with the edge of a teaspoon.

1)   2)

CUTTING TOMATOES (*left-hand version continued*)

3)

Hold a tomato half, cut side down, on the cutting board with your right hand, with your fingertips positioned straight down toward the cutting board. Position a sharp chef's knife, held with a pinch grip, so the flat of the blade rests against the flat side of the tip of your forefinger. This way, your forefinger serves as a guide for the knife. Start each cut with the tip of the blade in contact with, or near, the cutting board, with the handle angled up. As you bring the knife down, slide it forward so the edge of the blade is moving right through the tomato as you produce the slice. After each cut, move your forefinger to the right a distance equal to the desired thickness of the next cut. As you do this, it is important that the flat of the blade always remain in contact with the flat surface of your forefinger (3).

4)

Stack the strips of tomato and rotate 90 degrees. Hold the stack with your right hand, with your fingertips positioned straight down toward the board. Once again, position a sharp chef's knife, held with a pinch grip, so the flat of the blade rests against the flat side of the tip of your forefinger. Start each cut with the tip of the blade in contact with, or near, the cutting board, with the handle angled up. As you bring the knife down, slide it forward so the edge of the blade is moving through the tomato as you produce the dice. After each cut, move your forefinger to the right a distance equal to the desired thickness of the next cut. As you do this, it is important that the flat of the blade always remain in contact with the flat surface of your forefinger (4). This method is generally used for quickly and coarsely chopping tomatoes and the result is sometimes referred to as a *concassé*. The dicing method below is used for a more uniform cut.

Seeding a Tomato

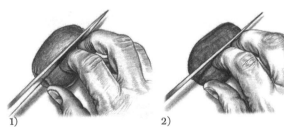

1)   2)

Place a whole, peeled tomato on the cutting board, and hold it with the fingertips of your right hand. Hold the chef's knife with a pinch grip in your left hand, and make a cut through the axis of the tomato to split it into two halves (1). Repeat this operation on each of the halves to make four wedges. (If the tomato is quite large, cut it into six or eight wedges.) Be sure to place each half cut side down when splitting it (2).

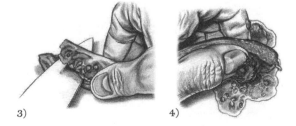

3)   4)

Work with each wedge separately. Lay the wedge cut side up on the cutting board. Hold the tomato with the thumb and forefinger of your right hand. Using the chef's knife held with a pinch grip in your left hand, with the blade almost parallel to the cutting board, cut out the seeds and the core (3). In some tomatoes, these will come out cleanly. In others, it will be necessary to use your left thumb to strip any tenacious seeds from the tomato (4).

Shredding a Tomato

Place a cleaned tomato wedge on the cutting board. Hold it firmly with your right hand, with your fingertips positioned straight down toward the board. Position a sharp chef's knife, held with a pinch grip, so the flat of the blade rests against the flat side of the tip of your forefinger. This way, your forefinger serves as a

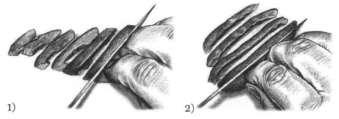

1)　　　　　　　　　2)

guide for the knife. The cuts should be made at about a 45-degree angle if the strips are to be the final result (1). If they are to be diced, the cuts should be made parallel to the long axis of the tomato wedge. Start each cut with the tip of the blade in contact with, or near, the cutting board, with the handle angled up. As you bring the knife down, slide it forward so the edge of the blade is moving right through the tomato as you produce a slice. After each cut, move your forefinger to the right a distance equal to the desired thickness of the next cut. Ideally, the thickness of this cut should be equal to the thickness of the tomato flesh, so the resulting strips have a square cross section. It is important that the flat of the blade always remain in contact with the flat surface of your forefinger (2).

Dicing a Tomato

Gather the tomato strips from the previous step together into a stack on the cutting board. Hold the stack firmly with your right hand, with your fingertips positioned straight down toward the cutting board. Position the chef's knife, held with a pinch grip, so the flat of the blade rests against the flat side of the tip of your forefinger. This way, your forefinger serves as a guide for the knife. Start each cut with the tip of the blade in contact with, or near, the cutting board, with the handle angled up. As you bring the knife down, slide it forward so

the edge of the blade is moving through the tomato as you produce the cubes. After each cut, move your forefinger to the right a distance equal to the desired thickness of the next cut. Ideally, the thickness of this cut should be equal to the thickness of the strips, so the resulting dice will be uniform. As you do this, it is important that the flat of the blade always remain in contact with the flat surface of your forefinger.

CUTTING AVOCADOS

MY FAVORITE WAY TO EAT AN AVOCADO IS TO CUT IT IN HALF, REMOVE THE seed, sprinkle a little salt on the flesh, and eat it out of its skin with a spoon. The best avocado I've ever eaten was at a fruit and vegetable stand in downtown Adelaide in Australia. I bought the avocado, split it with my wife's Swiss Army knife, and sat on a nearby bench and savored it. It was amazing. Creamy and sweet. No salt required.

Avocados are also great in salads, pureed into soup, and even as sashimi. Cutting a perfectly ripe avocado requires a little skill, but it's possible to do it without any waste.

When purchasing avocados, select ones that are not quite ripe or still hard. Avoid any with any soft spots or cuts or that are missing the stem remnant. (If the remnant is missing, the avocado can start rotting from the hole remaining in the skin where the stem was attached.) Keep avocados at room temperature until ripe, then store them in the refrigerator until ready to use them.

CUTTING AVOCADOS (*right-hand version*)

Pitting an Avocado

Hold an avocado firmly in the palm of your left hand as shown in the illustration. If there is still a remnant of stem attached to the avocado, remove it with your fingers. Using a sharp chef's knife held in a pinch grip in your right hand, make a single cut into the side of the avocado. The cut should be directly on a longitudinal plane through the fruit so that it will pass through the point where the

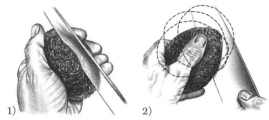

1)   2)

stem was attached (1). Once the knife hits the pit, use your left hand to rotate the avocado against the blade, and turn the avocado completely over in your left hand to extend the cut entirely around the avocado (2). Remove the knife from the avocado. Holding one half of the fruit in each hand, carefully twist the halves to separate them.

Holding the half of the avocado containing the pit in your left hand, use the chef's knife in a chopping motion to embed the edge of the blade solidly in the pit. Twist the knife from side to side, as indicated by the arrow in the illustration, to release the pit from the avocado half (3). Discard the pit.

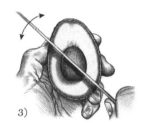

3)

Peeling an Avocado

There are two ways to peel an avocado. The quickest method, especially if the flesh is very soft, is to slide a large spoon between the flesh and the skin of each half: hold the avocado half firmly, but not too tightly, in the palm of your left hand. Starting at the right edge of the avocado half, gradually slide the spoon inside the skin toward the left (1). Always staying in contact with the skin, move the spoon around until the flesh is fully released from the skin. If any flesh remains on the skin, scrape it out with the spoon.

1)

The second peeling method is preferable if the avocado is still a bit hard. Hold an avocado half cut side down in the palm of your left hand. Using a paring knife with a sharp tip held in a pinch grip, make two or three cuts the full length of the fruit, just through the skin (2). Then, with your forefinger and middle finger wrapped around the

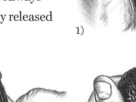

2)   3)

blade, slide the tip of the blade just under the skin at the upper right edge. Firmly hold the skin against the flat side of the blade, near the tip, with your thumb. Pull off the skin and discard (3). Continue removing the skin, each time turning the avocado toward the knife so new skin is exposed.

CUTTING AVOCADOS (*right-hand version continued*)

Slicing an Avocado

Place a peeled avocado half cut side down on a cutting board. Hold it in place with the fingertips of your left hand. Use a sharp chef's knife held in your right hand with a pinch grip to make successive cuts through the avocado. Start each cut with the tip of the blade in contact with the cutting board, with the handle angled up, and pull the blade toward you, always keeping the tip in contact with the board, until the slice is completed. The avocado can be sliced in whichever direction your recipe calls for.

Cutting an Avocado into Wedges

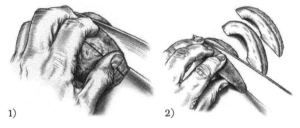

1)   2)

Place a peeled avocado half cut side down on a cutting board. Hold it in place with the fingertips of your left hand. Use a sharp chef's knife held in your right hand with a pinch grip to make to make a cut down the center of the avocado piece to cut it in half. Start the cut with the tip of the blade in contact with the cutting board, with the handle angled up, and pull the blade toward you, always keeping the tip in contact with the board, until the cut is completed (1). In the same manner, cut the quarter to your right into two wedges. Flip the quarter to your left onto its right side and cut it into wedges in the same manner as the first (2).

Dicing an Avocado

Place a peeled avocado half cut side down on a cutting board. Hold it in place with the fingertips of your left hand. Position a chef's knife, held with a pinch grip, so the blade is parallel to the cutting board and a distance above it equal to the size of the intended dice. Draw the blade fully through the avocado (1). Make additional horizontal cuts through the avocado to slice evenly. Keep the slices intact, maintaining shape of the avocado half, as you make each slice.

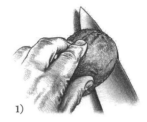

1)

Rotate the avocado so it is positioned for making lengthwise slices. Use the chef's knife held with a pinch grip in your right hand to make to make successive vertical cuts the length of the avocado. Start each cut with the tip of the blade in contact with the cutting board, with the handle angled up, and pull the blade toward you, always keeping the tip in contact with the board, until the slice is completed (2). As you pull the blade, reach over it with the forefinger of your left hand to keep each slice on the right of the blade from moving. Make the slices as even as possible (3).

2)   3)

Rotate the avocado so it is positioned for making crosswise slices. Use the chef's knife held in your right hand with a pinch grip to make to make successive vertical cuts across the avocado. Start each cut with the tip of the blade in contact with the cutting board, with the handle angled up, and pull the blade toward you, always keeping the tip in contact with the board, until the slice is completed. Make the slices as even as possible (4).

4)

CUTTING AVOCADOS (*left-hand version*)

Pitting an Avocado

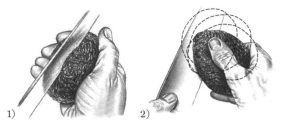

1) 2)

Hold an avocado firmly in the palm of your right hand as shown in the illustration. If there is still a remnant of stem attached, remove it with your fingers. Using a sharp chef's knife held in a pinch grip in your left hand, make a single cut into the side of the avocado. The cut should be directly on a longitudinal plane through the fruit so that it will pass through the point where the stem was attached (1). Once the knife hits the pit, use your right hand to rotate the avocado against the blade, and turn the avocado completely over in your right hand to extend the cut entirely around the avocado (2). Remove the knife from the avocado. Holding one half of the fruit in each hand, carefully twist the halves to separate them.

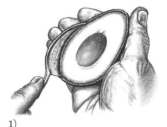

3)

Holding the half of the avocado containing the pit in your right hand, use the chef's knife in a chopping motion to embed the edge of the blade solidly in the pit. Twist the knife from side to side, as indicated by the arrow in the illustration, to release the pit from the avocado half (3). Discard the pit.

Peeling an Avocado

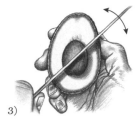

1)

There are two ways to peel an avocado. The quickest method, especially if the flesh is very soft, is to slide a large spoon between the flesh and the skin of each half: hold the avocado half firmly, but not too tightly, in the palm of your right hand. Starting at the left edge of the avocado half, gradually slide the spoon inside the skin toward the right (1). Always staying in contact with the skin, move the spoon around until the flesh is fully released from the skin. If any flesh remains on the skin, scrape it out with the spoon.

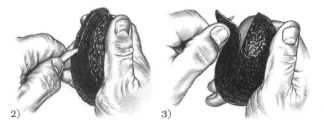

2) 3)

The second peeling method is preferable if the avocado is still a bit hard. Hold an avocado half cut side down in the palm of your right hand. Using a paring knife with a sharp tip held in a pinch grip, make two or three cuts the full length of the fruit, just through the skin (2). Then, with your forefinger and middle finger wrapped around the blade, slide the tip of the blade just under the skin at the upper left edge. Firmly hold the skin against the flat side of the blade, near the tip, with your thumb. Pull off the skin and discard (3). Continue removing the skin, each time turning the avocado toward the knife so new skin is exposed.

Slicing an Avocado

Place a peeled avocado half cut side down on a cutting board. Hold it in place with the fingertips of your right hand. Use a sharp chef's knife held in your left hand with a pinch grip to make successive cuts through the avocado. Start each cut with the tip of the blade in contact with the cutting board, with the handle angled up, and pull the blade toward you, always keeping the tip in contact with the board, until the slice is completed. The avocado can be sliced in whichever direction your recipe calls for.

Cutting an Avocado into Wedges

Place a peeled avocado half cut side down on a cutting board. Hold it in place with the fingertips of your right hand. Use a sharp chef's knife held in your left hand with a pinch grip to make to make a cut down the center of the avocado piece to cut it in half. Start the cut with the tip of the blade in contact with the cutting board, with the handle angled up, and pull the blade toward you, always keeping the tip in contact with the board, until the cut is completed (1). In the same manner, cut the quarter to your left into two wedges. Flip the quarter to your right onto its left side and cut it into wedges in the same manner as the first (2).

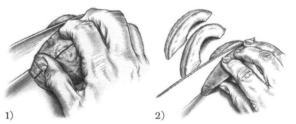

1)   2)

CUTTING AVOCADOS *(left-hand version continued)*

Dicing an Avocado

1)

Place a peeled avocado half cut side down on a cutting board. Hold it in place with the fingertips of your right hand. Position a chef's knife, held with a pinch grip, so the blade is parallel to the cutting board and a distance above it equal to the size of the intended dice. Draw the blade fully through the avocado (1). Make additional horizontal cuts through the avocado to slice it evenly. Keep the slices intact, maintaining shape of the avocado half, as you make each slice.

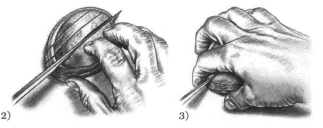

2)   3)

Rotate the avocado so it is positioned for making lengthwise slices. Use the chef's knife held with a pinch grip in your left hand to make to make successive vertical cuts the length of the avocado. Start each cut with the tip of the blade in contact with the cutting board, with the handle angled up, and pull the blade toward you, always keeping the tip in contact with the board, until the slice is completed (2). As you pull the blade, reach over it with the forefinger of your right hand to keep each slice on the left of the blade from moving. Make the slices as even as possible (3).

4)

Rotate the avocado so it is positioned for making crosswise slices. Use the chef's knife held in your left hand with a pinch grip to make to make successive vertical cuts across the avocado. Start each cut with the tip of the blade in contact with the cutting board, with the handle angled up, and pull the blade toward you, always keeping the tip in contact with the board, until the slice is completed. Make the slices as even as possible (4).

CUTTING APPLES AND PEARS

APPLES AND PEARS ARE OFTEN EATEN RAW OUT OF HAND, BUT FOR RECIPES, THEY usually are peeled and cut. Although they are distinctly different fruits, they can be cut in essentially similar ways.

When purchasing apples, look for fruit that is firm and unblemished and feels heavy for its size. Avoid any with visible bruises or flat spots, which may be a result of being dropped. Store apples in the refrigerator.

When buying pears, select ripe fruit that has a slight give near the stem. Avoid any with soft spots. Unripe fruit should be left at room temperature until it ripens. Ripe fruit can be stored in the refrigerator.

The peeled and cut surfaces of both pears and apples will discolor when exposed to air. If the fruit isn't going to be used immediately, place the pieces in acidulated water. Acidulated water is made by adding acid to water. Common acids are white vinegar, which should be added at a ratio of 1½ tablespoons per quart of cold water, or lemon juice, added at a ratio of 3 tablespoons per quart of water.

CUTTING APPLES AND PEARS (*right-hand version*)

Peeling an Apple or a Pear

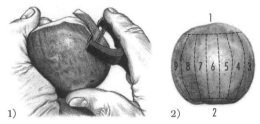

1)   2)

Whether peeling an apple or a pear, the process is the same. The technique here is illustrated with an apple. The fruit can be peeled whole or halved. In either case, the method is the same. A yoke-type peeler, shown in the illustration, is my preferred tool. Hold the fruit firmly in your left hand and the peeler in your right. Support your right hand against the fruit with your thumb (1). Start by peeling a circular area at both ends of the fruit. Then, peel the fruit in strips from top to bottom. After each strip, rotate the fruit toward you to expose a new section of skin. The suggested order of peeling is shown in the illustration (2).

Halving an Apple or a Pear

Stand an apple or pear on a cutting board with the stem up. Hold the fruit firmly in place with the fingertips of your left hand. Before you cut, look carefully at the piece of fruit. Turn the apple or pear until the axis of each end is in a plane with the blade of your knife. Using a sharp chef's knife held with a pinch grip in your right hand, start the cut at the stem and cut straight down through the fruit. If the stem is missing, cut through the hole where the stem was.

Coring an Apple or a Pear

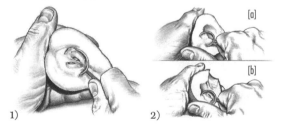

1)   2)

Although the core of either fruit can be removed with a sharp paring knife once it is halved, a baller makes for a neater result. Use a baller that's about 1 inch across. Hold the fruit firmly in your left hand, with its cut side facing you, and the baller in your right hand. Press the baller into the surface of the pear or apple near the center of the core, and twist the handle in a circular motion to cut out a hemispherically shaped piece of core (1). Then use the baller as a scoop to remove the ends of the core that remain. To do this, hold the baller in your right hand with your forefinger and middle finger wrapped around the shaft. With the thumb on your right hand providing opposing force on the fruit, scoop out one end of the core (2a). Turn the fruit around and remove the other end of the core in the same way (2b).

Slicing an Apple or a Pear

Place an apple or pear half on the cutting board, cut side down, so the cored groove runs from your lower left to upper right. Hold the fruit firmly with your left hand, with your forefinger pointing straight down toward the cutting board. Position the chef's knife, held in a pinch grip, so the flat of the blade rests against the flat side of the tip of your forefinger. This way, your forefinger serves 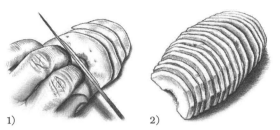 as a guide for the knife. Because of the height of the fruit, begin each cut with the edge of the blade horizontal, approximately parallel to the cutting board. Move the knife forward and backward in a sawing motion to produce each slice. After each cut, move your forefinger to the left, a distance equal to the desired thickness of the next cut. As you do this, it is important that the flat of the blade always remain in contact with the flat surface of your forefinger (1). With care, the slices will be of uniform thickness and still in the order in which they were cut. They can then be arranged neatly for their intended use (2).

Julienning an Apple or a Pear

To cut an apple or pear half into julienne or dice, first place it on the cutting board, cut side down, so the cored groove runs from your upper left to lower right. Firmly grip the edges of the fruit with the thumb and forefinger of your left hand. Use the chef's knife held with a pinch grip in your right hand to cut the half into two quarters (1). (If you need wedges of fruit, use this same method to cut the halves into wedges.)

Working with one quarter at a time, place it on the board with one cut edge down and the other facing right. Hold the quarter firmly with your left hand with your fingertips positioned straight down toward the board. Position the chef's knife, held with a pinch grip, so the flat of the blade rests against the flat side of the tip of your forefinger. This way, your forefinger serves as a guide for the knife. Because of the height of the fruit, begin each cut with the edge of the blade horizontal, approximately parallel to the cutting  board. Move the knife forward and backward in a sawing motion to produce each slice. After each cut, move your forefinger to the left a distance equal to the desired thickness of the next cut. As you do this, it is important that the flat of the blade always remain in contact with the flat surface of your forefinger. With care, the slices will be of uniform thickness and in the order in which they were cut (2). (Continue to julienne this quarter before slicing any of the other quarters.)

CUTTING APPLES AND PEARS (*right-hand version continued*)

3)

Stack the slices neatly and in order on the cutting board. Hold the stack firmly with your left hand, with your fingertips positioned straight down toward the cutting board. Position the chef's knife, held with a pinch grip, so the flat of the blade rests against the flat side of the tip of your forefinger. This way, your forefinger serves as a guide for the knife. Because of the height of the fruit, begin each cut with the edge of the blade horizontal, approximately parallel to the cutting board. Move the knife forward and backward in a sawing motion to produce each slice. After each cut, move your forefinger to the left a distance equal to the desired thickness of the next cut. As you do this, it is important that the flat of the blade always remain in contact with the flat surface of your forefinger. With care, the strips will have a square cross section (3).

Dicing an Apple or a Pear

Gather the julienned strips from the previous step together into a stack. Hold the stack firmly with your left hand, with your fingertips positioned straight down toward the board. Position the chef's knife, held with a pinch grip, so the flat of the blade rests against the flat side of the tip of your forefinger. This way, your forefinger serves as a guide for the knife. Begin each cut with the edge of the blade horizontal, approximately parallel to the cutting board. Move the knife forward and backward in a sawing motion to produce each slice. After each cut, move your forefinger to the left a distance equal to the desired thickness of the next cut. As you do this, it is important that the flat of the blade always remain in contact with the flat surface of your forefinger. With care, the cubes will be uniform.

Cutting a Pear Fan

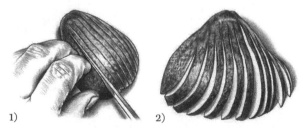

1)   2)

To make the decorative cut called an *éventail*, or fan, place a pear half cut side down on the cutting board. Hold the fruit firmly with your left hand, with your fingertips positioned straight down toward the cutting board. Position a sharp chef's knife, held with a pinch grip, so the flat of the blade rests against the flat side of the tip of your forefinger. This way, your forefinger serves as a guide for the knife. With care, the cuts will be spaced the same. Working from right to left, make a series of lengthwise cuts through the fruit: start each cut near the stem end of the pear. Pierce the flesh with the tip of the knife and, keeping the tip in contact with the cutting board, draw the knife toward you. Be careful to keep the slices attached to one another at the stem end. After each cut, move your forefinger to the left a distance equal to the desired width of the next cut. As you do this, it is important that the flat of the blade always remain in contact with the flat surface of your forefinger (1, 2). This technique is often used with cooked fruit, which is more pliable.

CUTTING APPLES AND PEARS *(left-hand version)*

Peeling an Apple or a Pear

Whether peeling an apple or a pear, the process is the same. The technique here is illustrated with an apple. The fruit can be peeled whole or halved. In either case, the method is the same. A yoke-type peeler, shown in the illustration, is my preferred tool. Hold the fruit firmly in your right hand and the peeler in your left. Support your left hand against the fruit with your thumb (1). Start by peeling a circular area at both ends of the fruit. Then, peel the fruit in strips from top to bottom. After each strip, rotate the fruit toward you to expose a new section of skin. The suggested order of peeling is shown in the illustration (2).

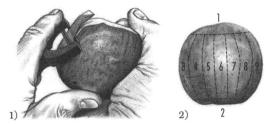

Halving an Apple or a Pear

Stand an apple or pear on a cutting board with the stem up. Hold the fruit firmly in place with the fingertips of your right hand. Before you cut, look carefully at the piece of fruit. Turn the apple or pear until the axis of each end is in a plane with the blade of the knife. Using a sharp chef's knife held with a pinch grip in your left hand, start the cut at the stem and cut straight down through the fruit. If the stem is missing, cut through the hole where the stem was.

Coring an Apple or a Pear

Although the core of either fruit can be removed with a sharp paring knife once it is halved, a baller makes for a neater result. Use a baller that's about 1 inch across. Hold the fruit firmly in your right hand, with its cut side facing you and the baller in your left hand. Press the baller into the surface of the pear or apple near the center of the core, and twist the handle in a circular motion to

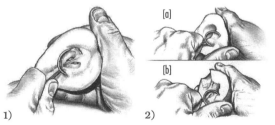

cut out a hemispherically shaped piece of core (1). Then use the baller as a scoop to remove the ends of the core that remain. To do this, hold the baller in your left hand with your forefinger and middle finger wrapped around the shaft. With the thumb on your left hand providing opposing force on the fruit, scoop out one end of the core (2a). Turn the fruit around and remove the other end of the core in the same way (2b).

CUTTING APPLES AND PEARS (*left-hand version continued*)

Slicing an Apple or a Pear

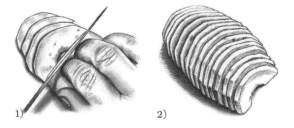

1) 2)

Place an apple or pear half on the cutting board, cut side down, so the cored groove runs from your lower right to upper left. Hold the fruit firmly with your right hand, with your forefinger pointing straight down toward the cutting board. Position the chef's knife, held in a pinch grip, so the flat of the blade rests against the flat side of the tip of your forefinger. This way, your forefinger serves as a guide for the knife. Because of the height of the fruit, begin each cut with the edge of the blade horizontal, approximately parallel to the cutting board. Move the knife forward and backward in a sawing motion to produce each slice. After each cut, move your forefinger to the right a distance equal to the desired thickness of the next cut. As you do this, it is important that the flat of the blade always remain in contact with the flat surface of your forefinger (1). With care, the slices will be of uniform thickness and still in the order in which they were cut. They can then be arranged neatly for their intended use (2).

Julienning an Apple or a Pear

1)

To cut an apple or pear half into julienne or dice, first place it on the cutting board, cut side down, so the cored groove runs from your upper right to lower left. Firmly grip the edges of the fruit with the thumb and forefinger of your right hand. Use the chef's knife held with a pinch grip in your left hand to cut the half into two quarters (1). (If you need wedges of fruit, use this same method to cut the halves into wedges.)

2)

Working with one quarter at a time, place it on the board with one cut edge down and the other facing left. Hold the quarter firmly with your right hand with your fingertips positioned straight down toward the board. Position the chef's knife, held with a pinch grip, so the flat of the blade rests against the flat side of the tip of your forefinger. This way, your forefinger serves as a guide for the knife. Because of the height of the fruit, begin each cut with the edge of the blade horizontal, approximately parallel to the cutting board. Move the knife forward and backward in a sawing motion to produce each slice. After each cut, move your forefinger to the right a distance equal to the desired thickness of the next cut. As you do this, it is important that the flat of the blade always remain in contact with the flat surface of your forefinger. With care, the slices will be of uniform thickness and in the order in which they were cut (2). (Continue to julienne this quarter before slicing any of the other quarters.)

Stack the slices neatly and in order on the cutting board. Hold the stack firmly with your right hand, with your fingertips positioned straight down toward the cutting board. Position the chef's knife, held with a pinch grip, so the flat of the blade rests against the flat side of the tip of your forefinger. This way, your forefinger serves as a guide for the knife. Because of the height of the fruit, begin each cut with the edge of the blade horizontal, approximately parallel to the cutting board. Move the knife forward and backward in a sawing motion to produce each slice. After each cut, move your forefinger to the right a distance equal to the desired width of the next cut. As you do this, it is important that the flat of the blade always remain in contact with the flat surface of your forefinger. With care, the strips will have a square cross section (3).

1) 3)

Dicing an Apple or a Pear

Gather the julienned strips from the previous step together into a stack. Hold the stack firmly with your right hand, with your fingertips positioned straight down toward the board. Position the chef's knife, held with a pinch grip, so the flat of the blade rests against the flat side of the tip of your forefinger. This way, your forefinger serves as a guide for the knife. Begin each cut with the edge of the blade horizontal, approximately parallel to the cutting board. Move the knife forward and backward in a sawing motion to produce each slice. After each cut, move your forefinger to the right a distance equal to the desired thickness of the next cut. As you do this, it is important that the flat of the blade always remain in contact with the flat surface of your forefinger. With care, the cubes will be uniform.

Cutting a Pear Fan

To make the decorative cut called an *éventail*, or fan, place a pear half cut side down on the cutting board. Hold the fruit firmly with your right hand, with your fingertips positioned straight down toward the cutting board. Position a sharp chef's knife, held with a pinch grip, so the flat of the blade rests against the flat side of the tip of your forefinger. This way, your

1) 2)

forefinger serves as a guide for the knife. With care, the cuts will be spaced the same. Working from left to right, make a series of lengthwise cuts through the fruit: start each cut near the stem end of the pear. Pierce the flesh with the tip of the knife and, keeping the tip in contact with the cutting board, draw the knife toward you. Be careful to keep the slices attached to one another at the stem end. After each cut, move your forefinger to the right a distance equal to the desired width of the next cut. As you do this, it is important that the flat of the blade always remain in contact with the flat surface of your forefinger (1, 2). This technique is often used with cooked fruit, which is more pliable.

CUTTING CITRUS FRUITS

L EMONS, LIMES, ORANGES, AND GRAPEFRUITS DIFFER FROM EACH OTHER IN SIZE, color, and sometimes shape, but their structure is essentially the same, so they can all be handled the same way. In all four, the individual parts—zest, flesh, and juice—tend to be used separately in recipes.

It is not uncommon to need only the zest—the colored part of the peel—from a lemon or an orange. If this is the case, wrap the remaining fruit tightly in couple of layers of plastic wrap. This will form a new seal to keep the flesh of the lemon or orange from drying out in the refrigerator.

When sectioning an orange or grapefruit in the manner described in this section, don't discard the remaining membranes without first squeezing the juice from them. They can hold an amazing amount.

CUTTING CITRUS FRUITS (*right-hand version*)

Grating Citrus Zest

To produce the finest zest from citrus fruit, use a Microplane-type grater. Hold the fruit in your left hand and the grater in your right. Grate the zest from one part of the fruit, moving only the grater, then rotate the fruit before making the next pass with the grater. In this manner, the amount of bitter white pith grated will be minimized. Continue around the fruit with the grater held above fruit. Holding the grater above the fruit keeps the grated zest in the hollow of the grater and also allows you to see what part of the fruit you have already grated.

Julienning Citrus Zest

To produce fine julienned or minced zest, peel the fruit with a peeler. A yoke-type peeler, shown in the illustration, is my preferred tool. Hold the fruit tightly in your left hand and the peeler in your right. Peel the fruit from top to bottom. After each strip of skin is peeled, rotate the fruit toward you to expose a new section (1).

1)

Next, one at a time, place each piece of peel pith side up on the cutting board. Hold the peel absolutely flat with the extended fingers of your left hand. Using a sharp chef's knife held with a pinch grip in your right hand, with the blade of the knife positioned parallel to and as close as possible to the cutting board, saw back and forth with the knife to separate the pith from the zest. Keep the blade flat against the peel throughout the entire cut. You should be able to remove most of the pith, leaving just a hint of white on the zest (2).

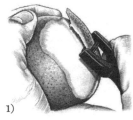

2)

To julienne the zest, stack a couple of pieces of the cleaned zest, pith side down, on the cutting board. Hold the stack firmly with your left hand, with your fingertips positioned straight down toward the board. Position a sharp chef's knife, held with a pinch grip, so the flat of the blade rests against the flat side of the tip of your forefinger. This way, your forefinger serves as a guide for the knife. Start each cut with the tip of the blade in contact with the cutting board, with the handle angled slightly up. As you bring the knife down,

3)

slide it forward so the edge of the blade is moving left through the zest as you produce the julienne. After each cut, move your forefinger to the left a distance equal to the desired thickness of the next cut. Ideally, the thickness of this cut should be the same as the thickness of the previous slice, probably less than $\frac{1}{32}$ inch, so the resulting strips have a perfectly square cross section. As you do this, it is important that the flat of the blade always remain in contact with the flat surface of your forefinger (3).

CUTTING CITRUS FRUITS (*right-hand version continued*)

Mincing Citrus Zest

Gather the julienned strips from the previous step together into a stack. Hold the stack firmly with your left hand, with your fingertips positioned straight down toward the board. Position the chef's knife, held with a pinch grip, so the flat of the blade rests against the flat side of the tip of your forefinger. This way, your forefinger serves as a guide for the knife. Start each cut with the tip of the blade in contact with the cutting board, with the handle angled slightly up. As you bring the knife down, slide it forward so the edge of the blade is moving left through the zest as you produce the mince. After each cut, move your forefinger to the left a distance equal to the desired thickness of the next cut. Ideally, the thickness of this cut should be the same as the thickness of the previous cut, probably less than $\frac{1}{32}$ inch, so the resulting mince will be uniform. As you do this, it is important that the flat of the blade always remain in contact with the flat surface of your forefinger.

Peeling Citrus

Lay the fruit on the cutting board with its central axis running from left to right. Hold the fruit firmly with your left hand and hold a sharp chef's knife with a pinch grip in your right. Trim off both ends of the peel by cutting straight down. Be careful to remove only the peel; do not cut into the flesh of the fruit. Turn the fruit upright so it sits on one of its cut ends. Hold it firmly with your left hand and hold a sharp chef's knife with a pinch grip in your right. Start the first cut at the point where the peel meets the surface of the fruit. Use a sawing motion. While making the cut, continuously change the angle of the blade so that it remains parallel to the surface of the fruit at the point of contact. Peel the fruit from top to bottom, being careful not to penetrate the flesh. After removing each strip, rotate the fruit toward you to expose a new section. Finally, trim any remaining areas where the peel was not totally removed.

Sectioning Citrus

To separate the individual sections of the fruit, hold the peeled fruit in your left hand. Using the chef's knife held with a pinch grip in your right hand, cut along the right side of a wedge as close as possible to the membrane that separates it from the next wedge to the right, cutting to the center of the fruit. Then make a similar cut along the left side of the wedge, as close as possible to the membrane, cutting deep enough to allow the wedge to fall away from the fruit. Continue cutting out the remaining wedges in this fashion.

CUTTING CITRUS FRUITS (*left-hand version*)

Grating Citrus Zest

To produce the finest zest from citrus fruit, use a Microplane-type grater. Hold the fruit in your right hand and the grater in your left. Grate the zest from one part of the fruit, by moving only the grater, then rotate the fruit before making the next pass with the grater. In this manner, the amount of bitter white pith grated will be minimized. Continue around the fruit with the grater above the fruit. Holding the grater above the fruit keeps the grated zest in the hollow of the grater and also allows you to see what part of the fruit you have already grated.

Julienning Citrus Zest

To produce fine julienned or minced zest, peel the fruit with a peeler. A yoke-type peeler, shown in the illustration, is my preferred tool. Hold the fruit tightly in your right hand and the peeler in your left. Peel the fruit from top to bottom. After each strip of skin is peeled, rotate the fruit toward you to expose a new section (1).

1)

Next, one at a time, place each piece of peel pith side up on the cutting board. Hold the peel absolutely flat with the extended fingers of your right hand. Using a sharp chef's knife held with a pinch grip in your left hand with the blade of the knife positioned parallel to and as close as possible to the cutting board, saw back and forth with the knife to separate the pith from the zest. Keep the blade flat against the peel throughout the entire cut. You should be able to remove most of the pith, leaving just a hint of white on the zest (2).

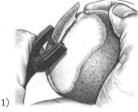

saw back and forth

2)

To julienne the zest, stack a couple of pieces of the cleaned zest, pith side down, on the cutting board. Hold the stack firmly with your right hand, with your fingertips positioned straight down toward the board. Position a sharp chef's knife, held with a pinch grip, so the flat of the blade rests against the flat side of the tip of your forefinger. This way, your forefinger serves as a guide for the knife. Start each cut with the tip of the blade in contact with the cutting board, with the handle angled slightly up. As you bring the knife down, slide it forward so the edge of the blade is moving right through the zest as you produce the julienne. After each cut, move your forefinger to the right a distance equal to the desired thickness of the next cut. Ideally, the thickness of this cut should be the same as the thickness of the previous slice, probably less than $\frac{1}{32}$ inch, so the resulting strips have a perfectly square cross section. As you do this, it is important that the flat of the blade always remain in contact with the flat surface of your forefinger (3).

3)

CUTTING CITRUS FRUITS (*left-hand version continued*)

Mincing Citrus Zest

Gather the julienned strips from the previous step together into a stack. Hold the stack firmly with your right hand, with your fingertips positioned straight down toward the board. Position the chef's knife, held with a pinch grip, so the flat of the blade rests against the flat side of the tip of your forefinger. This way, your forefinger serves as a guide for the knife. Start each cut with the tip of the blade in contact with the cutting board, with the handle angled slightly up. As you bring the knife down, slide it forward so the edge of the blade is moving right through the zest as you produce the mince. After each cut, move your forefinger to the right a distance equal to the desired thickness of the next cut. Ideally, the thickness of this cut should be the same as the thickness of the previous cut, probably less than $\frac{1}{32}$ inch, so the resulting mince will be uniform. As you do this, it is important that the flat of the blade always remain in contact with the flat surface of your forefinger.

Peeling Citrus

Lay the fruit on the cutting board with its central axis running from right to left. Hold the fruit firmly with your right hand and hold a sharp chef's knife with a pinch grip in your left. Trim off both ends of the peel by cutting straight down. Be careful to remove only the peel; do not cut into the flesh of the fruit. Turn the fruit upright so it sits on one of its cut ends. Hold it firmly with your right hand and hold a sharp chef's knife with a pinch grip in your left. Start the first cut at the point where the peel meets the surface of the fruit. Use a sawing motion. While making the cut, continuously change the angle of the blade so that it remains parallel to the surface of the fruit at the point of contact. Peel the fruit from top to bottom, being careful not to penetrate the flesh. After removing each strip of peel, rotate the fruit toward you to expose a new section. Finally, trim any remaining areas where the peel was not totally removed.

Sectioning Citrus

To separate the individual sections of the fruit, hold the peeled fruit in your right hand. Using the knife held with a pinch grip in your left hand, cut along the left side of a wedge as close as possible to the membrane that separates it from the next wedge to the left, cutting to the center of the fruit. Then make a similar cut along the right side of the wedge, as close as possible to the membrane, cutting deep enough to allow the wedge to fall away from the fruit. Continue cutting out the remaining wedges in this fashion.

CUTTING PINEAPPLE

THE PINEAPPLE HAS LONG BEEN A SYMBOL OF HOSPITALITY AS WELL AS A VERY tasty fruit. Although it can be found packed in cans everywhere, it is available in its fresh form year-round in many locales. Whether packed in syrup or its own juice, canned pineapple has little to offer when compared to a beautifully ripe, fresh pineapple. Now that growers have perfected low-acid varieties, the taste of fresh pineapple is better than ever.

The unique shape of the pineapple, which does resemble a pinecone in some ways, often scares the novice cook. How do you approach a pineapple? Where do you start? Start with eyes. The pineapple should be fresh and plump. Its leaves should be green. The stem end should smell sweet. There should be no visible bruises on the skin. It should give slightly when you push on it, but there should be no soft spots that cave in. Pineapples do not ripen further after picking, and color may not be an indicator of ripeness or flavor.

CUTTING PINEAPPLE (*right-hand version*)

Peeling a Pineapple

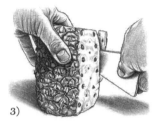

1)

2)

Some chefs recommend twisting off the crown of the pineapple before cutting into the fruit, but this is an unnecessary extra step. Simply lay the pineapple on its side on a cutting board so the crown is to your right. Hold the pineapple steady with your left hand. Using a sharp chef's knife held with a pinch grip, cut a thin slice from the top of the pineapple, just enough to remove the skin and crown (1). Then turn the pineapple around and cut off the base in a similar fashion (2).

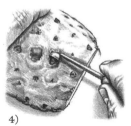

3)

To peel the pineapple, stand it on the cutting board on one of its cut ends. Hold the pineapple firmly in your left hand and hold a sharp chef's knife with a pinch grip in your right. With a sawing motion, slice off a section of the pineapple skin from top to bottom. In removing the skin, you have the option of either cutting just enough skin off to reveal the round eyes or shaving off thin strips of flesh until the eyes are completely gone. After cutting off each strip of skin, rotate the pineapple toward you to expose a new section (3).

4)

If you have left the eyes in place, there are several methods for removing them. One is to scoop out each eye with a small baller. Hold the pineapple with your left hand and hold the baller in your right hand, using it to encircle and remove each eye. Use a small baller that is only slightly larger than the eyes themselves (4).

A second method uses an Asian-style V-shaped gouge designed for vegetable carving to make spiral grooves around the entire pineapple. Lay the pineapple on its side. Hold the gouge in your right hand at a slightly left-pointing angle, and use your left hand to rotate the pineapple into the gouge. Start at the right end of the pineapple and continue making a single spiral groove until you reach the left end (5). Make as many additional grooves as necessary to remove all the eyes. This method results in more waste than the first but produces a more attractive result.

5)

Slicing a Pineapple

Hold a peeled pineapple against the cutting board with your left hand. Hold a sharp chef's knife with a pinch grip in your right hand. Because of the size of the pineapple, the cutting edge of the blade is held approximately parallel to the cutting board. Move the knife forward and backward in a sawing motion to make each slice (1).

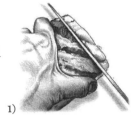
1)

The tough core can be removed from each slice with a small sharp knife, but a small biscuit or other round cutter about the size of the core will do the job much more neatly. Place the cutter over the core in each slice and press it through the slice with your right hand. It may be necessary to press down on the cutter with your palm instead of your fingers if the cutter is dull or the pineapple is a little tough. In either case, the resulting hole will be smooth and round (2).

2)

Wedge-Cutting a Pineapple

Begin by cutting a pineapple into long wedges. This can be done with a peeled or an unpeeled pineapple, depending on how you plan to use the pieces. With unpeeled wedges, the skin can be used as a kind of serving tray. After the crown and base have been removed, stand the pineapple on one of its cut ends, supporting it with your left hand. Use the chef's knife held with a pinch grip in your right hand to make the cuts. Using the tip of the knife, cut into the center of the core and then push down with the knife. Cut wedges the full length of the pineapple, as though you were cutting a pie. The wedges should be about an

1)

inch wide at the skin end. Lay each wedge flat on the cutting board with the core to your right. Hold the wedge firmly in place with the fingers of your left hand and, using the chef's knife held with a pinch grip in your right hand, slice the core from the wedge using a slight sawing motion (1).

Place the wedge skin side down the cutting board. Hold the wedge with the thumb and forefinger of your left hand. Using the chef's knife held in a pinch grip in your right hand, make a series of vertical cuts parallel to one another down the length of the wedge: if the skin is attached, cut only to the skin, not through it. If the wedge is peeled, cut all the way through it (2).

2)   3)

Then, if the skin is still attached to the wedge, turn the blade so it is parallel to the cutting board and, cutting as close to the skin as possible, carefully separate the flesh from the skin using the tip of the blade. If done carefully, the pieces will remain almost in place. If necessary, they can be repositioned on the skin for serving (3).

CUTTING PINEAPPLE (*left-hand version*)

Peeling a Pineapple

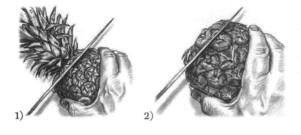

1)

2)

Some chefs recommend twisting off the crown of the pineapple before cutting into the fruit, but this is an unnecessary extra step. Simply lay the pineapple on its side on a cutting board so the crown is to your left. Hold the pineapple steady with your right hand. Using a sharp chef's knife held with a pinch grip, cut a thin slice from the top of the pineapple, just enough to remove the skin and crown (1). Turn the pineapple around and cut off the base in a similar fashion (2).

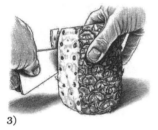

3)

To peel the pineapple, stand it on the cutting board on one of its cut ends. Hold the pineapple firmly in your right hand and hold a sharp chef's knife with a pinch grip in your left. With a sawing motion, slice off a section of the pineapple skin from top to bottom. In removing the skin, you have the option of either cutting just enough skin off to reveal the round eyes or shaving off thin strips of flesh until the eyes are completely gone. After cutting off each strip of skin rotate the pineapple toward you to expose a new section (3).

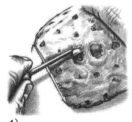

4)

If you have left the eyes in place, there are several methods for removing them. One is to scoop out each eye with a small baller. Hold the pineapple with your right hand and hold the baller in your left hand, using it to encircle and remove each eye. Use a small baller that is only slightly larger than the eyes themselves (4).

5)

A second method uses an Asian-style V-shaped gouge designed for vegetable carving to make spiral grooves around the entire pineapple. Lay the pineapple on its side. Hold the gouge in your left hand at a slightly right-pointing angle, and use your right hand to rotate the pineapple into the gouge. Start at the left end of the pineapple and continue making a single spiral groove until you reach the right end (5). Make as many additional grooves as necessary to remove all the eyes. This method results in more waste than the first but produces a more attractive result.

Slicing a Pineapple

Hold a peeled pineapple against the cutting board with your right hand. Hold a sharp chef's knife with a pinch grip in your left hand. Because of the size of the pineapple, the cutting edge of the blade is held approximately parallel to the cutting board. Move the knife forward and backward in a sawing motion to make each slice (1).

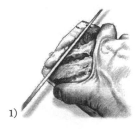

1)

The tough core can be removed from each slice with a small sharp knife, but a small biscuit or other round cutter about the size of the core will do the job much more neatly. Place the cutter over the core in each slice and press it through the slice with your left hand. It may be necessary to press down on the cutter with your palm instead of your fingers if the cutter is dull or the pineapple is a little tough. In either case, the resulting hole will be smooth and round (2).

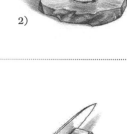

2)

Wedge-Cutting a Pineapple

Begin by cutting a pineapple into long wedges. This can be done with a peeled or an unpeeled pineapple, depending on how you plan to use the pieces. With unpeeled wedges, the skin can be used as a kind of serving tray. After the crown and base have been removed, stand the pineapple on one of its cut ends, supporting it with your right hand. Use the chef's knife held with a pinch grip in your left hand to make the cuts. Using the tip of the knife, cut into the center of the core and then push down with the knife. Cut

1)

wedges the full length of the pineapple, as though you were cutting a pie. The wedges should be about an inch wide at the skin end. Lay each wedge flat on the cutting board with the core to your left. Hold the wedge firmly in place with the fingers of your right hand and, using the chef's knife held with a pinch grip in your left hand, slice the core from the wedge using a slight sawing motion (1).

Place the wedge skin side down on the cutting board. Hold the wedge with the thumb and forefinger of your right hand. Using the chef's knife held in a pinch grip in your left hand, make a series of vertical cuts parallel to one another down the length of the wedge: if the skin is attached, cut only to the skin, not through it. If the wedge is peeled, cut all the way

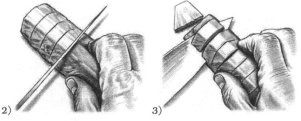

2)   3)

through it (2). Then if the skin is still attached to the wedge, turn the blade so it is parallel to the cutting board and, cutting as close to the skin as possible, carefully separate the flesh from the skin using the tip of the blade. If done carefully, the pieces will remain almost in place. If necessary, they can be repositioned on the skin for serving (3).

chapter 3

MEAT, FISH, & POULTRY

INSIDE THIS CHAPTER

CUTTING POULTRY

FROM A STRUCTURAL STANDPOINT, THERE'S NOT MUCH DIFFERENCE BETWEEN A chicken, a turkey, a duck, a goose, a quail, and a squab. Apart from the size difference between a thirty-pound turkey and a six-ounce quail, all birds are pretty much the same when viewed from a physiological perspective. If you become proficient at cutting up one, the others will be easy.

When you buy a cut-up chicken at the grocery store, chances are it was butchered at a factory that processes thousands of birds each day. In fact, the package you buy may contain parts from different chickens. At the factory, the employee doing the cutting was more concerned with speed than producing an evenly matched set of chicken parts. Learning how to disjoint a chicken yourself allows you to control the process. And because whole chickens are less expensive than chicken parts, you also save money—quite a bit if you eat chicken often.

Many people are afraid of handling poultry because they fear bacterial contamination. It is important to understand that the four major food-borne pathogens (*Salmonella enteritidis, campylobacter jejuni, Escherichia coli 0157:H7,* and *listeria monocytogenes*) only exist on the surface of the poultry. As part of the slaughtering process, the bird is bathed in hot water or steam to quickly kill these pathogens. In your home, there is not much you have to do to keep poultry or any meat from becoming contaminated. Number one, wash your hands thoroughly before handling the chicken. Number two, wash your cutting board with very hot water and a brush before and after using it for poultry (see page 33 for more on sanitizing cutting boards). If

you are not planning to cook the poultry within an hour or two after cutting it, be sure refrigerate it. In either case, cover the poultry with some plastic wrap to prevent it from becoming contaminated.

Since the pathogens exist only on the surface of the meat, it is only necessary to bring the surface up to a temperature of 165 °F for 15 seconds to kill them. It is not necessary to bring the entire piece of meat up to that temperature. Poultry should be cooked just until the texture changes from raw to cooked. Color is not a good judge of doneness for poultry raised by modern methods that produce a marketable bird in half the normal time. The meat in these birds may still appear pink even when cooked to a very high internal temperature.

Since the physiological makeup is essentially the same no matter what type of poultry you are cutting, it is important to make mental notes about how the carcass is put together whenever you cut up a bird. That way, the more you cut one type of poultry apart, the easier other types will be. You'll learn to cut in just the right places to make the process quick, efficient, and neat. Learning how to cut up raw poultry will also help you later when you carve cooked poultry.

CUTTING POULTRY (*right-hand version*)

Cutting Poultry into Eight Pieces

Place the bird on a cutting board, back side down and the left side toward you. Pull the bird's left leg outward toward you with your left hand to stretch the skin between the thigh and the breast (1). Using a sharp paring knife held with a pinch grip in your right hand, cut through only the stretched skin with the tip of the knife (2).

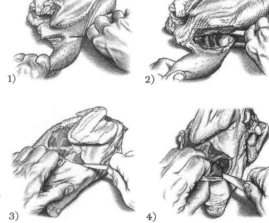

1) 2)

Roll the bird over onto its right side. Continue cutting around to the bird's back, slicing through the skin and muscle until you reach the bone (3). On the back, you will come to a circular piece of meat, sometimes referred to as the oyster. Use your knife to scrape this off the bone, leaving it as a single piece still attached to the leg section (4).

3) 4)

Continue cutting through the skin and meat attached to the back, working toward the tail end. The entire leg section should now be attached to the body only by the white ligaments at the joint (5).

5) 6) 7)

These ligaments could be torn apart by spreading the entire piece out toward the bird's back, but it is easier and more elegant simply to bend the leg outward until you can see the first ligament and then cut it with the tip of the paring knife. That will enable you to see the next ligament (6, 7). Continue cutting until the leg section is totally free from the body.

Remove the bird's right leg in the same manner (8, 9, 10).

8) 9) 10)

CUTTING POULTRY (*right-hand version continued*)

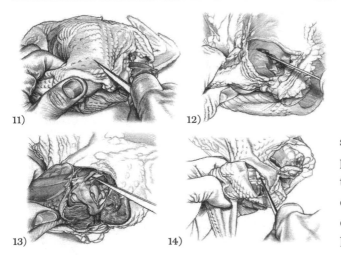

11)

12)

13)

14)

Continue to work with the now-legless bird again back side down. Hold the left wing with your left hand, just outside the point where it is attached to the body. Feel for the location of the joint with your right index finger in order to get an idea of precisely where the bones are connected. You will feel two distinct bumps below the skin. Place the blade of a sharp paring knife, held with a pinch grip, between the two bumps and start slicing through the skin and muscle (11, 12, 13). By pulling down on the wing, you can see the ligament that connects the wing to the breast. Cut through this ligament with the tip of your knife (14). Then continue cutting all the way around the joint, slicing through any remaining attachments, until the wing is entirely free from the body. Remove the bird's right wing in the same manner.

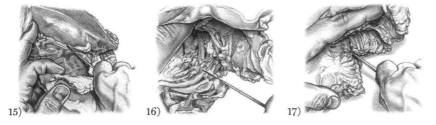

15)

16)

17)

To separate the back from the breast, lay the carcass on its left side with its back toward your left. Just below the breast there is a thin, almost transparent section of tissue. Using the tip of the paring knife held with a pinch grip, cut through this tissue near the rib bones all the way to its loose edge (15). Next, hold the carcass upright with the cut tissue facing you. Notice that the rib bones on the carcass's front side are connected on either side to the ribs on the back by a short band of white cartilage (16). Cut down through the cartilage on one side to separate the breast ribs from the back ribs; very little force is required if you cut through the cartilage instead of bone (17). Repeat the same cuts on the other side of the carcass.

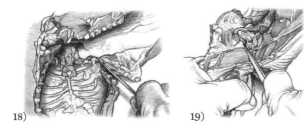

18)

19)

Grab the back of the carcass in your left hand and the breast in your right, and pull them apart so they are attached only at the shoulders. With the paring knife held in a pinch grip, cut through each shoulder joint to separate the breast and back pieces completely (18, 19). Discard the back, or save to make stock.

To remove the wishbone, place the breast, rib side down, on the cutting board, with the neck end toward you. The wishbone is beneath the breast meat at the neck opening. If you run your finger around the neck opening, along the breast muscles, you can easily feel the hard edge of the wishbone. With the tip of a sharp paring knife held in your right hand with a pinch grip, cut along the bone from the center down and out toward the end of each "arm." Work as close as possible to the neck opening so you remove as little of the breast meat as possible (20). Once you expose a small section of the wishbone, the rest of it should be easy to see and free up with the knife tip (21). At each end of the two

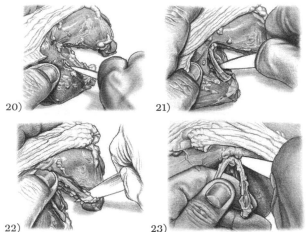

20)   21)

22)   23)

"arms" of the wishbone is a short ligament. Cut through both ligaments and lift the wishbone up slightly (22). At the center, the "arms" of the wishbone join together into a flat disk of bone that is in turn connected to the keel bone by a broad ligament. Cut around the disk of bone with the tip of your knife to locate the ligament and then cut through it (23). You can now remove the wishbone from the carcass. Discard, or save to make stock.

To divide the whole breast into two halves, place it, rib side down, with the neck end toward you, on the cutting board. Stabilize the breast by pressing down on either side of the keel bone with the thumb and forefinger of your left hand. Using a sharp chef's knife held with a pinch grip, cut through the skin and muscle directly above the keel bone, in the center of the breast (24). The top of the keel bone is round, so the knife will slide to one side or the other. Forcefully slice all the way through the breast meat and bone to divide it into two halves keeping the knife as close to the side of the keel bone as you can so you lose as little meat as possible, and using the palm of your left hand to

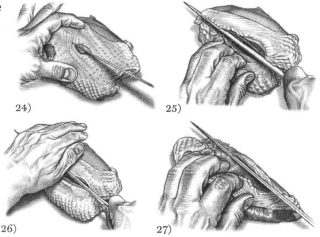

24)   25)

26)   27)

push the blade through the bones (25, 26). Then select the half that still has the keel bone attached, and cut through the meat and bone on the second side of the keel bone in the same way that you cut through the other side (27). The keel bone will now be entirely separated from both halves. Discard it, or save to make stock.

CUTTING POULTRY (*right-hand version continued*)

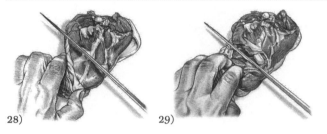

28)   29)

To separate the drumsticks from the thighs, place each leg, skin side down, on the cutting board. Hold the drumstick against the cutting board with your left hand. There is a thin line of fat running across the muscle over the joint where the thigh and the drumstick are attached. The "sweet spot," where there will be the least resistance in the joint, is usually very slightly toward the drumstick from the fat line (28). Using the chef's knife held with a pinch grip, slice through the joint (29).

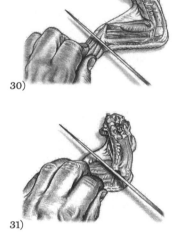

30)

To disjoint the wing, hold each wing tip against the cutting board with your left hand. Using the chef's knife held with a pinch grip, slice through the joint between the wing tip and the second section of the wing (30). Discard the wing tip, or save to make stock.

31)

Depending on how you plan to cook the poultry pieces and your own personal taste, you may wish to disjoint the wings further. Hold the second section of each one against the cutting board with your left hand. Using the chef's knife held with a pinch grip, slice through the joint between the first and second sections of the wing (31). Discard the second joint, or save to make stock.

Cutting Poultry into Twelve Pieces

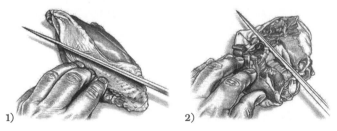

1)   2)

At this point your bird has been cut into eight portions: two legs, two thighs, two breast halves, and two wings—either whole or just the shoulder sections. If the whole bird weighed more than four or five pounds, the breast and thigh sections can be cut into two pieces each to yield a total of twelve portions. Thus, a large bird can be divided into four approximately equal servings of three pieces each. For both the breast half and the thigh, support the meat against the cutting board with your left hand while making the cut, and use the chef's knife held with a pinch grip in your right hand. Place each breast half bone side down and make the cut through the meat and bone on a slight diagonal (1). For the thighs, place each one skin side down on the cutting board, and make the cut along the bone on the side that appears to have more meat (2).

Butterflying Poultry

To butterfly a bird, lay it on its back with the neck toward you. Grasp the body firmly with your left hand—insert your thumb into the neck cavity to get a good firm grip. Carefully

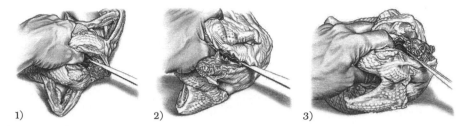

1)   2)   3)

insert the tip of a sharp chef's knife held with a pinch grip in your right hand a short distance into the carcass (1). Cut through the rib bones where they attach to the spine. Cut as close as you can to the spine down its entire length, all the way to the tail; after the cut is partially completed, it may be easier to rotate the bird slightly away from you (2). After completing the cut on one side of the spine, cut down the other side in the same manner (3). Discard the spine, or save to make stock.

Once butterflied, a whole bird will lie flat for grilling, roasting, or braising (4).

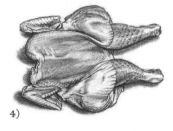

4)

Boning a Breast

To remove a boneless breast half from a whole bird, start by removing the wing. Work with the bird placed back side down. Hold the left wing in your left hand, just outside the point where it is attached to the body. Feel for the location of the joint with your right index finger in order to get an idea of where the bones are connected. You will feel two distinct bumps below the skin. Place the blade of a sharp paring knife, held in your right hand with a pinch grip, between the two bumps and start slicing through the skin and

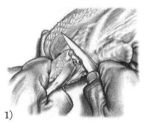

1)

muscle. By pulling down on the wing, you can see the ligament that connects the wing bone to the breastbone. Cut through this ligament with the tip of your knife. Then continue cutting all the way around the joint, slicing through any remaining attachments, until the wing is free from the body. Remove the other wing from the body in the same manner (1).

CUTTING POULTRY (*right-hand version continued*)

Support the bird with your left hand against the cutting board. Using a sharp paring knife held with a pinch grip, cut lightly through the skin down the entire length of the keel bone. Slide the skin back with your left hand to hold it out of the way. Next, cut along the keel bone with your paring knife, making a 2- or 3-inch-long cut between the breast meat and the keel bone (2). Insert the thumb of your right hand into the cut and slide your thumb along the bone in both directions and then progressively down below the meat to separate it from the underlying bone (3). Continue until the entire half breast is peeled off the bone (4). Finally, to free the breast from the carcass, use the paring knife held with a pinch grip and cut through the skin from the inner side out at the point where it holds the breast meat to the carcass. Proceed in the same manner for the other half breast (5).

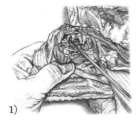

With care, it is possible to remove the breast with the skin still attached to it. The breast consists of two muscles: a large muscle, usually referred to as the breast, and a smaller muscle, called the tenderloin, or just the tender (6). It is not uncommon for the smaller muscle to separate from the larger muscle when the breast is removed from the carcass.

Creating a *Suprême*

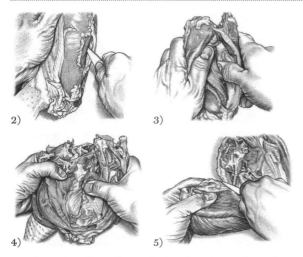

A *suprême* is a boneless breast similar to the one above, but with a portion of the wing still attached. Place the bird, back side down, on the cutting board. Hold the left wing in your left hand, just outside the point where it is attached to the body. Feel for the location of the joint with your right index finger in order to get an idea of where the bones are connected. You will feel two distinct bumps below the skin. Place the blade of a sharp paring knife, held in your right hand with a pinch grip, between the two bumps and make a short cut through the skin and muscle. By pulling down on the wing, you will see the ligament that connects the wing bone to the breastbone. Cut through this ligament with the tip of your knife. Next, cut through any remaining attachments in the joint, but leave the muscle holding the wing to the breast on the back side of the wing intact (1). Then remove the breast from the carcass in the method described above for boning a breast. Remove the wing-breast combination from the other side in the same manner as the first side.

To finish the *suprême*, lay each wing-breast combination, skin side up, on the cutting board. Supporting the wing with your left hand, use the heel of a sharp chef's knife held with a pinch grip in your right hand to cut through the wing bone just above the elbow (2). Although the

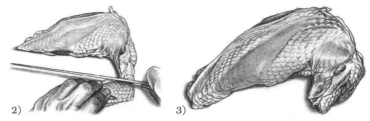

suprême will lay flat when raw, cooking will cause the muscles to contract, and the wing will stand up (3).

Boning a Thigh

Place the thigh, skin side down, on the cutting board. Hold it against the board with your left hand. Using either a sharp paring knife or chef's knife held with a pinch grip in your right hand, cut through the muscle directly over the bone. Make your cut along the bone and all the way through to the bone. The muscle is not very thick at this point. Scrape the meat off the bone along its entire length (1).

Slide the index finger of your right hand under the bone. Move your finger along the length of the bone to separate the meat from it (2), leaving the meat attached only at one end (3). To separate the meat entirely, swing

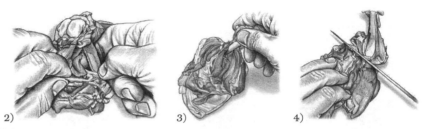

the bone up and over and cut through the connecting tissue as close to the bone as possible with a chef's or paring knife (4). Check the boned thigh for any remaining cartilage, and cut it away.

Creating a Pocket in a Breast for Stuffing

To cut a pocket for stuffing into a boned breast, place the breast on the cutting board with its thinner side toward your right. Hold the breast against the board with the flat of your left hand, keeping your fingers as straight as possible, and, using a sharp chef's knife held with a pinch grip in your right hand, with the blade parallel to the cutting board, cut

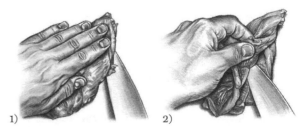

through the middle of the thin edge of the breast with the tip of the knife (1). (If your knife is not very long, it will be necessary to place the breast close to the edge of the cutting board so you can hold and maintain the blade in a horizontal position.) Continue making shallow cuts along the length of the breast until a pocket is formed (2). For a perfect pocket, be careful to keep the knife in the center of the breast so that the meat above the slit is equal in thickness to the meat below. Also be careful not to cut through the opposite side or the ends.

CUTTING POULTRY (*right-hand version continued*)

Butterflying a Boned Breast

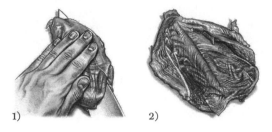

1)
2)

To butterfly a boned breast, place the breast on the cutting board with the thinner edge toward your right. Hold the breast against the board with the flat of your left hand, keeping your fingers as straight as possible, and, using a sharp chef's knife held with a pinch grip in your right hand, with the blade parallel to the cutting board, slice through the middle of the edge of the breast with a sawing motion (1). (If your knife is not very long, it will be necessary to place the breast close to the edge of the cutting board so you can hold and maintain the blade in a horizontal position.) Continue cutting through the length of the breast until the knife is close to the opposite edge. For a perfect butterfly, be careful to keep the knife in the center of the breast so that the meat above the cut is equal in thickness to the meat below. Also be careful not to cut through the opposite edge. Open the breast out flat, and check that you have cut close to the opposite edge (2). If not, a small ridge of meat will stand up along the center of the breast. If you haven't cut far enough, it is usually possible to just cut a little further down the center of the ridge to open the breast fully.

Preparing Poultry for Roasting

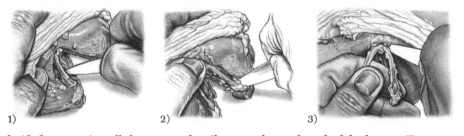

1)
2)
3)

The clavicle, or what is commonly called the wishbone, can be a hindrance when carving poultry because, since it extends past the plane of the breast, it prevents the carving knife from cutting all the way to the ribs near the neck end of the breast. To remove the wishbone, place the bird, breast side up, on the cutting board, with the neck end toward you. The wishbone is beneath the breast meat at the neck opening. If you run your finger around the neck opening, along the breast muscles, you can easily feel the hard edge of the wishbone. With the tip of a sharp paring knife held with a pinch grip in your right hand, cut along the bone from the center down and out toward the end of each "arm." Work as close as possible to the neck opening so you remove as little of the breast meat as possible (1). Once you expose a small section of the wishbone, the rest of it should be easy to see and free up with the knife tip. At each end of the two "arms" of the wishbone is a short ligament. Cut through both ligaments and lift the wishbone up slightly (2). At the center, the "arms" of the wishbone join together into a flat disk of bone that in turn is connected to the keel bone by a broad ligament. Cut around the disk of bone with the tip of your knife to locate the ligament and then cut through it (3). You can now remove the wishbone from the bird.

CUTTING POULTRY (*left-hand version*)

Cutting Poultry into Eight Pieces

Place the bird on a cutting board, back side down and the right side toward you. Pull the bird's right leg outward toward you with your right hand to stretch the skin between the thigh and the breast (1). Using a sharp paring knife held with a pinch grip in your left hand, cut through only the stretched skin with the tip of the knife (2).

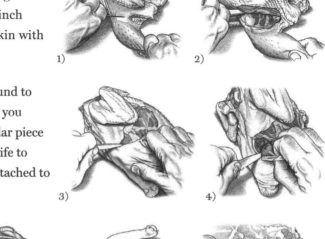

1) 2)

Roll the bird over onto its left side. Continue cutting around to the bird's back, slicing through the skin and muscle until you reach the bone (3). On the back, you will come to a circular piece of meat, sometimes referred to as the oyster. Use your knife to scrape this off the bone, leaving it as a single piece still attached to the leg section (4).

3) 4)

Continue cutting through the skin and meat attached to the back, working toward the tail end. The entire leg section should now be attached to the body only by the white ligaments at the joint (5). These ligaments could be torn apart by spreading the entire piece out toward the bird's back, but it is easier and more elegant simply to bend the leg outward until you can see the first ligament and then cut it with the tip of the paring knife. That will enable you to see the next ligament (6, 7). Continue cutting until the leg section is totally free from the body.

5) 6) 7)

Remove the bird's left leg in the same manner (8, 9, 10).

8) 9) 10)

CUTTING POULTRY (*left-hand version continued*)

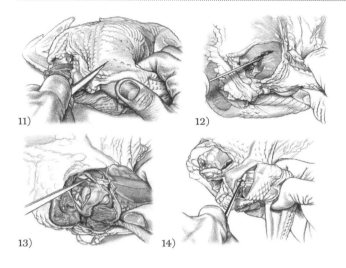

11)

12)

13)

14)

Continue to work with the now-legless bird again back side down. Hold the right wing with your right hand, just outside the point where it is attached to the body. Feel for the location of the joint with your left index finger in order to get an idea of precisely where the bones are connected. You will feel two distinct bumps below the skin. Place the blade of a sharp paring knife, held with a pinch grip, between the two bumps and start slicing through the skin and muscle (11, 12, 13). By pulling down on the wing, you can see the ligament that connects the wing to the breast. Cut through this ligament with the tip of your knife (14). Then continue cutting all the way around the joint, slicing through any remaining attachments, until the wing is entirely free from the body. Remove the bird's left wing in the same manner.

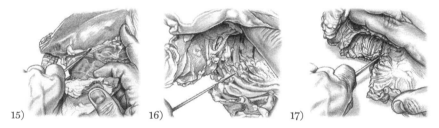

15)

16)

17)

To separate the back from the breast, lay the carcass on its right side with its back toward your right. Just below the breast there is a thin, almost transparent section of tissue. Using the tip of the paring knife held with a pinch grip, cut through this tissue near the rib bones all the way to its loose edge (15). Next, hold the carcass upright with the cut tissue facing you. Notice that the rib bones on the carcass's front side are connected on either side to the ribs on the back by a short band of white cartilage (16). Cut down through the cartilage on one side to separate the breast ribs from the back ribs; very little force is required if you cut through the cartilage instead of bone (17). Repeat the same cuts on the other side of the carcass.

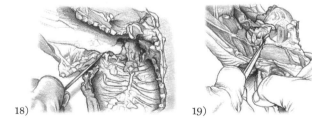

18)

19)

Grab the back of the carcass in your right hand and the breast in your left, and pull them apart so they are attached only at the shoulders. With the paring knife held in a pinch grip, cut through each shoulder joint to separate the breast and back pieces completely (18, 19). Discard the back, or save to make stock.

To remove the wishbone, place the breast, rib side down, on the cutting board, with the neck end toward you. The wishbone is beneath the breast meat at the neck opening. If you run your finger around the neck opening, along the breast muscles, you can easily feel the hard edge of the wishbone. With the tip of a sharp paring knife held in your left hand with a pinch grip, cut along the bone from the center down and out toward the end of each "arm." Work as close as possible to the neck opening so you remove as little of the breast meat as possible (20). Once you expose a small section of the wishbone, the rest of it should be easy to see and free up with the knife tip (21). At each end of the two

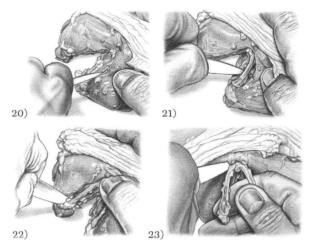

20) 21)

22) 23)

"arms" of the wishbone is a short ligament. Cut through both ligaments and lift the wishbone up slightly (22). At the center, the "arms" of the wishbone join together into a flat disk of bone that is in turn connected to the keel bone by a broad ligament. Cut around the disk of bone with the tip of your knife to locate the ligament and then cut through it (23). You can now remove the wishbone from the carcass. Discard, or save to make stock.

To divide the whole breast into two halves, place it, rib side down, with the neck end toward you, on the cutting board. Stabilize the breast by pressing down on either side of the keel bone with the thumb and forefinger of your right hand. Using a sharp chef's knife held with a pinch grip, cut through the skin and muscle directly above the keel bone, in the center of the breast (24). The top of the keel bone is round, so the knife will slide to one side or the other. Forcefully slice all the way through the breast meat and bone to divide it into two halves, keeping the knife close to the side of the keel bone as you can so you lose as little meat as possible,

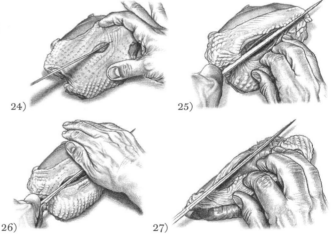

24) 25)

26) 27)

and using the palm of your right hand to push the blade through the bones (25, 26). Then select the half that still has the keel bone attached, and cut through the meat and bone on the second of the keel bone in the same way that you cut through the other side (27). The keel bone will now be entirely separated from both halves. Discard it, or save to make stock.

CUTTING POULTRY (*left-hand version continued*)

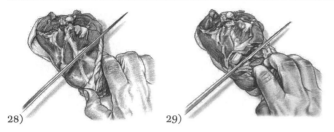

28) 29)

To separate the drumsticks from the thighs place each leg, skin side down, on the cutting board. Hold the drumstick against the cutting board with your right hand. There is a thin line of fat running across the muscle over the joint where the thigh and the drumstick are attached. The "sweet spot," where there will be the least resistance in the joint, is usually very slightly toward the drumstick from the fat line (28). Using the chef's knife held with a pinch grip, slice through the joint (29).

30)

To disjoint the wing, hold each wing tip against the cutting board with your right hand. Using the chef's knife held with a pinch grip, slice through the joint between the wing tip and the second section of the wing (30). Discard the wing tip, or save to make stock.

31)

Depending on how you plan to cook the poultry pieces and your own personal taste, you may wish to disjoint the wings further. Hold the second section of each one against the cutting board with your right hand. Using the chef's knife held with a pinch grip, slice through the joint between the first and second sections of the wing (31). Discard the second joint, or save to make stock.

Cutting Poultry into Twelve Pieces

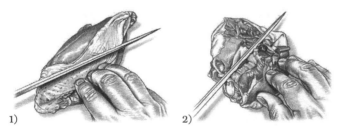

1) 2)

At this point your bird has been cut into eight portions: two legs, two thighs, two breast halves, and two wings—either whole or just the shoulder sections. If the whole bird weighed more than four or five pounds, the breast and thigh sections can be cut into two pieces each to yield a total of twelve portions. Thus, a large bird can be divided into four approximately equal servings of three pieces each. For both the breast half and the thigh, support the meat against the cutting board with your right hand while making the cut, and use the chef's knife held with a pinch grip in your left hand. Place each breast half bone side down and make the cut through the meat and bone on a slight diagonal (1). For the thighs, place each one skin side down on the cutting board, and make the cut along the bone on the side that appears to have more meat (2).

Butterflying Poultry

To butterfly a bird, lay it on its
back with the neck toward you.
Grasp the body firmly with
your right hand—insert your
thumb into the neck cavity to
get a good firm grip. Carefully

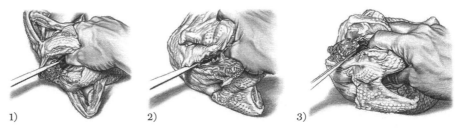

1)   2)   3)

insert the tip of a sharp chef's knife held with a pinch grip in your left hand a short distance into the carcass (1).
Cut through the rib bones where they attach to the spine. Cut as close as you can to the spine down its entire
length, all the way to the tail; after the cut is partially completed, it may be easier to rotate the bird slightly away
from you (2). After completing the cut on one side of the spine, cut down the other side in the same manner (3).
Discard the spine, or save to make stock.

Once butterflied, a whole bird will lie flat for grilling, roasting or braising (4).

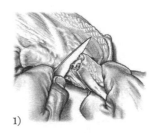

4)

Boning a Breast

To remove a boneless breast half from a whole bird, start by removing the wing. Work
with the bird placed back side down. Hold the right wing in your right hand, just
outside the point where it is attached to the body. Feel for the location of the joint with
your left index finger in order to get an idea of where the bones are connected. You will
feel two distinct bumps below the skin. Place the blade of a sharp paring knife, held in
your left hand with a pinch grip, between the two bumps and start slicing through the

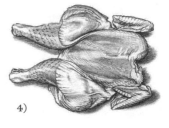

1)

skin and muscle. By pulling down on the wing, you can see the ligament that connects the wing bone to the
breastbone. Cut through this ligament with the tip of your knife. Then continue cutting all the way around the
joint, slicing through any remaining attachments, until the wing is free from the body. Remove the other wing
from the body in the same manner (1).

CUTTING POULTRY *(left-hand version continued)*

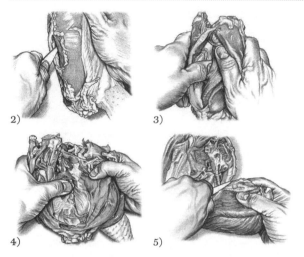

2) 3) 4) 5)

Support the bird with your right hand against the cutting board. Using a sharp paring knife held with a pinch grip, cut lightly through the skin only down the entire length of the keel bone. Slide the skin back with your right hand to hold it out of the way. Next, cut along the keel bone with your paring knife, making a 2- or 3-inch-long cut between the breast meat and the keel bone (2). Insert the thumb of your left hand into the cut and slide your thumb along the bone in both directions and then progressively down below the meat to separate it from the underlying bone (3). Continue until the entire half breast is peeled off the bone (4). Finally, to free the breast from the carcass, use the paring knife held with a pinch grip and cut through the skin from the inner side out at the point where it holds the breast meat to the carcass. Proceed in the same manner for the other half breast (5).

6)

With care, it is possible to remove the breast with the skin still attached to it. The breast consists of two muscles: a large muscle, usually referred to as the breast, and a smaller muscle, called the tenderloin, or just the tender (6). It is not uncommon for the smaller muscle to separate from the larger muscle when the breast is removed from the carcass.

Creating a *Suprême*

1)

A *suprême* is a boneless breast similar to the one above, but with a portion of the wing still attached. Place the bird, back side down, on the cutting board. Hold the right wing in your right hand, just outside the point where it is attached to the body. Feel for the location of the joint with your left index finger in order to get an idea of where the bones are connected. You will feel two distinct bumps below the skin. Place the blade of a sharp paring knife, held in your left hand with a pinch grip, between the two bumps and make a short cut through the skin and muscle. By pulling down on the wing, you can see the ligament that connects the wing bone to the breastbone. Cut through this ligament with the tip of your knife. Next, cut through any remaining attachments in the joint, but leave the muscle holding the wing to the breast on the back side of the wing intact (1). Then move the breast from the carcass in the method described above for boning a breast. Remove the wing-breast combination from the other side in the same manner as the first side.

To finish the *suprême*, lay each wing-breast combination, skin side up, on the cutting board. Supporting the wing with your right hand, use the heel of a sharp chef's knife held with a pinch grip in your left hand to cut through the wing bone just above the elbow (2). Although the *suprême* will lay flat when raw, cooking will cause the muscles to contract, and the wing will stand up (3).

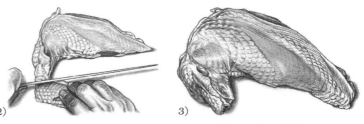

Boning a Thigh

Place the thigh, skin side down on the cutting board. Hold it against the board with your right hand. Using either a sharp paring knife or chef's knife held with a pinch grip in your left hand, cut through the muscle directly over the bone. Make your cut along the bone and all the way through to the bone. The muscle is not very thick at this point. Scrape the meat off the bone along its entire length (1).

Slide the index finger of your left hand under the bone. Move your finger along the length of the bone to separate the meat from it (2), leaving the meat attached only at one end (3). To separate the meat entirely, swing the bone up and over and cut through the connecting tissue as close to the bone as possible with a chef's or paring knife (4). Check the boned thigh for any remaining cartilage, and cut it away.

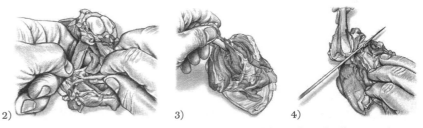

Creating a Pocket in a Breast for Stuffing

To cut a pocket for stuffing into a boned breast, place the breast on the cutting board with its thinner side toward your left. Hold the breast against the board with the flat of your right hand, keeping your fingers as straight as possible, and, using a sharp chef's knife held with a pinch grip in your left hand, with the blade parallel to the cutting board, cut through the middle of the thin edge of the breast with the tip of the knife (1). (If your knife is not very long, it will be necessary to place the breast close to the edge of the cutting board so you can hold and maintain the blade in a horizontal position.) Continue making shallow cuts along the length of the breast until a pocket is formed (2). For a perfect pocket, be careful to keep the knife in the center of the breast so that the meat above the slit is equal in thickness to the meat below. Also be careful not to cut through the opposite side or the ends.

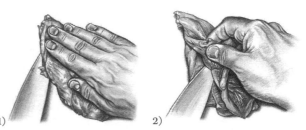

CUTTING POULTRY *(left-hand version continued)*

Butterflying a Boned Breast

1)
2)

To butterfly a boned breast, place the breast on the cutting board with the thinner edge toward your left. Hold the breast against the board with the flat of your right hand, keeping your fingers as straight as possible, and, using a sharp chef's knife held with a pinch grip in your left hand, with the blade parallel to the cutting board, slice through the middle of the edge of the breast with a sawing motion (1). (If your knife is not very long, it will be necessary to place the breast close to the edge of the cutting board so you can hold and maintain the blade in a horizontal position.) Continue cutting through the length of the breast until the knife is close to the opposite edge. For a perfect butterfly, be careful to keep the knife in the center of the breast so that the meat above the cut is equal in thickness to the meat below. Also be careful not to cut through the opposite edge. Open the breast out flat, and check that you have cut close to the opposite edge (2). If not, a small ridge of meat will stand up along the center of the breast. If you haven't cut far enough, it is usually possible to just cut a little further down the center of the ridge to open the breast fully.

Preparing Poultry for Roasting

1)
2)
3)

The clavicle, or what is commonly called the wishbone, can be a hindrance when carving poultry because, since it extends past the plane of the breast, it prevents the carving knife from cutting all the way to the ribs near the neck end of the breast. To remove the wishbone, place the bird, breast side up, on the cutting board, with the neck end toward you. The wishbone is beneath the breast meat at the neck opening. If you run your finger around the neck opening, along the breast muscles, you can easily feel the hard edge of the wishbone. With the tip of a sharp paring knife held with a pinch grip in your left hand, cut along the bone from the center down and out toward the end of each "arm." Work as close as possible to the neck opening so you remove as little of the breast meat as possible (1). Once you expose a small section of the wishbone, the rest of it should be easy to see and free up with the knife tip. At each end of the two "arms" of the wishbone is a short ligament. Cut through both ligaments and lift the wishbone up slightly (2). At the center, the "arms" of the wishbone join together into a flat disk of bone that in turn is connected to the keel bone by a broad ligament. Cut around the disk of bone with the tip of your knife to locate the ligament and then cut through it (3). You can now remove the wishbone from the bird.

CUTTING FISH

MOST OCEAN-CAUGHT FISH TODAY ARE CLEANED AND FILLETED FAR OUT AT SEA, a few minutes after being caught, and then quickly frozen. This process allows the ships to remain away from port for several days until their cargo holds are full. It no longer is necessary to return to port nightly to off-load the day's catch. The result is that we can often buy "fresher" fish processed on these floating factories than what used to be available from small local fishing vessels—assuming that you lived close enough to the ocean to purchase part of the day's catch. (I live forty-five minutes from the ocean, and most of the "fresh" fish sold locally is in reality two to three days out of the water.) Even farm-raised seafood—such as salmon, trout, tilapia, and bass—often comes from halfway around the world as frozen fillets, rather than whole fish.

If you live in the right location, fish is often available on the bone, and some people are lucky enough to catch their own fish. It is therefore valuable to know how to prepare whole fish for cooking. The advantage of filleting a fish yourself instead of allowing your fishmonger do it for you is that you are motivated to produce a better result. When you buy a whole fish to be filleted at the market, the price is based on the fish before filleting, and often even before gutting. So the fishmonger has no incentive to produce fillets that leave the minimum amount of meat wasted on the bone. He simply wants to fillet your fish as fast as possible and move on to the next customer. You, however, will want to minimize waste and produce the largest fillets possible. It may take a few attempts for you to perfect your technique, but the process is not especially difficult. Even if you purchase your fish as steaks or fillets, you may want to cut these into different shapes and sizes to use in a variety of recipes. And most of this is possible with the same knives used for cutting fruits and vegetables.

CUTTING FISH (*right-hand version*)

Filleting a Whole Flatfish

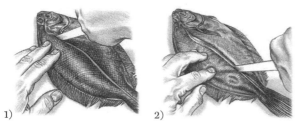

Lay a scaled flatfish top (dark) side up on your cutting board with the head pointed away and to your left. While supporting the fish with your left hand, starting at the head end of the fish, make a cut through the skin with a boning knife held in a pinch grip in your right hand (1). (The knife should have a flexible blade.) The cut should be right on the line in the skin that denotes the midpoint of this side of the fish and go all the way through to the bones. Extend the cut all the way from the head to the tail, cutting right through to the bones in the center of the fish (2).

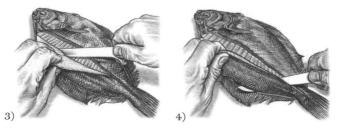

To remove the fillet that lies toward your left, turn your knife over so the blade is parallel to the bones and cutting toward your left. Holding the edge of the blade against the bones and slightly downward, make long cuts from the head to tail (3). As you cut, lift the fillet away from the bones with your left hand for a better view. When you get near the edge of the fillet, where it meets the fins, push the tip of your knife through the skin to separate the fillet from the body of the fish. Set this fillet aside (4).

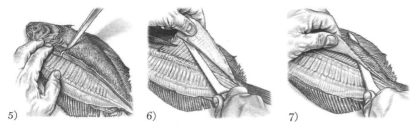

To remove the other fillet on the top side of the fish, first make a cut through the skin at the head end just at the edge of the cavity that holds the internal organs. Cut all the way through the skin and flesh to the bones with your knife held in a pinch grip in your right hand; do not cut into the cavity (5). Then turn your knife over so the blade is parallel to the bones and cutting toward your right and slightly away. Holding the edge of the blade against the bones and slightly downward, make long cuts from the cavity to the tail (6). Unless your wrist has a high degree of rotation, it will be necessary to hold the knife in a sword grip with your thumb on top of the blade near the bolster. As you cut, lift the fillet away from the bones with your left hand for a better view. When you get near the edge of the fillet, where it meets the fins, push the tip of your knife through the skin and to separate the fillet from the body of the fish (7). Set the fillet aside.

8)   9)   10)

Flip the fish over and remove the other two fillets using the techniques described above. Discard the head and bones or reserve for stock (8, 9, 10).

One at a time, place the boned-out fillets on your cutting board, with the tail end to the left and toward you and the other end to your right. Hold the skin at the tail tightly against the board with the fingers of your left hand. Working from left to right, slide the boning knife between the skin and the flesh; the side of the blade should be flat against the skin. Apply a slight sawing motion as you push the blade down the length of the skin (11).

11)

Each skinned fillet will probably have some ragged fin meat attached to the main fillet. While holding the fillet in your right hand, gently pull the fin meat away with your left hand (12). Discard the fin meat or save for stock.

12)

CUTTING FISH (*right-hand version continued*)

Filleting a Whole Round Fish

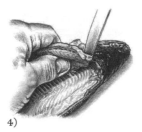

Trim the dorsal fin from the back of the fish with a pair of heavy-duty scissors (1).

1)

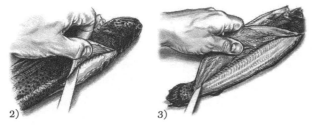

Lay the fish on the cutting board with its back toward you and the head away from you and to the right. Using a sharp boning knife held with a pinch grip in your right hand and supporting the fish with your left, make a long cut down through the back of the fish from the head to the tail. The knife should glide directly on top of the bones (2). Cut just to the spine in the center of the fish (3).

2)   3)

Lift up the loose portion of the fillet with your left hand and make a vertical cut just behind the head of the fish. Cut just to the bones—don't cut the head off (4).

4)

Cut the fillet off the bones around the belly of the fish until the fillet is freed (5). On some fish, the meat at the base of the belly is very fatty. If this is the case, slice this strip of flesh from the fillet (6).

5)   6)

7) 8) 9)

Flip the fish over, with the head down and to your left. Remove the second fillet in the same manner as the first (7, 8, 9).

To skin the fillets, one at a time, place each one, skin side down, near the edge of the cutting board. Hold the skin at the tail tightly to the board with the fingers of your left hand. Working from left to right, slide the boning knife between the skin and the flesh, holding the side of the blade flat against the skin. Apply a slight sawing motion as you push the blade down the length of the fillet (10).

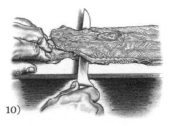

10)

Move the index finger of your left hand up and down the length of each skinned fillet to find the small pin bones (11). One by one, pull each bone out of the fillet with a pair of small pliers or fish tweezers (12). The bones are usually easiest to remove when pulled toward the head end of the fillet.

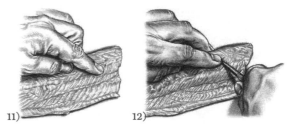

11) 12)

CUTTING FISH (*right-hand version continued*)

Boning a Whole Trout

1)

Place the gutted trout on the cutting board so the tail is pointed down and to the left. Hold the fish in place with your left hand. Use a sharp boning knife held with a pinch grip in your right hand to slit the skin from the anus to the tail (1).

2)

Open the belly of the trout with your left hand and insert the knife just below the bones on the far side. Use the spine of the knife, not the cutting edge, to "pull" the bones free from the belly. Pull parallel to the cutting board and toward the belly of the fish. After the first group of bones is pulled free, insert the tip of the knife under a new set of bones toward the tail and repeat the process. Continue until all the belly bones are free on the first side of the fish (2).

3)

Using the cutting edge of the knife, peel the meat free from the upper set of bones on the side of the fish you have been working on. Do not cut the bones themselves, but guide the knife along the bones to cut the meat off them in one piece (3).

4)

5)

Repeat the same process on the other side of the fish (4). At this point, the spine will be attached only at the head and the tail (5).

Use a pair of heavy-duty scissors to cut through the spine at the head and tail (6).

6)

Slide the index finger of your left hand up and down the entire length of each fillet to find the small pin bones. One by one, pull each bone out of the fillet with a pair of small pliers or fish tweezers. The bones are usually easiest to remove when pulled toward the head (7).

7)

Trim the remnant of the dorsal fin from the middle of the back of the fish with a pair of heavy-duty scissors (8).

8)

Slicing a Fish Fillet

To cut thin slices of fish, lay a fillet on the cutting board so the tail end is pointed toward your lower left. If the fillet still has its skin attached, place the fillet skin side down. With your left hand, hold the fillet firmly with your fingertips extended and slightly up. Position a sharp chef's knife or slicer so the flat of

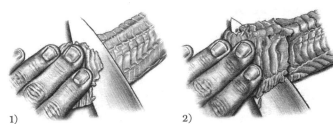

1)   2)

the blade is almost parallel to the cutting board—the blade should be parallel and in a plane slightly below your fingers. Be sure to hold the knife with a pinch grip (1). Using a sawing motion, make cuts through the fillet to produce thin slices. After each cut, move the slice onto a stack elsewhere on the cutting board. It is important that the flat of the blade always remain parallel to and in a plane slightly below your fingers (2).

Julienning a Fish Fillet

To julienne the fish, stack three or four slices at a time on the cutting board. Hold the stack firmly in place with your left hand by pressing down on top of it with your fingertips, in a vertical position. Position the chef's knife, held with a pinch grip, so the flat of the blade rests against the flat side of the tip of your forefinger. This way, your forefinger serves as a guide for the knife. Start each cut with the tip of the blade in contact with, or near, the cutting board, with the handle angled up. As you bring the

knife down, slide it forward so the edge of the blade moves through the meat as you produce the julienne. After each cut, move your forefinger to the left a distance equal to the desired width of the next cut. Ideally, the width of this cut should be the same as the thickness of the slices, so the resulting strips have a perfectly square cross section. As you do this, it is important that the flat of the blade always remain in contact with the flat surface of your forefinger.

CUTTING FISH (*right-hand version continued*)

Dicing a Fish Fillet

To dice the fish, gather the julienned strips into a stack, with all the strips parallel to one another. With the fingertips of your left hand in a vertical position, hold the stack firmly in place. Position the chef's knife, held with a pinch grip, so the flat of the blade rests against the flat side of the tip of your forefinger. This way, your forefinger serves as a guide for the knife. Start each cut with the tip of the blade in contact with, or near, the cutting board, with the handle angled up. As you bring the knife down, slide it forward so the edge of the blade moves through the meat as you produce the cubes. After each cut, slide your forefinger to the left a distance equal to the desired width of the next cut. Ideally, the width of this cut will be equal to the thickness of the strips, so the resulting dice will be perfect cubes. It is important that the flat of the blade always remain in contact with the flat surface of your forefinger.

Boning a Salmon Steak and Forming It into a Large Disk

1)   2)   3)

Lay the steak on the cutting board with the back part toward your left. With a sharp paring knife held with a pinch grip in your right hand, bone the steak: start by pushing the tip of your knife into the steak parallel to the backbone so that the spine of the knife is at the back of the fish and the cutting edge points at the spine of the fish. Slide the knife along the backbone with a slight sawing motion until the edge reaches the spine (1). Then rotate the cutting edge to continue separating the flesh from the bones. Partway around the spine you'll probably encounter resistance from the small pin bones. Cut through them and continue around the spine. Continue cutting along the bones that cover the belly until you reach the base of those bones (2). There is often a small area of fat at the end of the belly section. When you reach this section, turn the cutting edge of the knife outward and cut through the skin. Repeat the process on the other side of the steak (3).

4)

You now have a piece of fish that is boneless, except for the pin bones. Gently rub the surface of the meat on both sides with your fingers to find the remaining pin bones, and remove them with a small pair of pliers or fish tweezers (4). The bones should be easy to remove. Be sure not to leave any behind. If the fish steak has part of the dorsal fin attached, cut this off close to the back with a pair of heavy-duty scissors.

Stand the salmon steak near the edge of the cutting board so that it rests on the skin of one side of the belly. Support the inside of the belly section with your left hand. With the paring knife held in your right hand with a pinch grip, slide the blade between the skin and flesh directly below the point where the spine once was. The blade should be flat against the skin and the cutting edge pointed toward the belly end. Slide the knife down toward the belly so the skin is cut from the flesh. Do this on only one side of the salmon steak (5).

5)

Lay the steak flat on the cutting board. Roll the belly flesh from the side you just skinned inward. Tuck the belly flesh from the other side around the outside of the first side and under the loosened flap of skin. Pull the loosened skin flap tight around the second side to form a round disk. Push two skewers through the center of the disk to hold it together during cooking: start the first skewer at the end of the loosened piece of skin flap, to hold it firmly in place, and be sure to pull the skin tight as you push the skewer through the fish. Start the second skewer about 90 degrees from where the tip of the other side of the belly is tucked under the skin, in order to hold the whole steak firmly together (6). Cook this steak the same way as you would any fish steak. Remove the skewers before serving.

6)

CUTTING FISH (*left-hand version*)

Filleting a Whole Flatfish

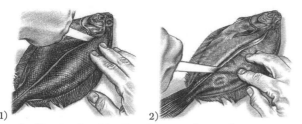

1) 2)

Lay a scaled flatfish top (dark) side up on your cutting board with the head pointed away and to your right. While supporting the fish with your right hand, starting at the head end of the fish, make a cut through the skin with a boning knife held in a pinch grip in your left hand (1). (The knife should have a flexible blade.) The cut should be right on the line in the skin that denotes the midpoint of this side of the fish and go all the way through to the bones. Extend the cut all the way from the head to the tail, cutting right through to the bones in the center of the fish (2).

3) 4)

To remove the fillet that lies toward your right, turn your knife over so the blade is parallel to the bones and cutting toward your right. Holding the edge of the blade against the bones and slightly downward, make long cuts from the head to tail (3). As you cut, lift the fillet away from the bones with your right hand for a better view. When you get near the edge of the fillet, where it meets the fins, push the tip of your knife through the skin to separate the fillet from the body of the fish. Set this fillet aside (4).

5) 6) 7)

To remove the other fillet on the top side of the fish, first make a cut through the skin of the fish at the head end just at the edge of the cavity that holds the internal organs. Cut all the way through the skin and flesh to the bones with your knife held in a pinch grip in your left hand; do not cut into the cavity (5). Then turn your knife over so the blade is parallel to the bones and cutting toward your left and slightly away. Holding the edge of the blade against the bones and slightly downward, make long cuts from the cavity to the tail (6). Unless your wrist has a high degree of rotation, it will be necessary to hold the knife in a sword grip with your thumb on top of the blade near the bolster. As you cut, lift the fillet away from the bones with your right hand for a better view. When you get near the edge of the fillet, where it meets the fins, push the tip of your knife through the skin and to separate the fillet from the body of the fish (7). Set the fillet aside.

8) 9) 10)

Flip the fish over and remove the other two fillets using the techniques described above. **Discard the head and bones or reserve for stock** (8, 9, 10).

One at a time, place the boned-out fillets on your cutting board, with the tail end to the right and toward you and the other end to your left. Hold the skin at the tail tightly against the board with the fingers of your right hand. Working from right to left, slide the boning knife between the skin and the flesh; the side of the blade should be flat against the skin. Apply a slight sawing motion as you push the blade down the length of the skin (11).

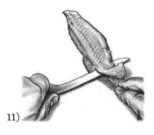

11)

Each skinned fillet will probably have some ragged fin meat attached to the main fillet. While holding the fillet in your left hand, gently pull the fin meat away with your right hand (12). Discard the fin meat or save for stock.

12)

CUTTING FISH (*left-hand version continued*)

Filleting a Whole Round Fish

Trim the dorsal fin from the back of the fish with a pair of heavy-duty scissors (1).

1)

2)

3)

Lay the fish on the cutting board with its back toward you and the head away from you and to the left. Using a sharp boning knife held with a pinch grip in your left hand and supporting the fish with your right, make a long cut down through the back of the fish from the head to the tail. The knife should glide directly on top of the bones (2). Cut just to the spine in the center of the fish (3).

4)

Lift up the loose portion of the fillet with your right hand and make a vertical cut just behind the head of the fish. Cut just to the bones—don't cut the head off (4).

5)

6)

Cut the fillet off the bones around the belly of the fish until the fillet is freed (5). On some fish, the meat at the base of the belly is very fatty. If this is the case, slice this strip of flesh from the fillet (6).

7) 8) 9)

Flip the fish over, with the head down and to your right. Remove the second fillet in the same manner as the first (7.8.9).

To skin the fillets, one at a time, place each one, skin side down, near the edge of the cutting board. Hold the skin at the tail tightly to the board with the fingers of your right hand. Working from right to left, slide the boning knife between the skin and the flesh, holding the side of the blade flat against the skin. Apply a slight sawing motion as you push the blade down the length of the fillet (10).

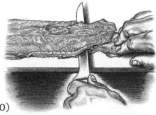

10)

Move the index finger of your right hand up and down the length of each skinned fillet to find the small pin bones (11). One by one, pull each bone out of the fillet with a pair of small pliers or fish tweezers (12). The bones are usually easiest to remove when pulled toward the head end of the fillet.

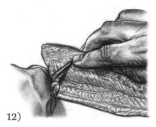

11) 12)

CUTTING FISH (*left-hand version continued*)

Boning a Whole Trout

1)

Place the gutted trout on the cutting board so the tail is pointed down and to the right. Hold the fish in place with your right hand. Use a sharp boning knife held with a pinch grip in your left hand to slit the skin from the anus to the tail (1).

2)

Open the belly of the trout with your right hand and insert the knife just below the bones on the far side. Use the spine of the knife, not the cutting edge, to "pull" the bones free from the belly. Pull parallel to the cutting board and toward the belly of the fish. After the first group of bones is pulled free, insert the tip of the knife under a new set of bones toward the tail and repeat the process. Continue until all the belly bones are free on the first side of the fish (2).

3)

Using the cutting edge of the knife, peel the meat free from the upper set of bones on the side of the fish you have been working on. Do not cut the bones themselves, but guide the knife along the bones to cut the meat off them in one piece (3).

4)

5)

Repeat the same process on the other side of the fish (4). At this point, the spine will be attached only at the head and the tail (5).

6)

Use a pair of heavy-duty scissors to cut through the spine at the head and tail (6).

Slide the index finger of your right hand up and down the entire length of each fillet to find the small pin bones. One by one, pull each bone out of the fillet with a pair of small pliers or fish tweezers. The bones are usually easiest to remove when pulled toward the head (7).

7)

Trim the remnant of the dorsal fin from the middle of the back of the fish with a pair of heavy-duty scissors (8).

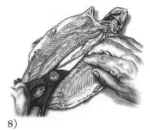

8)

Slicing a Fish Fillet

To cut thin slices of fish, lay a fillet on the cutting board so the tail end is pointed toward your lower right. If the fillet still has its skin attached, place the fillet skin side down. With your right hand, hold the fillet firmly with your fingertips extended and slightly up. Position a sharp chef's knife or slicer so the flat of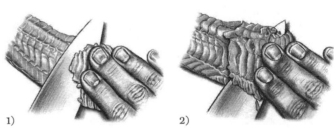
the blade is almost parallel to the cutting board—the blade should be parallel to and in a plane slightly below your fingers. Be sure to hold the knife with a pinch grip (1). Using a sawing motion, make cuts through the fillet to produce thin slices. After each cut, move the slice onto a stack elsewhere on the cutting board. It is important that the flat of the blade always remain parallel to and in a plane slightly below your fingers (2).

Julienning a Fish Fillet

To julienne the fish, stack three or four slices at a time on the cutting board. Hold the stack firmly in place with your right hand by pressing down on top of it with your fingertips in a vertical position. Position the chef's knife, held with a pinch grip, so the flat of the blade rests against the flat side of the tip of your forefinger. This way, your forefinger serves as a guide for the knife. Start each cut with the tip of the blade in contact with, or near, the cutting board, with the handle angled up. As you bring the
knife down, slide it forward so the edge of the blade moves through the meat as you produce the julienne. After each cut, move your forefinger to the right a distance equal to the desired width of the next cut. Ideally, the width of this cut should be the same as the thickness of the slices, so the resulting strips have a perfectly square cross section. As you do this, it is important that the flat of the blade always remain in contact with the flat surface of your forefinger.

CUTTING FISH (*left-hand version continued*)

Dicing a Fish Fillet

To dice the fish, gather the julienned strips into a stack, with all the strips parallel to one another. With the fingertips of your right hand in a vertical position, hold the stack firmly in place. Position the chef's knife, held with a pinch grip, so the flat of the blade rests against the flat side of the tip of your forefinger. This way, your forefinger serves as a guide for the knife. Start each cut with the tip of the blade in contact with, or near, the cutting board, with the handle angled up. As you bring the knife down, slide it forward so the edge of the blade moves through the meat as you produce the cubes. After each cut, slide your forefinger to the right a distance equal to the desired width of the next cut. Ideally, the width of this cut will be equal to the thickness of the strips, so the resulting dice will be perfect cubes. It is important that the flat of the blade always remain in contact with the flat surface of your forefinger.

Boning a Salmon Steak and Forming It into a Large Disk

1)   2)   3)

Lay the steak on the cutting board with the back part toward your right. With a sharp paring knife held with a pinch grip in your left hand, bone the steak: start by pushing the tip of your knife into the steak parallel to the backbone so that the spine of the knife is at the back of the fish and the cutting edge points at the spine of the fish. Slide the knife along the backbone with a slight sawing motion until the edge reaches the spine (1). Then rotate the cutting edge to continue separating the flesh from the bones. Partway around the spine, you'll probably encounter resistance from the small pin bones. Cut through them and continue around the spine. Continue cutting along the bones that cover the belly until you reach the base of those bones (2). There is often a small area of fat at the end of the belly section. When you reach this section, turn the cutting edge of the knife outward and cut through the skin. Repeat the process on the other side of the steak (3).

4)

You now have a piece of fish that is boneless except for the pin bones. Gently rub the surface of the meat on both sides with your fingers to find the remaining pin bones, and remove them with a small pair of pliers or fish tweezers (4). The bones should be easy to remove. Be sure not to leave any behind. If the fish steak has part of the dorsal fin attached, cut this off close to the back with a pair of heavy-duty scissors.

Stand the salmon steak near the edge of the cutting board so that it rests on the skin of one side of the belly. Support the inside of the belly section with your right hand. With the paring knife held in your left hand with a pinch grip, slide the blade between the skin and flesh directly below the point where the spine once was. The blade should be flat against the skin and the cutting edge pointed toward the belly end. Slide the knife down toward the belly so the skin is cut from the flesh. Do this on only one side of the salmon steak (5).

5)

Lay the steak flat on the cutting board. Roll the belly flesh from the side you just skinned inward. Tuck the belly flesh from the other side around the outside of the first side and under the loosened flap of skin. Pull the loosened skin flap tight around the second side to form a round disk. Push two skewers through the center of the disk to hold it together during cooking: start the first skewer at the end of the loosened piece of skin flap, to hold it firmly in place, and be sure to pull the skin tight as you push the skewer through the fish. Start the second skewer about 90 degrees from where the tip of the other side of the belly is tucked under the skin, in order to hold the whole steak firmly together (6). Cook this steak the same way as you would any fish steak. Remove the skewers before serving.

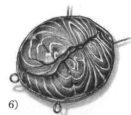

6)

CUTTING MEAT

THESE DAYS IT IS MOST LIKELY THAT THE MEAT YOU BUY WILL COME FROM A supermarket—sitting in a Styrofoam tray sealed in plastic film. Unless you live near a "real" butcher, all your meat is sold prepackaged as someone else's idea of how large a portion should be. Often enough these pieces are just what you need, but sometimes a recipe calls for a different shape or cut from what is in your local supermarket. In that case, it's helpful to know how to break down a large cut of meat into smaller portions. For example, you may be preparing a stew. I prefer to buy meat for stew in large pieces from my butcher for two reasons: First, store-produced stew meat is crudely "hacked" from large pieces—with no effort to remove sinew, fat, or gristle. Second, the size of the store-produced "chunks" is rarely the size I need for the dish I'm preparing. By cutting the meat myself, I can start the recipe with meat clean of all unwanted features and cut to just the right size.

With a little knife work, you can fashion many of the cuts you want from large, less expensive pieces of meat. For example, you can buy a boneless pork loin and cut it into individual boneless loin pork chops of just the desired thickness. Or, you can buy a whole beef inner round and portion it into 2-inch-thick London broils for the number of guests you plan to feed. Add a grinder to your armamentarium, and you can produce ground meat with the fat content and flavor you like rather than being stuck with ground scraps from the local market.

CUTTING MEAT (*right-hand version*)

Basic Meat Cutting

The real secret of butchering is "dividing" meat. What does this mean? The next time you have a piece of raw meat in your hand, notice that—assuming the piece is not too small— it is actually made up of multiple sections of different muscles. Usually you will be looking at a cross section of a group of muscles. If you tug slightly at the meat, you'll see the individual muscles attached to each other by some rather flimsy membranes (1). Each muscle is actually wrapped in a membrane, and the membranes are lightly bonded to 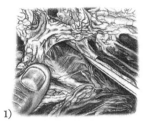 each other. When a muscle is pulled, the membrane is exposed. If you cut into the membrane with the tip of a small knife, the membrane will break away and the muscles will separate. The process requires almost no force on the knife, and the edges of the muscles are left intact. Much of butchery is based on this concept.

The thick membrane commonly called silver skin is the start of the tendon that attaches the muscle to the bone. It is extremely tough and hard to cut. To remove it, 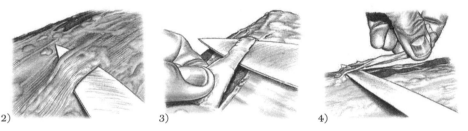 hold the piece of meat firmly with your left hand and insert the tip of a sharp chef's knife just under a strip of the silver skin, so the knife is between it and the meat (2). Then slide the blade to your right along the silver skin, with the blade tipped slightly into it. Once you have created a gap, lift the silver skin with your left index finger to create a little more tension on the silver skin (3). Next, reverse the knife and separate the strip of silver skin from the meat in the opposite direction, i.e., toward your left (4). Usually it is possible to remove only about a half-inch-wide strip of silver skin with each pass of your knife. Continue the process until all of the silver skin has been removed.

CUTTING MEAT (*right-hand version continued*)

Butterflying a Large Piece of Meat

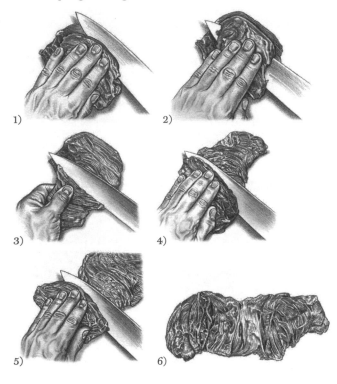

1)
2)
3)
4)
5)
6)

To butterfly a large piece of meat, start with one that has "straight" ends. The piece does not need to be perfectly cylindrical, but straight ends will produce a more rectangular result. Boneless loins work well. Hold the meat flat against the cutting board with your left hand. With a sharp chef's knife held with a pinch grip in your right hand, make a shallow cut near the top of one side of the meat, using a sawing motion and cutting parallel to the top and about a quarter inch below it (1). Continue cutting until you are close to the opposite side (2). Peel back the cut portion with your left hand and rotate the knife so the blade stays parallel to the outside of the meat (3). When the cutting edge is about a quarter inch above the board, swing the meat around so the flap is off to your right and continue cutting, now with the knife close to the cutting board and parallel to it (4). In this manner, continue cutting as you "unroll" the piece of meat (5, 6).

Thinly Slicing Meat

To cut thin slices of meat, lay a large piece on the cutting board so the grain is running from upper right to lower left. With your left hand, hold the meat firmly with your fingertips extended out and slightly up. Position a sharp chef's knife, held with a pinch grip, so the flat of the blade is almost parallel to the cutting board; the blade should be parallel to and in a plane slightly below your extended fingers. Using a sawing motion, make cuts through the meat. After each cut, move the slice onto a stack elsewhere on the cutting board. It is important that the flat of the blade always remain parallel to and in a plane slightly below your fingers.

Julienning Meat

To julienne the meat, stack three or four slices at a time on the cutting board. Hold the stack firmly in place with your left hand by pressing down on top of it with your fingertips in a vertical position. Position the chef's knife, held with a pinch grip, so the flat of the blade rests against the flat side of the tip of your forefinger. This way, your forefinger serves as a guide for the knife. Start each cut with the tip of the blade in contact with, or near, the cutting board, with the handle angled up. As you bring the  knife down, slide it forward so the edge of the blade moves through the meat as you produce the julienne. After each cut, move your forefinger to the left a distance equal to the desired width of the next cut. Ideally, the width of this cut should be the same as the thickness of the slices, so the resulting strips have a perfectly square cross section. As you do this, it is important that the flat of the blade always remain in contact with the flat surface of your forefinger.

Dicing Meat

To dice the meat, gather the julienned strips into a stack, with all the strips parallel to one another. With the fingertips of your left hand in a vertical position, hold the stack firmly in place. Position the chef's knife, held with a pinch grip, so the flat of the blade rests against the flat side of the tip of your forefinger. This way, your forefinger serves as a guide for the knife. Start each cut with the tip of the blade in contact with, or near, the cutting board, with the handle angled up. As you bring the  knife down, slide it forward so the edge of the blade moves through the meat as you produce the cubes. After each cut, slide your forefinger to the left a distance equal to the desired width of the next cut. Ideally, the width of this cut will be equal to the thickness of the strips, so the resulting dice will be perfect cubes. It is important that the flat of the blade always remain in contact with the flat surface of your forefinger.

CUTTING MEAT (*right-hand version continued*)

Preparing a Rack of Lamb for Roasting

Rack of lamb is usually sold already dressed, but if you happen to purchase a rack that is fully intact, you can easily butcher it yourself. At the neck end of the rack, there may be a remnant of the shoulder blade between the overlying fat and the main muscle. If it is there, pull it from the rack with your left hand and cut it from its attachment with a boning knife or paring knife held with a pinch grip in your right hand (1). Discard this piece of bony cartilage.

If the rack still has the chine bone attached, it will be necessary to remove this set of bones so that the meat is easy to carve after roasting. The chine bone—actually a portion of the spine comprised of eight or so vertebral sections—can be very thick or very thin, depending on how the butcher separated the rack from the main portion of the lamb's spine. Place the rack, rib side down, on your cutting board with the chine bone to your right and the tips of the ribs to your left. Use the fingers of your left hand to pull the fat and meat away from the chine bone. Hold a boning knife in a pinch grip with your right hand, and slide the blade down the length of the chine bone. Keep the knife angled slightly toward the bone so as little meat is left attached to the bone as possible. Make long cuts from the far end to the near end so the meat is trimmed neatly. Pulling the meat away from the bone with your left hand as you make each new pass with the blade will provide you with the best possible view. Cut down along the bone until you can visualize where the ribs are attached to it (2).

Stand the rack on end so the chine bone is vertical and to your right. Hold the ribs with your left hand so the meat side is away from you, pulling the meat away from the chine bone as you do this. Use a heavy-duty chef's knife or meat cleaver held in a pinch grip in your right hand to chop through the ribs where they attach to the chine bone: do this very carefully, and be sure to keep your left hand out of the way of the blade. Use sufficient force to chop through two or three ribs at a time. The harder you chop, the cleaner the cut will be (3). Once the two pieces are separated, wipe off any small pieces of bone that are stuck to the ribs with a clean towel. Discard the chine bone or save it for stock. (If used for stock, the bone should be chopped into four or five pieces.)

Look at each end of the rack to see where the main piece of meat ends on the side toward the ribs. Make a small cut through the skin at each end to mark the junctions. Place the rack, rib side down, on your cutting board with the spine edge toward your upper right. Hold the rack stable with the fingers of your left hand. Using a boning knife held in a 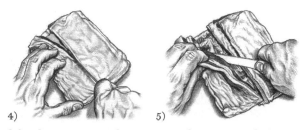 pinch grip in your right hand, make a cut through the skin and fat that connects the two cuts that you made in the skin, cutting all the way to the ribs (4). Then rotate the knife so the edge of the blade points to your left, and cut the skin and fat off the ribs (5). Discard the piece you just removed or reserve it for use in a sauce to accompany the finished rack of lamb. (Some chefs leave this piece in place when they prepare a rack of lamb.)

The next step is to remove the meat between the rib bones. Hold the bare-rib end of the rack with your left hand so the ribs are off your cutting board, supporting the meat end on the board. Using  a boning knife or a paring knife held in your right hand, puncture the meat between each pair of ribs, making the punctures in line with the fat and skin cut in the previous step (6). Then, with the rack still supported with your left hand, cut down along each rib, with the knife held with a pinch grip, to remove the small piece of meat between the ribs (7). Alternatively, you can cut down one side and up the other, rotating the knife at the bottom, and skip the puncture step (8). Discard the meat just removed or reserve with the meat removed earlier.

Place the rack of lamb rib side down on your cutting board, with the just-denuded rib bones pointing toward you. Support the rack with your left hand. Use a paring knife held in a pinch grip in your right hand to scrape away any meat or membranes still covering the rib bones (9). This step is strictly for aesthetics: most of the tissue remaining on the bones will burn off during roasting if it has not been scraped away.

Flip the rack of lamb over so it is skin side down on your cutting board. Near the edge where the skin meets the meat, on the end away from the ribs, is a band of tough, elastic, white tissue that must be removed. Locate the band and carefully cut it away from the meat using a boning knife or paring knife held with a pinch grip. Start at one end, and as you separate the band from the meat, pull the loose end with your left hand. The band should separate from the meat very easily without damaging the meat (10). Discard the band.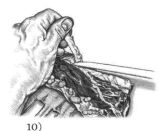

CUTTING MEAT (*right-hand version continued*)

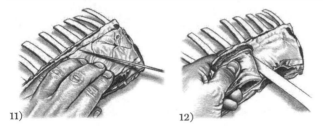

11)   12)

The rack of lamb can be roasted with the skin in place or without it. Place the rack rib side down on your cutting board with the skin edge toward you. If you plan to leave the skin in place, lightly score the skin with a coarse diamond pattern with the tip of a boning knife or sharp paring knife held with a pinch grip (11).

If you want to remove the skin and some of the fat attached to it, use a boning knife held with a pinch grip to separate the skin and fat from the rack by cutting with the blade parallel to the board and from right to left. There is a natural break between the fat attached to the skin and the fat attached to the meat, so this piece should come away very easily (12).

Preparing a Leg of Lamb for Roasting

1)

Some people prefer to roast lamb with the layer of fat that covers the outside still in place, while others wish to remove it. Those who leave the fat in place claim that the cooked meat is juicier. Those who remove it claim that the results are less greasy. As usual, this is a matter of personal taste. If you choose to remove it, use a sharp boning knife held with a pinch grip in your right hand to progressively cut off sections of fat, using a sawing motion (1).

If the hip bone has not already been removed from the leg, it will be necessary to do so at this point. A sharp boning knife with a flexible blade works best for this. Lay the leg, inner side up, with the hip bone to your right, on your cutting board. Support the leg with your left hand, and cut the meat from the bone (2). Change your grip as required to keep the knife at the proper angle with respect to the meat and bone, and move the leg around with your left hand so you are always cutting in a comfortable position (3). Use the tip of the knife to cut the meat while keeping the cutting edge in contact with the bone, following the surface of the bone (4). Work all around the bone until it is attached only at the joint with the femur, then cut the ligaments that hold the two bones together (5). Discard the hip bone or save it for stock. You should now have a somewhat loose flap of meat that was previously attached to the hip bone. You may want to remove this flap so the leg is more uniform in appearance.

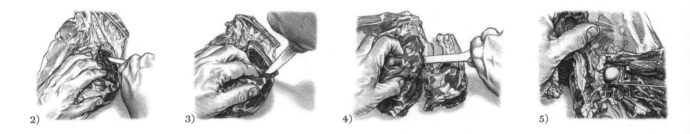

2)   3)   4)   5)

Using the boning knife, held with a pinch grip, cut all around the shank bone about 2 to 3 inches above its sawed-off end (6). Scrape the bone to remove any remaining meat. This gives a neater appearance to the finished piece of lamb. The bone can be used as a handle when the lamb is carved.

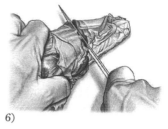

6)

Boning a Leg of Lamb

To butterfly a lamb leg, if necessary, remove the hip bone and trim the shank end as described above. Lay the leg on the cutting board with its outer surface down, with the femur end be toward your left and the shank end toward your right. Support the meat with your left hand. Using a sharp boning knife held with a pinch grip in your right hand, make a slit-like cut directly over the femur down its entire length (1). Insert the tip of your knife under one side of the muscle flap created by your slit and gradually work your blade down the entire length of the flap to loosen it from the bone, working with the tip of the knife in contact with and parallel to the bone (2). Once the flap is loosened, run

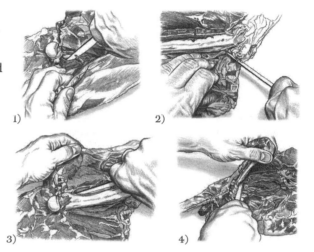

1)   2)

3)   4)

the knife around the bone more deeply two or three times in order to free most of the first side from the bone (3). Then proceed in the same manner with the flap on the other side. Once you have worked your way entirely around the bone, first from one side and then from the other, most of the meat should now be freed from the bone. Then work in a similar manner to separate the meat from around the knee. A loose piece of cartilage, the kneecap, may come off with the meat; if this happens, simply cut it out from the meat around it. Once the knee is free, continue to cut the remainder of the meat from the femur. Finally, cut the meat from the shank bone. It should come off quite easily (4). Discard the bones, or save to make stock.

The meat from one side of the bone will be thicker than the meat from the other side. If you intend to cook the meat splayed flat, lay the boned leg outer side down on the cutting board with the thicker muscle to your left. Hold it down with your left hand. Using a sharp chef's knife held with a pinch grip in your right hand, holding the blade parallel to the cutting board, make a single cut, moving from right to left, partway through the thicker part of the meat so it can be "unfolded" to the thickness of the rest of the meat. Do not cut all the way through the meat (5).

5)

CUTTING MEAT (*right-hand version continued*)

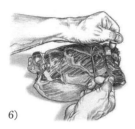 

6) 7)

To roll and tie the meat into a roast, form the meat into a cylindrical shape on the cutting board, then tightly tie it with butcher's twine at about 1-inch intervals (6, 7).

CUTTING MEAT (*left-hand version*)

Basic Meat Cutting

The real secret of butchering is "dividing" meat. What does this mean? The next time you have a piece of raw meat in your hand, notice that—assuming the piece is not too small—it is actually made up of multiple sections of different muscles. Usually you will be looking at a cross section of a group of muscles. If you tug slightly at the meat, you'll see the individual muscles attached to each other by some rather flimsy membranes (1). Each muscle is actually wrapped in a membrane and the membranes are lightly bonded to each other. When a muscle is pulled, the membrane is exposed. If you cut into the membrane with the tip of a small knife, the membrane will break away and the muscles will separate. The process requires almost no force on the knife and the edges of the muscles are left intact. Much of butchery is based on this concept.

1)

The thick membrane commonly called silver skin is the start of the tendon that attaches the muscle to the bone. It is extremely tough and hard to cut. To remove it,

2)   3)   4)

hold the piece of meat firmly with your right hand and insert the tip of a sharp chef's knife just under a strip of the silver skin, so the knife is between it and the meat (2). Then slide the blade to your left along the silver skin, with the blade tipped slightly into it. Once you have created a space, lift the silver skin with your right index finger to create a little more tension on the silver skin (3). Next, reverse the knife and separate the strip of silver skin from the meat in the opposite direction, i.e., toward your right (4). Usually it is possible to remove only about a half-inch-wide strip of silver skin with each pass of your knife. Continue the process until all of the silver skin has been removed.

CUTTING MEAT (*left-hand version continued*)

Butterflying a Large Piece of Meat

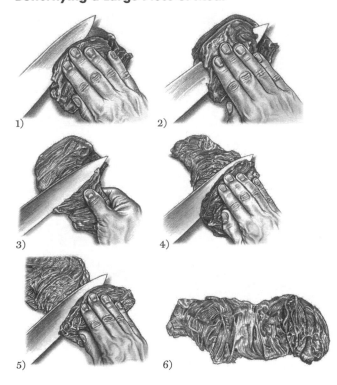

1)

2)

3)

4)

5)

6)

To butterfly a large piece of meat, start with one that has "straight" ends. The piece does not need to be perfectly cylindrical, but straight ends will produce a more rectangular result. Boneless loins work well. Hold the meat flat against the cutting board with your right hand. With a sharp chef's knife held with a pinch grip in your left hand, make a shallow cut near the top of one long side of the meat, using a sawing motion, and cutting parallel to the top and about a quarter inch below it (1). Continue cutting until you are close to the opposite side (2). Peel back the cut portion with your right hand and rotate the knife so the blade stays parallel to the outside of the meat (3). When the cutting edge is about a quarter inch above the board, swing the meat around so the flap is off to your left and continue cutting, now with the knife close to the cutting board and parallel to it (4). In this manner, continue cutting as you "unroll" the piece of meat (5, 6).

Thinly Slicing Meat

To cut thin slices of meat, lay a large piece on the cutting board so the grain is running from upper left to lower right. With your right hand, hold the meat firmly with your fingertips extended out and slightly up. Position a sharp chef's knife, held with a pinch grip, so the flat of the blade is almost parallel to the cutting board; the blade should be parallel to and in a plane slightly below your extended fingers. Using a sawing motion, make cuts through the meat. After each cut, move the slice onto a stack elsewhere on the cutting board. It is important that the flat of the blade always remain parallel to and in a plane slightly below your fingers.

Julienning Meat

To julienne the meat, stack three or four slices at a time on the cutting board. Hold the stack firmly in place with your right hand by pressing down on top of it with your fingertips, in a vertical position. Position the chef's knife, held with a pinch grip, so the flat of the blade rests against the flat side of the tip of your forefinger. This way, your forefinger serves as a guide for the knife. Start each cut with the tip of the blade in contact with, or near, the cutting board, with the handle angled up. As you bring the  knife down, slide it forward so the edge of the blade moves through the meat as you produce the julienne. After each cut, move your forefinger to the right a distance equal to the desired width of the next cut. Ideally, the width of this cut should be the same as the thickness of the slices, so the resulting strips have a perfectly square cross section. As you do this, it is important that the flat of the blade always remain in contact with the flat surface of your forefinger.

Dicing Meat

To dice the meat, gather the julienned strips into a stack, with all the strips parallel to one another. With the fingertips of your right hand in a vertical position, hold the stack firmly in place. Position the chef's knife, held with a pinch grip, so the flat of the blade rests against the flat side of the tip of your forefinger. This way, your forefinger serves as a guide for the knife. Start each cut with the tip of the blade in contact with, or near, the cutting board, with the handle angled up. As you bring the  knife down, slide it forward so the edge of the blade moves through the meat as you produce the cubes. After each cut, slide your forefinger to the right a distance equal to the desired width of the next cut. Ideally, the width of this cut will be equal to the thickness of the strips, so the resulting dice will be perfect cubes. It is important that the flat of the blade always remain in contact with the flat surface of your forefinger.

CUTTING MEAT (*left-hand version continued*)

Preparing a Rack of Lamb for Roasting

1)

Rack of lamb is usually sold already dressed, but if you happen to purchase a rack that is fully intact, you can easily butcher it yourself. At the neck end of the rack, there may be a remnant of the shoulder blade between the overlying fat and the main muscle. If it is there, pull it from the rack with your right hand and cut it from its attachment with a boning knife or paring knife held with a pinch grip in your left hand (1). Discard this piece of bony cartilage.

2)

If the rack still has the chine bone attached, it will be necessary to remove this set of bones so that the meat is easy to carve after roasting. The chine bone—actually a portion of the spine comprised of eight or so vertebral sections—can be very thick or very thin, depending on how the butcher separated the rack from the main portion of the lamb's spine. Place the rack, rib side down, on your cutting board with the chine bone to your left and the tips of the ribs to your right. Use the fingers of your right hand to pull the fat and meat away from the chine bone. Hold a boning knife in a pinch grip with your left hand, and slide the blade down the length of the chine bone. Keep the knife angled slightly toward the bone so as little meat is left attached to the bone as possible. Make long cuts from the far end to the near end so the meat is trimmed neatly. Pulling the meat away from the bone with your right hand as you make each new pass with the blade will provide you with the best possible view. Cut down along the bone until you can visualize where the ribs are attached to it (2).

3)

Stand the rack on end so the chine bone is vertical and to your left. Hold the ribs with your right hand so the meat side is away from you, pulling the meat away from the chine bone as you do this. Use a heavy-duty chef's knife or meat cleaver held in a pinch grip in your left hand to chop through the ribs where they attach to the chine bone: do this very carefully, and be sure to keep your right hand out of the way of the blade. Use sufficient force to chop through two or three ribs at a time. The harder you chop, the cleaner the cut will be (3). Once the two pieces are separated, wipe off any small pieces of bone that are stuck to the ribs with a clean towel. Discard the chine bone or save it for stock. (If used for stock, the bone should be chopped into four or five pieces.)

Look at each end of the rack to see where the main piece of meat ends on the side toward the ribs. Make a small cut through the skin at each end to mark the junctions. Place the rack, rib side down, on your cutting board with the spine edge toward your upper left. Hold the rack stable with the fingers of your right hand. Using a boning knife held in a

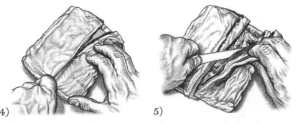

4)   5)

pinch grip in your left hand, make a cut through the skin and fat that connects the two cuts that you made in the skin, cutting all the way to the ribs (4). Then rotate the knife so the edge of the blade points to your right, and cut the skin and fat off the ribs (5). Discard the piece you just removed or reserve it for use in a sauce to accompany the finished rack of lamb. (Some chefs leave this piece in place when they prepare a rack of lamb.)

The next step is to remove the meat between the rib bones. Hold the bare-rib end of the rack with your right hand so the ribs are off your cutting board, supporting the meat end on the board. Using

6)   7)   8)

a boning knife or a paring knife held in your left hand, puncture the meat between each pair of ribs, making the punctures in line with the fat and skin cut in the previous step (6). Then, with the rack still supported with your right hand, cut down along each rib, with the knife held with a pinch grip, to remove the small piece of meat between the ribs (7). Alternatively, you can cut down one side and up the other, rotating the knife at the bottom, and skip the puncture step (8). Discard the meat just removed or reserve with the meat removed earlier.

Place the rack of lamb rib side down on your cutting board, with the just-denuded rib bones pointing toward you. Support the rack with your right hand. Use a paring knife held in a pinch grip in your left hand to scrape away any meat or membranes still covering the rib bones (9). This step is strictly for aesthetics: most of the tissue remaining on the bones will burn off during roasting if it has not been scraped away.

9)

Flip the rack of lamb over so it is skin side down on your cutting board. Near the edge where the skin meets the meat, on the end away from the ribs, is a band of tough, elastic, white tissue that must be removed. Locate the band and carefully cut it away from the meat using a boning knife or paring knife held with a pinch grip. Start at one end, and as you separate the band from the meat, pull the loose end with your right hand. The band should separate from the meat very easily without damaging the meat (10). Discard the band.

10)

CUTTING MEAT (*left-hand version continued*)

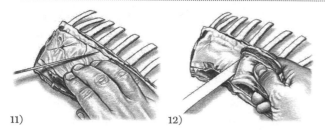

11)

12)

The rack of lamb can be roasted with the skin in place or without it. Place the rack rib side down on your cutting board with the skin edge toward you. If you plan to leave the skin in place, lightly score the skin with a coarse diamond pattern with the tip of a boning knife or sharp paring knife held with a pinch grip (11). If you want to remove the skin and some of the fat attached to it, use a boning knife held with a pinch grip to separate the skin and fat from the rack by cutting with the blade parallel to the board and from left to right. There is a natural break between the fat attached to the skin and the fat attached to the meat, so this piece should come away very easily (12).

Preparing a Leg of Lamb for Roasting

1)

Some people prefer to roast lamb with the layer of fat that covers the outside still in place, while others wish to remove it. Those who leave the fat in place claim that the cooked meat is juicier. Those who remove it claim that the results are less greasy. As usual, this is a matter of personal taste. If you choose to remove it, use a sharp boning knife held with a pinch grip in your left hand to progressively cut off sections of fat, using a sawing motion (1).

If the hip bone has not already been removed from the leg, it will be necessary to do so at this point. A sharp boning knife with a flexible blade works best for this. Lay the leg, inner side up, with the hip bone to your left, on your cutting board. Support the leg with your right hand and cut the meat from the bone (2). Change your grip as required to keep the knife at the proper angle with respect to the meat and bone, and move the leg around with your right hand so you are always cutting in a comfortable position (3). Use the tip of the knife to cut the meat while keeping the cutting edge in contact with the bone, following the surface of the bone (4). Work all around the bone until it is attached only at the joint with the femur, then cut the ligaments that hold the two bones together (5). Discard the hip bone or save it for stock. You should now have a somewhat loose flap of meat that was previously attached to the hip bone. You may want to remove this flap so the leg is more uniform in appearance.

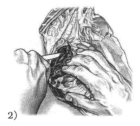

2)

3)

4)

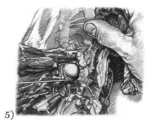

5)

Using the boning knife, held with a pinch grip, cut all around the shank bone about 2 to 3 inches above its sawed-off end (6). Scrape the bone to remove any remaining meat. This gives a neater appearance to the finished piece of lamb. The bone can be used as a handle when the lamb is carved.

6)

Boning a Leg of Lamb

To butterfly a lamb leg, if necessary, remove the hip bone and trim the shank end as described above. Lay the leg on the cutting board with its outer surface down, with the femur end toward your right and the shank end toward your left. Support the meat with your right hand. Using a sharp boning knife held with a pinch grip in your left hand, make a slit-like cut directly over the femur down its entire length (1). Insert the tip of your knife under one side of the muscle flap created by your slit and gradually work your blade down the entire length of the flap to loosen it from the bone, working with the tip of the knife in contact with and parallel to the bone (2). Once the flap is loosened, run the

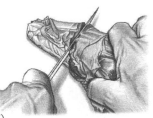

1)

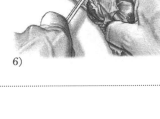

2)

3)

4)

knife around the bone more deeply two or three times in order to free most of the first side from the bone (3). Then proceed in the same manner with the flap on the other side. Once you have worked your way entirely around the bone, first from one side and then from the other, most of the meat should now be freed from the bone. Then work in a similar manner to separate the meat from around the knee. A loose piece of cartilage, the kneecap, may come off with the meat; if this happens, simply cut it out from the meat around it. Once the knee is free, continue to cut the remainder of the meat from the femur. Finally, cut the meat from the shank bone. It should come off quite easily (4). Discard the bones, or save to make stock.

The meat from one side of the bone will be thicker than the meat from the other side. If you intend to cook the meat splayed flat, lay the boned leg outer side down on the cutting board with the thicker muscle to your right. Hold it down with your right hand. Using a sharp chef's knife held with a pinch grip in your left hand, holding the blade parallel to the cutting board, make a single cut, moving from left to right, partway through the thicker part of the meat so it can be "unfolded" to the thickness of the rest of the meat. Do not cut all the way through the meat (5).

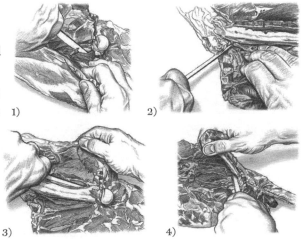

5)

CUTTING MEAT *(left-hand version continued)*

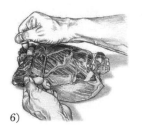

6)

7)

To roll and tie the meat into a roast, form the meat into a cylindrical shape on the cutting board, then tightly tie it with butcher's twine at about 1-inch intervals (6, 7).

CARVING MEAT AND POULTRY

I REMEMBER MY FATHER CARVING THE THANKSGIVING TURKEY SITTING AT THE TABLE with a large napkin wrapped around his neck as an apron. The guests would marvel as he struggled with the bird that always seemed too large for the platter. In the end, he always won, but sometimes the fight was long and hard. The carving set was beautiful to look at, but not well designed for its intended purpose. Working seated, he was at the wrong angle to perform his duty comfortably. By the time he was ready to pass the platter with the meat around the table, the rest of the dinner was becoming quite cool. Today I carve the Thanksgiving turkey in the kitchen and fill my guests' plates before sending them out to the dining room. For my father, carving was performance art. For me, carving is just one of the tasks required to fill my guests' plates. It doesn't mean that my results are less attractive than his; in fact mine are probably more consistent.

Carving in the kitchen allows you to hold the meat in a more casual manner—maybe with a towel instead of a fork—than required for a public performance. You can work faster and with fewer interruptions, and in a comfortable stance. And, most important, you can snack on a periodic scrap or two.

Just as with cutting poultry in preparation for cooking, carving a roast turkey, duck, or goose is, in essence, the same as carving a roast chicken. If you can carve a couple of roast chickens during the course of the year as practice, you will be prepared when Thanksgiving rolls around and you are confronted with carving a larger, but no more difficult, turkey.

CARVING MEAT AND POULTRY (*right-hand version*)

Carving Whole Poultry

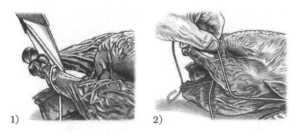

1)　　2)

To demonstrate this technique, I used a small turkey. The carving techniques are the same for a thirty-pound turkey or a one-pound squab. If the bird was trussed, whether with string or the producer's trussing straps, start by removing the string or straps (1, 2).

3)　　4)　　5)

Place the turkey on a cutting board, back side down and left side toward you. To remove the legs, first pull the left leg outward with your left hand to open a space between the leg and the breast. (If the leg is too hot, use a towel to grab its tip.) Using a sharp slicer or carving knife held with a pinch grip in your right hand, cut through just the skin between the thigh and the breast with the tip of the knife (3). Roll the bird over onto its right side. Continue cutting around to the bird's back, slicing through the skin and muscle until you reach the bone (4). On the back, you will come to a circular piece of meat, sometimes referred to as the oyster. Use your knife to scrape this off the bone, leaving it as a single piece still attached to the leg section. Continue cutting through the skin and meat attached to the back, working toward the tail end. The entire leg section should now be attached to the body only by the white ligaments at the joint. These ligaments can be easily torn apart by spreading the entire piece outward toward the bird's back (5). Remove the other leg in the same manner. Depending upon how you plan to serve the turkey, each leg can be left whole or cut into thigh and drumstick portions as shown for disjointing raw poultry on page 190.

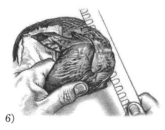

6)

Continuing to work with the turkey on its side, hold the wing in your left hand. (If the wing is too hot, use a towel to hold it.) Using the slicer or carving knife held with a pinch grip, cut through the shoulder joint where the wing is attached to the breast. If you gently pull the wing out from the body as you cut all the way around the joint, it will be easy to remove (6). Remove the other wing in the same manner. Depending upon how you plan to serve the turkey, each wing can be kept whole or cut into pieces as shown for disjointing raw poultry on page 190.

To slice the breast meat, place the turkey on its back on the cutting board. Push a meat fork, held in your left hand, through the breast just left of the keel bone to stabilize the bird. Using the slicer or carving knife held with a pinch grip in your right hand, cut along each side of the keel bone as deep as you can (7). Next, turn the blade to almost parallel to the cutting board and cut a series of thin horizontal slices from the breast on the right side of the turkey, using a sawing motion (8). Start at the top and progress down toward the cutting board (9). If the wishbone was removed before roasting, as shown on page 194, you'll be able to easily slice all the way to the breastbone. Continue slicing until all the breast meat on the first side has been removed. Then turn the bird around and slice the meat from the other side in the same manner.

Carving a Boneless Roast

Lay the roast on the cutting board. If the roast is tied with string, remove the string by cutting it with a pair of scissors. If the roast is in a netting, cut it away with scissors (1).

1)

Stabilize the meat on the cutting board with a meat fork held in your left hand or simply your left hand. Use a sharp slicer or carving knife, or a sharp chef's knife, held with a pinch grip in your right hand to cut vertical slices through the meat. Use a long sawing motion that takes advantage of the entire length of the blade to increase the efficiency of the cut (2, 3).

2)

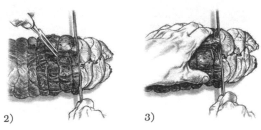
3)

CARVING MEAT AND POULTRY (*right-hand version continued*)

Slicing a Flank Steak or Other Thin Steak

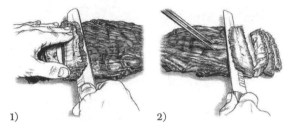

1)

2)

Place the steak on the cutting board. Because the meat is thin, for a nicer presentation, you will want to cut it into diagonal slices so each slice is wider than it would be if the meat were cut with the knife straight up and down. Use a sharp slicer, or a sharp chef's knife, held with a pinch grip in your right hand to cut diagonal slices through the meat: turn the blade so it is diagonal to the cutting board, and use a sawing motion that takes advantage of the entire length of the blade to increase the efficiency of the cut. Stabilize the meat with the fingertips of your left hand, pressing just enough to keep the meat from moving. The pinch grip will stabilize the slicer so you are less likely to slip and cut yourself when carving in this manner (1). With a little practice, you will find that you can rapidly cut very thin, even slices with this method. Alternatively, you can stabilize the meat with a meat fork held in your left hand. It will then be necessary to hold the slicer with an awkward grip, because it would be uncomfortable to rotate your right wrist enough to the left to use a pinch grip when cutting to your right (2).

Slicing a London Broil or Other Thick Steak

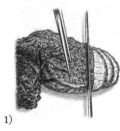

1)

2)

Place the meat on the cutting board. Stabilize the meat with a meat fork held in your left hand or simply with your left hand. Use a sharp slicer, or chef's knife, held with a pinch grip in your right hand to cut vertical slices through the meat. Use a long sawing motion that takes advantage of the entire length of the blade to increase the efficiency of the cut (1, 2).

Carving a Bone-In Leg of Lamb

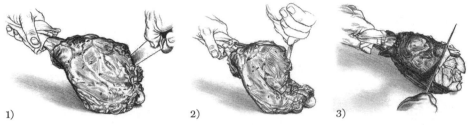

1)   2)   3)

Hold the cooked leg by the shank bone with your left hand (use a towel for a better grip): hold the leg, knee down, on the cutting board. Use a sharp slicer or carving knife held with a pinch grip in your right hand to cut thin slices from the muscle above the bone (1). Start at the hip end and work toward the shank, slicing at about a 45-degree angle to the bone (2, 3). After each slice, rotate the knife blade and make a slice along the bone, toward your left, to separate the slice from the leg.

When all the meat has been cut from the back of the leg, flip it over and slice the meat from the knee side in a similar manner (4).

4)

Alternatively, for a less traditional approach, cut the two whole muscles away from the leg and then slice them the same way you'd slice a boneless roast, as shown on page 239.

CARVING MEAT AND POULTRY (*left-hand version*)

Carving Whole Poultry

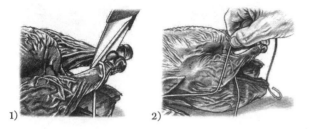

1) 2)

To demonstrate this technique, I used a small turkey. The carving techniques are the same for a thirty-pound turkey or a one-pound squab. If the bird was trussed, whether with string or the producer's trussing straps, start by removing the string or straps (1, 2).

3) 4) 5)

Place the turkey on a cutting board, back side down and right side toward you. To remove the legs, first pull the right leg outward with your right hand to open a space between the leg and the breast. (If the leg is too hot, use a towel to grab its tip.) Using a sharp slicer or carving knife held with a pinch grip in your left hand, cut through just the skin between the thigh and the breast with the tip of the knife (3). Roll the bird over onto its left side. Continue cutting around to the bird's back, slicing through the skin and muscle until you reach the bone (4). On the back, you will come to a circular piece of meat, sometimes referred to as the oyster. Use your knife to scrape this off the bone, leaving it as a single piece still attached to the leg section. Continue cutting through the skin and meat attached to the back, working toward the tail end. The entire leg section should now be attached to the body only by the white ligaments at the joint. These ligaments can be easily torn apart by spreading the entire piece out toward the bird's back (5). Remove the other leg in the same manner. Depending upon how you plan to serve the turkey, each leg can be left whole or cut into thigh and drumstick portions as shown for disjointing raw poultry on page 198.

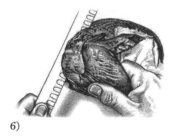

6)

Continuing to work with the turkey on its side, hold the wing in your right hand. (If the wing is too hot, use a towel to hold it.) Using the slicer or carving knife held with a pinch grip, cut through the shoulder joint where the wing is attached to the breast. If you gently pull the wing out from the body as you cut all the way around the joint, it will be easy to remove (6). Remove the other wing in the same manner. Depending upon how you plan to serve the turkey, each wing can be kept whole or cut into pieces as shown for disjointing raw poultry on page 198.

To slice the breast meat, place the turkey on its back on the cutting board. Push a meat fork, held in your right hand, through the breast just right of the keel bone to stabilize the bird. Using the slicer or carving knife

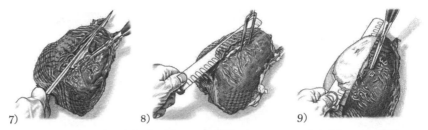

7) 8) 9)

held with a pinch grip in your left hand, cut along each side of the keel bone as deep as you can (7). Next, turn the blade to almost parallel to the cutting board and cut a series of thin horizontal slices from the breast on the left side of the turkey, using a sawing motion (8). Start at the top and progress down toward the cutting board (9). If the wishbone was removed before roasting, as shown on page 202, you'll be able to easily slice all the way to the breastbone. Continue slicing until all the breast meat on the first side has been removed. Then turn the bird around and slice the meat from the other side in the same manner.

Carving a Boneless Roast

Lay the roast on the cutting board. If the roast is tied with string, remove the string by cutting it with a pair of scissors. If the roast is in a netting, cut it away with scissors (1).

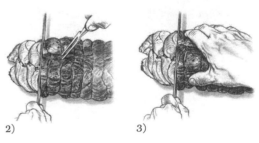

1)

Stabilize the meat on the cutting board with a meat fork held in your right hand or simply your right hand. Use a sharp slicer or carving knife, or a sharp chef's knife, held with a pinch grip in your left hand to cut vertical slices through the meat. Use a long sawing motion that takes advantage of the entire length of the blade to increase the efficiency of the cut (2, 3).

2) 3)

CARVING MEAT AND POULTRY *(left-hand version continued)*

Slicing a Flank Steak or Other Thin Steak

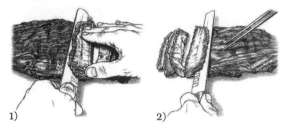

Place the steak on the cutting board. Because the meat is thin, for a nicer presentation, you will want to cut it into diagonal slices so each slice is wider than it would be if the meat were cut with the knife straight up and down. Use a sharp slicer, or a sharp chef's knife, held with a pinch grip in your left hand to cut diagonal slices through the meat: turn the blade so it is diagonal to the cutting board, and use a sawing motion that takes advantage of the entire length of the blade to increase the efficiency of the cut. Stabilize the meat with the fingertips of your right hand, pressing just enough to keep the meat from moving. The pinch grip will stabilize the slicer so you are less likely to slip and cut yourself when carving in this manner (1). With a little practice, you will find that you can rapidly cut very thin, even slices with this method. Alternatively, you can stabilize the meat with a meat fork held in your right hand. It will then be necessary to hold the slicer with an awkward grip, because it would be uncomfortable to rotate your left wrist enough to the right to use a pinch grip when cutting to your left (2).

Slicing a London Broil or Other Thick Steak

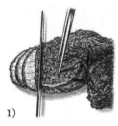

Place the meat on the cutting board. Stabilize the meat with a meat fork held in your right hand or simply with your right hand. Use a sharp slicer, or a chef's knife, held with a pinch grip in your left hand to cut vertical slices through the meat. Use a long sawing motion that takes advantage of the entire length of the blade to increase the efficiency of the cut (1, 2).

Carving a Bone-In Leg of Lamb

Hold the cooked leg by the shank bone with your right hand (use a towel for a better grip): hold the leg, knee down, on the cutting board. Use a sharp slicer or carving knife  held with a pinch grip in your left hand to cut thin slices from the muscle above the bone (1). Start at the hip end and work toward the shank, slicing at about a 45-degree angle to the bone (2, 3). After each slice, rotate the knife blade and make a slice along the bone, toward your right, to separate the slice from the leg.

When all the meat has been cut from the back of the leg, flip it over and slice the meat from the knee side in a similar manner (4).

Alternatively, for a less traditional approach, cut the two whole muscles away from the leg and then slice them the same way you'd slice a boneless roast, as shown on page 243.

ACKNOWLEDGMENTS

First and foremost, I wish to thank my life partner, Jill Chinen, for her ongoing support for my writing efforts, one of which led to this book. Without her continuous encouragement and assistance, none of my projects would ever be completed.

Secondly, I'd like to thank Bob Mecoy, my agent, who had the foresight to see a simple article on my website as a book on knife skills. If he hadn't called me out of the blue and spent an hour convincing me that a book was possible, it would still be just words on the Internet.

Thirdly, I am indebted to Alan Witschonke for his clear illustrations, which give life and color to the words of this book.

Lastly, I am beholden to the superb team at W. W. Norton, led by Maria Guarnaschelli, my editor, who turned this book into a reality.

INDEX